Titles continued overleaf

Please note that a sister series, *British History in Perspective*, is available which covers all the key topics in British political history.

Towns in Tudor and Stuart Britain

Sybil M. Jack

First published 1996 by
MACMILLAN PRESS LTD
Houndmills, Basingstoke, Hampshire RG21 6XS
and London
Companies and representatives
throughout the world

ISBN 0–333–61082–2 hardcover
ISBN 0–333–61083–0 paperback

A catalogue record for this book is available
from the British Library.

10   9   8   7   6   5   4   3   2   1
05   04   03   02   01   00   99   98   97   96

Printed in Hong Kong

CONTENTS

MAPS AND TABLES

Cities and Towns mentioned in Text

INTRODUCTION

Geographers in Afric maps
With savage pictures filled their gaps
And o'er uninhabitable downs
Placed elephants for want of towns.

Jonathan Swift

Why should one study urban history? Were towns the precipitating element for change in the human way of life? Historians of different persuasions have argued bitterly about the function of towns in the shifts of human ways of life and behaviour. Certainly, the town has always been a central focus of human history. A wide variety of social, political and economic needs were met where large numbers of people congregated together on a permanent basis. Perhaps for this reason, it has been described as 'one of the most exciting aspects of the adventure of humanity'.[1] Some see it as a measure of civilisation, others equally attack it as destructive of natural man. Some see it as a critical independent variable in social and economic development, others as merely an arena for developments caused by other factors. People have wondered whether different civilisations have different urban forms. In Greece and Rome the citizen was political; in the USA, mercantile. It has been suggested that 'in a great civilisation home, house, city and landscape are in perfect harmony'.[2] Scholars have argued about whether town life favoured or discouraged innovation.

The relationship between the city and society, politics and economy, is still unresolved. Some assume that towns have a central role in economic life; others see them as parasites. The relationship between town and state in the development of coercive state power has been seen either as crucial or irrelevant. Their wider role in world history is frequently seen as vital, particularly as cities and states appear at roughly the same moment. Their physical appearance is seen as embodying the contemporary political and social structure.

Is there indeed a common set of characteristics which make 'the town' a entity about which there can be useful generalisations? Does 'the town' exist or are there simply towns, places where a considerable number of people live in close proximity but which have no other common features? Is density of population an adequate description of a town or would one add other characteristics such as a specialised function or a distinctive physical appearance. What distinguishes a town from a city, is it simply size or the possession of a cathedral, making the town the centre of a religious diocese? The self-definition of a town in the early modern period was of a community living within established limits, whose circuit was jealously guarded. The annual 'riding' of those boundaries was both serious business and a festivity designed to promote the embodiment of a sense of identity. Detailed studies of individual towns often imply that the microcosm reflects the macrocosm but some historians would argue fiercely that a wider theory is necessary to make coherent sense; others that no such coherent theory has ever been produced. They have attempted to demolish the idea that certain activities presuppose permanent urban settlement.

Meeting places, after all, do not have to be towns. There can be places in the open fields such as Anglo-Saxon gathering places. The administrative centres of Scottish regalities were not necessarily towns. The centres of Gaelic lordships in Ireland and Wales were not usually towns. Even ports do not necessarily have towns around them. In nineteenth-century Australia some ports were only a jetty, pier or quay with a common storehouse attached. Towns, moreover, are not necessarily permanent. They can be created almost instantaneously by a company to provide for workers in a particular area and be dismantled and removed at the end of the work. Settlements may for a time have all the basic characteristics of a town but then, as the reason for them vanishes, they may disappear leaving only the relics which human scavengers have found too much trouble to remove.

What cannot be disputed is that the number of people who live in towns has soared since the Middle Ages. From a time when most people were rural dwellers, there has been a transition to a situation in which most live in urban or suburban conglomerates. This has profoundly altered human experience. The process is called urbanisation and there is ongoing investigation of what precipitated it, what caused it and what made it possible. The very variety of the town's potential functions makes it a difficult concept to pin down. Its historical significance in any specific period can vary and is frequently elusive. The factors which led to town growth have been variously seen, from Lewis Mumford's idea that it resulted from the balance between power and production[3] to those who see cities defined simply as large and significant towns, as organisational forces in their own right.[4]

What we are concerned with is the increasing tendency of humanity to live in large settled communities which meet certain religious, social and economic needs from the most basic need for protection against enemies and climate through to politics and colonisation. There is a danger of anthropomorphism, however, in approaching the town as if it was a distinct entity with a life of its own. It is essential to bear in mind that in the last analysis a town is a group of individual people clustered together and that from moment to moment, year to year and generation to generation, that cluster is constantly changing. As people are born and die, decide for their own reasons to come or go, to work at one task or another, the town becomes different. Towns are human artefacts – they do not move of themselves. They are a venue for human activity to which residents have a greater or lesser commitment according to their circumstances and endowing them with a persona is only convenient shorthand. The creation of a place with which individuals identify, sometimes passionately, is the result of implementing culturally specific architectural/philosophical concepts of space, place and time, spaciousness and crowding.[5]

At the same time not all historians see urban history as a separate subject. Some ask whether there is anything which is specific to urban history. Is the town a dependent or an independent variable? Can it in fact be separated from wider cultural movements? Does it have a history of its own? Other authors of overarching studies of the long run of urban history have stressed both the early arrival of towns, the relative stability of urban sites and, more contentiously, networks, and claim that from the start there was a relatively high percentage of the population who were town dwellers.[6] This underpins claims that the history of towns is critical to our understanding of the past, indeed, that towns have heralded most of the decisive changes in our history.

Taking this approach, towns have been divided in accordance with function and considerable importance has been attached to the development of links between towns. There is a stress on the idea of hierarchy and network. Briefly, a hierarchy involves a ranking of towns in order of size in which specialist goods flow down while raw materials, food and more standard goods flow up. Networks would see goods flowing from one town with a specialised function to another perhaps on the same level which had a different specialisation, in a more complicated connection of levels both in domestic and in international trade. The development of an integrated network has been seen as an essential prerequisite for the economic advances of the later industrialisation of Europe.

Towns in 1500 were much smaller than those of today, with a correspondingly smaller population. A town of 5000 was considered large and towns between 2500 and 5000 still sizeable. Most towns, including a number of county towns, were under 2500 but were still an important part of the social and economic fabric. By 1700 a number of towns were approaching 20 000 and the capitals had swelled to many times that size. Interpreting this change and its implications for the people who lived in them has become the main focus of recent historical work.

The History of Urban Historical Writing

The questions we shall be asking are different from those that preoccupied earlier urban historians. Historians write to make sense of the past for their contemporaries and a change of focus is a measure of ongoing change. Earlier accounts are generally associated with the creation of a sense of identity, be it individual, family, religious, or national and state identity. A brief account of earlier preoccupations may set the present study in context.

In the sixteenth and seventeenth centuries, Italian cities, most far larger than English towns, produced sophisticated histories modelled on classical authors such as Livy to express their grandeur. Early urban recording of events in Britain had the more limited aim of recording what was deemed useful. Early chronicles written in Reading and Lincoln, the King's Lynn 'Calendar' which recorded its practices, and Bristol's customs recorded at the end of the fifteenth century in a book of remembrance by its town clerk, Robert Ricard, show a consciousness of identity, but uniformly lacked sophistication. The monarch's sources were so limited that Henry VIII offered inducements to Leland to survey the state of the realm and his 'Itinerary' contains precious information on the state of the towns.[7]

The second half of the sixteenth century saw a rising interest in chorographical descriptions but although it produced works such as William Smith's *The Particular Description of England with the portraiture of Certaine of the Cheiffest Citties and Townes 1588*; William Harrison's *Description of England*; Camden's *Britannia* and Carew's *Survey of Cornwall* the focus was still on county rather than town. The appearance of town histories like Stow's *History of London* or William Aldersey's *Annals of Chester* may be a sign of growing urban self-consciousness.[8] Local town histories began to be written in greater numbers in the early seventeenth century. Nathanial Bacon, the recorder of Ipswich, compiled the *Annals of Ipswich* ostensibly to make available to the aldermen the precedents for the government of the city. To do so he used the town records which he combed with a lawyer's eye. In his introduction he spoke of records 'whereof no recollection hath bein formerly made, and therby lay buried up as it were in a heap of rubbish' which he sought to recover because few of the town's residents were aware of the true nature of its government. His underlying purpose, however, was to argue for the value of the participation of people in their own government. This is how he sees the elected town officials as opposed to the bailiffs who are described as Norman officers to control the town. The stress is on mutual consent and community. He disapproves of monarchs who intervened as 'touching too much as was thought, upon the prerogative of kings . . .'[9] Promoting their towns was the object of studies like Henry Manship at Yarmouth, John Twyn at Canterbury and John Hooker at Exeter.

In the later seventeenth century interest in this appears to have dwindled, and urban studies in the early eighteenth century were dominated by gentlemen and clerics with a fashionable interest in Roman remains, castles and churches rather than recent history. It reflects the increasing integration of the upper classes into town life and their appropriation of its interpretation.[10] A history like John Throsby's *History of Leicester* in 1791 claimed to be novel in that it avoided conjecture, speculation and wonder and confined itself to visible demonstrations of truth. The contents perhaps do not quite live up to these claims as he starts with King Leir and his daughters and devotes much time to scholarly (and now discredited) speculation about the Roman remains, but he does use information from leases and town records to amplify his illustration of the physical remains, from the charters to justify the town's role in defence, from parish registers to establish death rates and from the churchwardens' accounts to detail the reformation changes.[11]

His nineteenth-century successor James Thompson illustrates a swing towards a national perspective and an interest in social history. Much influenced by the French historian, Thierry, he believed that proof was a complete narration which assembled material scientifically and used art to breathe life into it.[12]

The political exploitation of urban histories can be seen in the Irish historiographical tradition from the eighteenth century. Published Irish town histories promoted an English vision of their history and role. Most of them have been described as mediocre and they concentrated on the fashionable interests of the day.

Scottish town histories have a similar national focus, providing a general history of the kingdom into which the occasional events of the town are fitted.[13]

As the nineteenth century advanced, 'professional' and academic histories became a separate genre from the more popular histories which included myth and anecdote and by the later nineteenth century were directed at a growing tourist market. Such popular works, like Walter Thornbury's *Old and New London*,[14] were often still organised topographically. They were not unscholarly but they recorded the stories which formed the common perception of the past. Professional historians were engaged in the establishment of history as a discipline and took every opportunity to denigrate popular or antiquarian works as inadequate or misleading. History was to be 'scientific' and 'objective', which tended to limit study to the technical and demonstrably factual.

Gradually a set pattern for the academic histories evolved which treated each town as a self-contained whole, independent of the world around it. They started with an account of the institutional structure and economic organisation. Most were tightly focused on the individual town and on the narrow issues of the formal authority and management of the corporation. The towns pressed on with publication of borough records like Mary Bateson's *Records of Leicester*. Comparative studies were limited to town administration or the gilds.

The writing of 'patriotic' histories of towns in which national events were external to the actions of the corporation continued for much of the first half of the twentieth century. There was a continuing demand for works which charted and dated matters relating to the ongoing physical and corporate life of the body. Interest in the town as a form of local community which might have significant regional variations, however, slowly grew in the interwar period with the work of historians like W. G. Hoskins and H. P. R. Finberg.

The post-Second World War period saw a significant shift of focus as the British Isles painfully adjusted to a changing status in the world. Early works such as Wallace MacCaffrey's study of Exeter for the first time started to look at the city as part of the wider polity both influential and influenced by the nation, by events outside any individual or corporate control such as the discovery of the Americas, and by imperatives such as religion. A more analytical approach revived interest in the social structure and social life of the people who inhabited the towns. Paul Slack and Peter Clark renewed interest in the history of the poor and the problems of disease in towns. Historians, influenced by architects and sociologists, started to look at the town as built environment which embodied the ideology and vision of the elite and the resistance of the poor. The rituals and symbolism which formed part of the means by which social and political order were maintained were subjected to anthropologically inspired dissection. Not all of these approaches were acceptable to every urban historian. Interest in ritual in particular was seen as breaching the invisible wall which limited historians to matters for which the evidence was direct and relatively unambiguous.

Scholars were increasingly anxious, however, to find means of explicitly addressing the problems of motivation and means. Historians like David Sacks and David Underdown concentrated on the dynamics of change: what enforced shifts in merchant thinking; what effects new trading demands had on the commercial structure of business. The evidence was at best indirect and conjectural but the importance of the subject was imperative. The approach to urban history, which saw each town as an isolated unit, had gone. Susan Brigden embarked upon a major attempt to integrate London and national religious experience of change in the early sixteenth century. Increasingly this is not enough as historians in the context of contemporary supranational developments need to set even national events in a global context.

The questions which historians are now addressing include the following. Was the urban system in Britain a relative failure or a comparative success? What was the level of urbanisation in Britain in 1500 and how had it changed by 1700? What were the dynamics of change? What drew people to towns and cities? What explains the appearance of new towns and the decline of once flourishing settlements. Was it a largely local phenomenon or part of a developing system? Was the growing size of some towns fuelled by new or considerably altered functions? Was it structurally associated with the increasing need for large-scale coordination of economic activities? Were there different ways of organising work? How significant were the interaction of government functions, the management of religion in the interests of social cohesion, the channelling of exchange and control and monopoly control of resources. Did the interplay between specialists living in close proximity with a resultant cross-cutting of social relationships create a new and more fluid community? Was a city more than simply the location in which otherwise significant events occur or did the town occupy a strategic position in the nation?

1

PLACE, SPACE AND TIME – THE BUILT ENVIRONMENT

Towns and cities are not alike, even if they share an underlying common structure and similar objectives. One of the most immediate factors which differentiates them is their physical appearance. The importance of this environment to a sense of urban identity was crucial. The importance of location to their success was fundamental.

The Location of Towns

Towns, if they were to prosper, had to draw the world towards them and so they had to be placed where they could, relatively conveniently, serve the needs of a more or less extensive hinterland. The location of a town was critical to its success. Some had the potential to serve a wide area; others, handicapped in one way or another, were never likely to have more than a local significance. This is the argument of locational theorists, who, however, work mainly on recent history and see a long-standing and predictable relationship which may not apply so neatly to an earlier period.

By 1500 considerations which were critical in the early location of towns, such as strategic, defensive and administrative needs, were becoming less important. Trade was retaining its importance or growing while service functions, religious functions, and a manufacturing role were also developing. Towns which served only a single need were most vulnerable to decline. As functions waxed and waned, the fortunes of individual towns certainly rose or faded, but the critical question remains whether in this period one set of determiners is largely replaced by another, affecting the whole distribution of towns in the islands.

The mixture of defence and trading functions can be seen particularly clearly in areas like North and South Wales where the early towns spread in a line along the coast, each located where a valley opened to the sea. The sites were chosen either for natural defensibility or conversely because strategically a bridge or ford or pass needed defence. Speed's description of Haverfordwest shows a desirable combination of these features. It was situated on a steep bank, guarded by the river Tyvy, which was passable only by a bridge under the castle, and its walls took advantage of the rising rocks.

Most of the more important towns had been ports from the start. Often positioned at the highest tidal point on a river through which they dominated the valleys and plains beyond, they provided access to cheap water transport. Inland towns like Worcester, Shrewsbury and Bridgnorth were also in some ways ports. Developed on the only three crossings of the Severn they flourished on the intersection of water and land routes. Lesser markets were usually on the margins of two different regions. If regions shifted such markets might fade. By 1500 most of these more obvious sites in Britain already served a small settlement although there would be a spate of 'new town' creation in Ireland, new towns were founded in Scotland and a few new ports were established on the North Western coast of England. Some new towns which appeared, or developed from insignificant villages in this period, did so as centres of new industry. This fits the location theory which claims that an industry using economies of scale would produce a concentration of economic activity in a small spatial location, that is, a town.

The Social Organisation of Urban Space

The extent to which urban life was enjoyable or even tolerable was very much governed by the degree of crowding which the available space required. Our concept of a crowded city may not apply to many of the smaller towns in Britain since their density of population may have been low both by medieval and modern standards. While density may have started low, however, fairly small numbers could rapidly build up to unacceptable levels of overcrowding as infilling and cramped additions to buildings destroyed the original town layout.

One of the major changes which took place between 1500 and 1700 was the physical reshaping of the built environment of the town. In the sixteenth century Britain lacked the glories of the European Renaissance city. Only after the Restoration were some towns rebuilt to embody the grandeur to which an increasingly gentrified residential class aspired. The reshaping signalled the enforcement of a new social order. Space was a political form. The socio-economic controls which regulated access to key positions, by which the powerless were relegated to the insalubrious areas in either formal or informal ghettos, were very much the product of building and town planning – an issue which the 'Chicago school' of urban studies made its focal point.

To its inhabitants and those that visited it the most immediate impact of a town came from its buildings, the physical environment they saw, heard and smelt; that in which they lived and conducted their business, ate, bathed, made love and war and to whose form they had to a greater or lesser extent contributed. The symbolism of its physical structure for the daily life of inhabitants was critical and often complex, particularly in the more populous towns with limited space. Catering for most human activities within this restricted space, which was often also constrained by the terrain, required careful functional divisions. Changing requirements over the period resulted in significant rebuilding or modification. Such alterations to the town environment affected the lives and perceptions of its inhabitants.

Town layouts had great representational and symbolic value. Consciously or unconsciously there was a ritual embodied in the architecture. The positioning of particular buildings privileged them in the chain of everyday life. The wealth and identity of a town were reflected in its walls and castles, churches and town-halls, gaols, schools and almshouses, public roads and sightlines. The imposing private houses, which were generally on its main streets, were the physical representation of its being. Many towns were dominated architecturally by the local landlord's house. In Carrickfergus this was the home of Sir Arthur Chichester which Brereton on his travels described as 'very stately or rather like a palace'.[1] At Whitehaven, a town deliberately designed on a grid-iron pattern, Lowther's hall was the focal point of the main axis.[2]

The external and internal layout of the buildings represented the practices of government, worship and family life. New histo-ricists draw symbolic meaning from the idea of outside and inside, chaos and order in building forms. Even though some of these differences, such as building materials, might be merely superficial, they too served to instal in the imagination of the indweller the distinctive character of the home town. Towns were not wholly urban, however, with the country often encroaching on the town which possessed common fields and pastures, and these too played their part in the creation of an urban image.

Contemporaries were aware of the importance of the physical environment. Leland routinely comments on position and ap-pearance and both were important to the community on a number of different levels. Few of the towns he visited were architecturally impressive in the 1530s. Only the cathedrals and a few churches had had resources lavished upon them. The castles associated with them had been built for strength and had not yet been replaced by palaces. Their amenities were limited. The most far-reaching practical effects of architecture, however, are not on a superficial visual level but are felt in terms of space and its use[3] which is destroyed by rebuilding. Archaeology, now, is helping us unveil the earlier urban life-style and while written records are patchy, we can see some towns as the authorities wanted them to appear.

A new way of presenting this material fabric emerged in the sixteenth century with the growing popularity of town maps. These order and present towns as planned structures centring on markets, cathedrals and castles. The increasing sophistication of map-making techniques gives us the image of the city which government sources were promoting, supplemented by early descriptions such as those in Camden's *Britannia*. Thus Camden wrote of Cork as 'of an oval figure surrounded by walls, environed and intersected by the river which is passable only by bridges and consisting of one straight street continued by a bridge . . . . a little trading town of great resort but so beset by rebellious neighbours as to require as constant watch as if continually besieged'.

Increasing numbers of maps provide a visual record of the changes to the physical presentation of the towns which had a revolutionary impact on perceptions of urban life. The maps show which structures were considered most important to the town. Generally in the sixteenth century they show town walls, churches with towers and steeple, the town-hall, market cross, schools and almshouses. Thus what Gutkind calls 'the language of form characteristic of a given period'[4] can tell us a great deal about the contemporary purpose for towns and its shifts over time. The tower houses which are prominent in so many early Irish town maps and the fortified warehouses at Ardglass and Galway are visual evidence of a society preoccupied with defence. By 1700 there has been a shift from defence to gracious living.

Town Plans

The basic arrangement of dwellings and other buildings in the town, their juxtaposition and means of access and the relationship of one to another had a profound effect on the way people conducted their lives, how frequently they met their neighbours, where they did their business, and where they spent their leisure. Anthropological studies of primitive settlement show that the orientation of houses has much to do with ease of access from one to another and little to do with regular alignment. A rough distinction may then be seen between such settlements and towns based on a regular Roman pattern. Much has been made of the distinction between the irregular, native town plans in Wales or Ireland, and the regular, deliberately designed and Renaissance-inspired plantation or settlement towns like Derry, whose rebuilders after 1608 were clearly influenced by continental theory, and copied the French city of Vitry le François.[5]

The winding alleys and haphazard building in the earlier towns like Kilkenny can, however, also be seen in early English settlement towns like Galway. The apparent irregularity of some plans is simply a different focus on a monastery or cathedral church as at Armagh or in medieval Canterbury. A regular plan makes military control easier. Dominance in a regular grid pattern is easier as the straight streets offer little shelter for urban guerilla warfare. A major restructuring of a town layout, however, indicates a shift of purpose. The layout of medieval Canterbury was destroyed by the construction of a main east-west thoroughfare involving a new gate and a street grid bypassing the cathedral, which shifted the town's focus away from the church.[6]

Where an older structure could not be easily reformed an effective 'new town' sometimes developed on a separate estate, as one did at Bewdley in the fourteenth century on the land of the Countess of March. Most long-existent towns are composite in form with a number of separate 'units' planned at different dates as town functions altered or expanded. A careful analysis of the size and shape of the building blocks can identify the early layout of the towns and the later infill and rebuilding and extensions. The town fields, often managed by the corporation, usually surrounded the built-up area but where town walls encompassed a greater area than was built on, some plots were within the walls. The value of the fields to the town is indicated by the reluctance of the authorities to surrender them for house buildings, so that they often came to form a *cordon sanitaire* beyond which building resumed.

Town layouts reflect social life. The existence of 'double towns' often points to racial divisions. Thus Limerick was divided between the English town or high town and the 'Irish town'.[7] In many English towns an early division between a free and villein settlement was obliterated and forgotten by the sixteenth century. Occasionally the division is reflected in the market place. Aberdeen had two market crosses, the High or Fleshe cross at the west end of Castlegate, and the Lesser or Fish Cross at the east end. Futtie quarter was almost a suburb populated by an independent community of fisherfolk in frequent conflict with the authorities over their rights with its own church dedicated to St Clement.

Some Common Features of Town Plans

Historical geographers consider that most towns started with a single street pattern ('linear') which then developed short cross streets, ('cruciform' or 'developed cruciform') which may become an irregular block. 'T form' or 'developed T form' may be imposed by the local morphology and become again an irregular block. A secondary street running parallel to the first may have developed in the larger towns. Frequently, however, this basic pattern had an infill of what is commonly described as a maze of lanes, in places like Yarmouth which were often too narrow for even a handcart to pass. Where there was population pressure, workshops and storehouses on back lanes were rebuilt as cottages often approached by insanitary alleys. Towns like Dartmouth built in narrow valleys had to adapt their housing to the space and often built upwards. Tall narrow houses corbelled over the street were common.

A true grid pattern tends to indicate a settlement town with military and administrative objectives. Walls were designed for military convenience and many towns such as Radnor, Rhuddlan, and Winchelsea never filled the area enclosed. Where town walls were constructed early they affected the original town plan. This marks a distinction between Ireland, where most significant towns were walled; Scotland, where walls were a late innovation; and England, where many towns were never walled. Nevertheless at least 108 English towns were walled in the Middle Ages mostly with the help of the right to collect a special tax. The building of defences had been common and by the later Middle Ages in some places these had turned into stone walls. Ireland had at least 56 towns, including all the most important, walled at some stage; Wales had 21 walled towns.

Dominant and Symbolic Features

Walled or unwalled, the heart of the British town in 1500 was the market place, often a triangular open space. Markets were a double-edged symbol since they represented voluntary exchange, or peaceful activities, but in as much as they were regulated also denoted acceptance of government authority. It was quite common and again symbolic, for the market place to adjoin the church, the second pillar of the realm and justifier of rule and obedience. Indeed, the churchyard might sometimes be an adjunct or substitute for the open space especially in Wales and in the smaller Scottish towns. The main streets usually converged on the markets. These open places notionally belonged to all, but were increasingly regulated in the interest of a particular idea of social control. At the same time the irregularities of back lanes, stairs and alleys gave opportunities for frequent, unstructured social intercourse. The importance of the market, however, was in decline by 1700. Ports with good harbours had a different focus and a particular structure centred on rivers, quays and a harbour, usually fortified.

The priority which a town's inhabitants gave in any period to providing or maintaining particular public works provides a clear indication of what they valued most. Where town walls were constructed there is both practical and symbolic significance. They are 'an indication of what the town thought it ought to be'. Magnificent walls indicated prosperity and self-confidence and maintaining them was a form of local patriotism.[8] Citizens were reminded of their separateness and their community of interest. The cost of this public face was considerable and the construction time could employ large numbers of labourers for years. When new walls were built for Derry in 1613–18 the 1700-yard circuit cost £10 357. Such walls in Britain seldom reached the size and impressiveness of continental walls but they were sufficient for their purpose.

Public Buildings

The form of public building embodies ideas of hierarchy. When as a result of a bequest Monmouth was able to build itself a court house, the interior was to have 'a fair board in manner of a Chequer' with benches and forms 'handsomely and decently appointed' and with a bar to keep out strangers.[9] The use of barriers, steps and canopies emphasised the idea of social distance and hierarchical position. Often the central seat in such a court had a tapestry with the royal coat of arms over it, to emphasise that the courts were the monarch's court and that the individual seated below was the representative of royalty.

This formal sense of hierarchy was reinforced in the church, particularly after the Reformation when the provision of pews and the allocation of pews to individuals, who usually paid pro rata for their position, introduced a visible record of an individual's standing. The town officials were prominent and if the monarch came to visit a special throne was erected and rows of seating moved to accommodate it. One of the ways in which the Yarmouth authorities slighted the Cinque Ports representatives when they came to hold their annual Herring Fair was a pointed failure to offer them the prominent seat which their public position required. Where seating plans survive for a period of years, the growing status of individuals can be measured by their gradual shift from a modest pew at the back to the prominent pews at the front.

On the other hand, the existence of formal public buildings was limited. In 1500 even in the largest towns there were comparatively few public buildings. In York although there were two council chambers there was no official residence for the mayor and only four craft halls.[10] The assertion of a town's prosperity could often be the construction of a new town hall or tollbooth, church or chapel. The existence of a formal mayoral residence was uncommon except in the greater towns. The mayor was expected to have a suitable residence of his own for his public duties. These might include entertaining royalty or important councillors, but more routinely included assize judges and visiting commissioners. The mayoral feast was also held there – often demanding more than one room.

This mixing of public and private extended to the inns, which were also often used for public activities, even the holding of courts, as was the case at Faringdon in Oxfordshire. Inns had a much wider role than the modern public house.[11] Ideally fronting the market place, they were the termini of public transport, the centres from which merchants did business in market and fair time, as well as places providing accommodation, food and drink, the focus of gossip and intrigue. They usually had a narrow frontage but several yards behind, frequently galleried, with stabling and warehousing at the back. The main buttery or bar area was at ground level in the front, but there were private rooms which could be rented. A good inn had extensive kitchens and cellars below. They were centres for entertainment such as plays, prize-fighting (if it was not outlawed by the authorities) and dancing.

Private Buildings

Private housing also had a public image. The rebuilding of a significant number of houses in a particular style implied the restructuring of a cultural image. Thus in 1615, at Armagh, a scheme for replacing some of the existing houses with two-storey houses of brick, stone or timber, with specified dimensions and an 'English' form had a clear political significance.[12] Town houses were gradually changing from the medieval pattern with a great hall either on the ground or first floor. Merchants' houses were increasingly narrow and tall with two or three rooms on each floor. Shop, kitchen and sometimes parlour were now usually on the ground floor with chambers above. Workshops were usually on the back streets. They might include butteries, brew houses, bolting houses, stables and barns as well as the space for the principal craft. In a port like King's Lynn the most desirable residences backed on to the river, giving direct access to the sea. Such houses evidently developed as soon as towns reached a certain size in every kingdom. As pressure on space grew the houses were built higher. Where a growing city did not spread beyond its walls the built area rapidly became crowded and the compression of a large number of people into a small area had both social and hygienic implications. The infilling aggravated problems of water, sewage and rubbish collection.

Prestige was also associated with a frontage to the main street. Norden's survey of Wrexham in the 1620s takes us down the High Street in which gentry like Sir Henry Salusbury and Hugh Meredith Esquire held impressive houses, while others who can be identified as the younger sons of local gentry families held houses in which they conducted merchant businesses. Such people were not merely neighbours. Many of them were also related by marriage. These private houses were becoming more affluent. A wealthy butcher's house in Leicester was handsomely furnished with painted cloths, tables, forms, chairs, carpets, joined bedsteads and even flower pots.[13] Location theory suggests that the narrow frontage and deep curtilage served the inhabitants well for swift access to market and business, courts and administration.

The distinction between the houses of the affluent and the poor was marked. In 1641 a civil survey in Ireland was conducted, which provides a house-to-house record of Cork, Limerick and Kilmalloch. The better houses were stone and slated, 'front' houses were usually three storeys plus attic, 'backhouses' two storeys and attic. Outside the walls there were cabins with mud walls and no chimneys. The stone houses averaged seven rooms usually on three storeys, the thatched tenements five, thatched houses four and cabins two.[14]

The Urban Scene

The urban scene within this setting of public and private space – streets, squares, town walls and bridges, churches and cathedrals, town halls and guildhalls, water and sewage, ports and dockyards – represented the reality of life for townspeople. The rights of the passing throng to walk abroad unmolested, to meet together in groups of different sizes, to linger, to play, to drink and eat, to worship and make love and bury their dead, were structured within this environment. Tangible forms were not the only compelling aspects which constrained them. The formal ringing of bells for victories, coronations, royal births and deaths were part of the structure of power. Glasgow had four bells, one of which was 'the old bell that ged throw the towne of auld at the buriall of the dead' and the 'skellat' bell which was used for inviting offers to purchase goods. Ceremonial was an important part of the fabric of urban life. Before the Reformation the hierarchy of urban society was expressed in frequent religious processions in which order was represented by the marching of officials and craftsmen in their livery. After the Reformation processions were more limited, but the carrying of emblems of authority, such as the town mace, and common worship partially replaced them. The symbols which formed the town's self-image changed but their importance continued.

This scene was fully fledged in the larger densely populated, often walled, town where the gates were shut at night and public space was at a minimum. Whether it was paralleled in small, unwalled market towns where a few hundred yards took the walker into the fields has yet to be investigated. Even in the smallest town, however, the allocation of city space – its spatial organisation – was determined by social and economic structuring which was constantly changing. Access to urban space was not equally allocated. The less privileged were excluded from certain areas.

Space had a temporal dimension – what was permitted at some hours might be prohibited at others. Nightwalking is the obvious example. Space could also be given different 'forms' for limited times, such as the creation of a 'fair' within marked boundaries, or the creation of a 'court', public and privileged, in a temporary location. There were areas to which all might normally have access, such as the market place, and areas to which access was restricted such as the church chancel and house interiors accessible only to members of the household or invited visitors. Some areas were forbidden to women and children.

These constraints affected the way in which daily life was conducted. House and street layouts affected the routine movements of people as they slept and woke, ate and defecated, worked, shopped, worshipped and played. In the common, better quality, side-entry type of house, with its multiple hearths and single long passage off which shop and main rooms had their entry, the movement of family, friends and clients can be envisaged. The best rooms were usually on the first floor and if they were let to lodgers it imposed frequent contact on the family as they passed back and forth from ground to second floor. The degree of control which husband or wife could exercise depended on the possibility of gate-keeping which the access permitted. In the smaller houses of the poor, a quite different pattern of movement is likely.

What is harder to determine is how many people lived in each house – the distinction between a family and a 'houseful' – and whether this varied from town to town or area to area within a town. Families might take in a lodger, or several lodgers, but in most tax records they would be treated as a separate group. Only the most careful and painstaking matching of records where houses and streets can be matched to tax 'units' can give some idea of the physical housing of tax groups. High rents and shortage of central space for building combined to push people into a familiar proximity. The precise nature of the relationship between spatial organisation and social life is difficult to tease out but it is important because domestication has been represented as a discourse of power[15] and profound changes may be concealed behind minor physical shifts.

Changing Urban Appearance

A number of significant changes in the physical layout of towns and the buildings and so of the life people led within them occurred. The greatest improvement forced upon town dwellers in the period was a change in building materials. In 1500 towns built mainly of stone like Stirling were the exception. Most towns throughout Britain were still built of timber, or wickerwork with an outer covering of clay, and a floor of clay and thatched roof. It was a matter for comment that a small town like Oundle was all stone built. Even in a big town like York many of the houses were single-storey thatched hovels of one or two rooms.

Frequent disastrous fires, often the result of the interleaving of domestic and industrial activity, caused town authorities every-where to attempt to regulate the building materials. Thatched roofs were gradually outlawed. Brick or stone was slowly replacing timber helped by the increasing scarcity of suitable wood. Power to coerce the property owners was, however, limited so the process was slow. Where they could, the town authorities were improving their town's facilities. Greater emphasis on water supplies and sanitation, better roads and safer building materials spread throughout the bigger towns. Improvement was part of regular town activities and competition to construct impressive public buildings in the most fashionable style was increasing.

The physical landmarks which distinguished a town were changing. Town walls and a castle were increasingly irrelevant everywhere except perhaps in Ireland. Their destruction opened the town to the countryside. The physical market place was losing its dominance as merchants dealt by sample and on consignment. What mattered was an imposing town hall, a suitable hospital, fine schools, well-paved and well-lit streets and if possible additional embellishments such as libraries and town walks which improved the overall amenities. Increasingly towns which lacked such adjuncts were scarcely to be honoured with the title. As Peter Borsay suggests, the town in 1714 would have been hardly recognisable to a Rip van Winkle from 1500.

The image of the larger town was no longer primarily defence and survival but civility and society. Workshops had been moved out of sight of the main concourse; instead there were the fashionable fully glazed enclosed shops with chairs for the clients, shelves and counters for display, looking glasses and other accessories first seen in London in the mid-seventeenth century. These smart shops transformed the shopping experience and introduced a new element to town life. A sense that style and presentation mattered, that vistas should be planned and managed undoubtedly related to the formalisation of hierarchical relations and a growing distinction of public and private. This is also reflected in a burst of enthusiasm for constructing town halls, which were the symbol of political control.

The restructuring of the town centre was accelerating changes to residential patterns. While these had always tended to be affected by topographical requirements such as the need for water which had resulted in the location of weavers, fullers and dyers near any rivers, brooks and streams, the distinctions were becoming more absolute. There was a growing tendency as towns grew in size and complexity for an originally undifferentiated distribution of rich and poor, in which people of many different conditions lived side-by-side, to give way to a development of some better favoured areas for the rich while the poor were relegated to more crowded and less congenial parts. Newcastle upon Tyne, one of the most prosperous cities in England, its fortunes securely based on an inexhaustible demand for coal, salt and glass, illustrates the process. The town itself was divided by internal walls into the upper and lower (or sandhills) towns. The Tyne keelmen lived east of the sandgate but most of the population were still within the walls, the majority in the lower town. Rich and poor were not sharply divided but while the labourers lived in the stairs or the alleys leading to the quay, the wealthy merchants lived near the cloth market and the gentry and clergy near the Westgate and in Pilgrim Street.

In Bristol, which prided itself on its reputation for fine buildings, clean streets and excellent water supply, the merchants lived in fashionable Small Street, while St Augustine the Less housed sailors and lightermen and other trades associated with boats and their building, and the Irish migrants huddled in the less salubrious areas. In most towns there were streets which were clearly wealthier and areas inhabited by the poor. Not surprisingly, perhaps, the poorer districts were those that suffered more in epidemics.

In general, in the sixteenth and seventeenth centuries, the richer districts tended to be central while the poorer suburbs were further from the centre and near the walls, if they existed. Alongside this differentiation, there was developing a greater likelihood that the workplace was or was becoming distinct from the home. This cannot be carried too far. Work like fishing had always taken the worker away from home. Some major crafts like masonry and carpentry were essentially peripatetic. Certain trades like milling had from an early period demanded separate purpose-built buildings with the miller living alongside.

The development of new large-scale manufactories for brewing and so on was increasing the percentage of people who travelled to work and the special needs of forges tended to separate them from the home, but many houses throughout the period were still being built as workplaces. This often meant that one or more rooms were designed for the specific trade of the occupant. In the textile trades, light was a vital consideration and the rooms were often set on the first-floor south-facing side to maximise natural light. Bakers' need for ovens equally required particular structures. The extent to which there was a division of home and workplace thus tended to differ according to the main trade in the particular town under investigation.

Public building in the Restoration period was matched by much rebuilding of houses particularly by the wealthier townsfolk. Even Welsh towns were being rebuilt on grander lines. The movement of the gentry into towns helped the process. In a town like Monmouth the building of a great house for the Earl of Worcester had spin-offs in improvements to the technological skills of local building tradesmen and so to the design and construction of lesser houses.[16] After the Great Fire, merchant houses in London were standardised: they were narrow-fronted brick buildings four storeys high on main streets; three on side streets and lanes; and two on bye-lanes; with two or three rooms a floor. Usually the shop or workshop would be on the ground floor, the kitchen/dining room on the first with bedrooms on the floors above. Dublin between 1680 and 1730 built similar gabled houses in the fashionable Dutch style in the centre and in the Liberties (enclaves exempt from town control). From 1660 well-built brick two- or three-storey houses with a garret for looms and cloth inspection were built round small squares. Many of the houses, however, were still the old 'cage work' style wooden buildings made so that they could be taken down and put up at will. Edinburgh's building was at this time was less elaborate and the furnishings more austere. The wealthier inhabitants of the provincial towns were imitating the pretensions of the capitals. Town gardens were beginning to be popular and were easier and cheaper outside the capitals.

How far the improvements extended is another question. Rebuilding in England was generally more advanced than building in the other kingdoms. Most Irish town property was still modest. An English house in Ireland usually meant a stone chimney. In Sligo a 1663 survey records that most two-storey houses were only 12–15 foot wide and 30–45 foot deep while the one-storey cabins on average covered even less ground.[17] Similarly houses in Welsh towns before 1660 were two storey but although stone-built, were usually even smaller. The rooms were often only 10 by 10 and the medieval style of a hall on the first floor continued, although fireplaces gradually came in.[18]

There has been a debate about whether comfort increased in the period. Certainly it seems to have done so for the better off as such things as glazing ceased to be an occasional luxury and became too routine even for separate mention in inventories. Conveniences such as the introduction of sash windows and better lighting were spreading and houses were becoming larger and more elaborately furnished. A house which was exceptional in the sixteenth century was, by 1700, built with better materials and, with increasing prosperity, quite common.

Where the humbler buildings can be identified, however, it seems that the poor still lived in wooden huts or hovels of lath and plaster, often only with two rooms, without a chimney and with little furniture. These houses, however, were less visible as towns were restructured so that their public face focused attention on selected areas. The wealthy then were able to purchase locational advantage while the poor remained locationally disadvantaged. Such segregation carried to extremes meant that a town might house many separate communities, some the result of religious migration, some of occupational activities, some economic and some social.

The increasing intervention of government in the use of space may be significant. Marxists tend to see urban form as reproducing capitalist relations in general and reflecting the commodification of the city.[19] Without adopting Marxism, one may see a process whereby a relatively homogenous social distribution with rich and poor intermingled gives way to a socially and economically differentiated spatial distribution as an indicator of an altering perception of human relations. The access of humbler people to the streets and shops of the wealthy may have been limited by problems of dress and manners. Policing was increasingly based on appearance and presentation. Divisions were appearing in recreations and sports, so that the myth of a common community associating young and old, rich and poor alike, was largely abandoned.

Conclusion

The shift in the dominant image between 1500 and 1700 is remarkable and reflects the shift in urban function. The tight-knit, defensible small cluster of unimpressive buildings focused on church and market place is giving way in the more prosperous towns to an open, organised street-based structure, dominated by town hall and great houses, competing for architectural distinction, looking outward towards other towns and cities. This was reinforcing a sense of hierarchy, distinguishing the city with its increasing density of population from the country town where population pressure was less, and from small towns where there had been little money and perhaps less incentive to alter the physical appearance of a settlement whose population growth had been slight in relative terms.

2

SOCIAL STRUCTURE AND SOCIAL EXPERIENCE IN THE TOWN

Towns drew people to them in part because they offered a richer and more varied social life. The strength of the attraction varied from period to period, but between 1500 and 1700 the pull seemed to be strengthening for both rich and poor. There was an urban dimension to the social process which came from the greater frequency of contact between people of all ranks.

For richer and poorer, young and old, honest and dishonest, there was a range of different activities and entertainments. The ways in which these varied between towns and over time is significant not only for the experience of the individual but for the power structure and economic controls which resulted from them. Understanding urban social structure is the key to under-standing much political change. Both economic determinists and Marxists, for example, have seen the growth of a gulf between rich and poor as important for the growth of capitalism. Another indicator of, and at the same time explanation for, urbanisation is the appearance of a sizeable economic 'middle group' in society, skilled individuals who promote activity and consume its product. The concentration of wealth is seen as attracting more and more activities to towns.

A great deal of historical effort has therefore been directed at establishing the structural aspects of town life. The increasing complexity of larger towns or cities has been co-related with greater specialisation and significant economic development. Until recently the survival or creation of smaller towns, which had a less specialised social structure in which one person might have a number of occupations, cultivating a share of the common fields to support or supplement the household food supply, brewing for domestic consumption or petty sale, as well as industrial activity, has been given less importance, although a fully articulated explanation needs to include them.

Forms of Analysis

Social structure can be envisaged in a number of different if overlapping ways. It can be analysed as a 'fixed' set of relationships between those of different education, status and wealth. Alternatively, it can be considered as a way in which people reproduce values, ideas and practices – material and religious culture. The people may then be studied as producing children, establishing social relationships inside and beyond the household with kin and with community, and producing the food, clothing, goods and services which maintain them. They may be seen as establishing an identity for themselves. An accepted occupation was, as Corfield has said, a badge of respectability and of an identified and approved position in the community. All of these things were part of a system of giving meaning to life, and questions as to whether urban attitudes varied significantly from rural ones have been much neglected for this period.

Interest in the fixed social composition of the country goes back to the late seventeenth century when the Royal Society was promoting investigation into many areas. Growing numeracy encouraged informal censuses. Gregory King in the 1690s attempted a 'scientific' analysis of the population based, as he claimed, on the evidence of taxes and surveys and personal investigation into average household size in different wealth and employment categories. Historians have demonstrated that his work was less thorough than he claimed, and have revised his social tables, increasing the numbers of shopkeepers and traders and inserting about 200 000 families living from manufacturing and building trades. William Petty provided some basic figures for late seventeenth century Ireland and from these and various taxation returns the internal social and occupational structure of British towns is being investigated. They varied enormously in complexity from the metropolis of London to Welsh towns, which were mostly small even by contemporary standards with a social structure which has been described as 'woefully shallow'. The few wealthy merchants were outnumbered by the many yeomen and husbandmen who were partly rural in their activities.[1]

Analysis of Social Structure

Questions which are asked of the static structure include the general composition of the population, age, sex ratio, life expectancy, employment, wealth and its distribution between different groups. Marrying the scanty sources to answer these questions is more difficult. Life-expectancy tables for the kingdoms are fraught with difficulties, and the production of separate urban tables involves massive assumptions. Certain peculiarities have been observed. The numbers of children in the larger towns was low, either from poor infant mortality or because they were sent away for nursing and education. Conversely, the percentage of young adults was disproportionately high as migrants of both sexes sought betterment and training. Not all of these incomers stayed in the towns, even if they survived, once they had saleable skills. The life expectancy of the poor was usually worse than that of the more comfortably off, the differential incidence of disease in separate parts of many cities suggesting that it was the poor who clustered in the less sanitary areas.[2] Women formed a higher percentage of town residents than men although on average they seem to have married younger than their rural counterparts.

Employment categories are hard to classify. Independent employers, skilled employees, and unskilled labourers do not conveniently cover all the forms of economic activity to be found in towns. The percentage of those who were independent employers varied from town to town, but rarely exceeded 15 per cent of the population. Such independence did not necessarily co-relate perfectly with wealth, as some respectable crafts like shoemaking did not produce a significant long-distance trading commodity. At the other end of the scale the unskilled might represent up to 40 per cent of the population. What constituted skilled employment is also debatable. Did it include domestic service? Where should apprentices be included – in the servant class or in the skilled employment to which they were aspiring?

The shape of the hierarchy is generally seen as pyramidal with the wealth concentrated in the hands of the top 5 to 10 per cent. Although different towns show significantly different percentages of people in the different bands, with some towns like Salisbury having larger numbers of poor and exempt people, early suggestions that an unbridgeable gap was developing between rich and poor do not seem to be borne out by analysis of tax records.

Over the period it looks as if a middle class of largely urban dwellers was coming into existence. The growing demand for the services of groups who saw themselves as professionals, such as lawyers, physicians, surgeons, apothecaries, and even the clergy, meant increasing numbers of a non-mercantile middle class living in at least the larger towns. They lived and described themselves as gentlemen and expected a comparable life-style which created employment for others. Merchants who had reached the top of the *cursus honorum* might also be accepted as gentlemen or even esquires.

There seems little evidence that the upper echelons in the towns were a closed and impermeable caste. English and Welsh towns generally saw a fairly rapid turnover in leading families as the descendants of families who had been successful retired to the country or moved on. Norwich was comparatively unusual in that in the sixteenth century its aldermanic body was dominated by eleven families most of whom were connected by marriage. In the seventeenth century, the families that replaced them were also increasingly connected to the leading county families which was more typical of all the major towns.

Townsmen and women in England had significant links with their hinterland at all levels of society. The wealthier York businessmen were connected to the local rural elite by birth or marriage.[3] The formal status of town dwellers, that is whether they were freemen, residents or 'foreigners' and whether they had achieved freeman status by inheritance, apprenticeship marriage or purchase, may conceal more significant elements in the social pattern. This is now viewed more as a network in which birth and connections partly determine position.

This pattern does not repeat itself in Ireland where there was more consciousness of difference. Many Irish towns, especially in the sixteenth century, had a small and apparently stable population with constant intermarriage between their chief families and limited opportunity for outsiders to join the magic circle. The continuity of a few dominant families is much more marked than in most English cities. Between 1558 and 1625 only 12 different surnames appear amongst the mayors of Cork with Tury, Roche and Galloways holding the mayoralty in half the years. A similar situation prevailed in Youghal and Galway.[4] In the lesser towns like Sligo, it is apparent that some of the more substantial merchant families had come from its bigger neighbour, Galway, while others were Scottish, and that all had links to Dublin. Although by 1680 there was no segregation – Old English, Irish, English and Scots living side by side in the same street – relations between Catholics and Protestants were difficult.[5]

Even though they might not participate in urban government, the towns' elites thus increasingly were not wholly composed of a merchant element. The significant professional residents – clergy and doctors, schoolmasters and lawyers and in garrison towns military or naval officers – were an influential part of the social structure and when assessed for taxes, also often in the top assessment bracket. A town like Lichfield, although small, was largely a professional centre well known for its educational facilities. By the late seventeenth century its wealthiest taxpayers were the clergy and gentry rather than the merchants.[6] Caernarvon was an administrative centre where the top rank were lawyers and gentlemen.[7]

Apprentices and Other Immigrants

While towns were developing these more complex social layers they were increasingly and measurably different from one another in terms of their *raison d'être*. The hierarchy inside the business community in any given town was largely related to its dominant economic and social bias, so that in a town like Leicester butchers were prominent. The dominant economic bias was reflected in the percentage of different businesses that were to be found and in the distribution of wealth between them. Position in the social hierarchy was largely determined by wealth. In most towns the wealthiest merchants were often the wholesale clothiers who effectively controlled the specialist trades like fullers and dyers. Goldsmiths were also likely to be wealthy, while there was a large middle group of trades from which people could expect to make a reasonable if not an affluent living, including tanning and saddle-making, cutlers and pewterers. Weavers were rarely more than comfortably off. These rankings were not immutable. The demand for particular products varied. The cost of apprenticeship to a particular craft at any given moment is a good indication of the current estimate of their profitability. At the same time, many of these trades were interdependent, creating a network of commercial relationships.

The attraction of apprenticeship was one factor which drew migrants to the town, maintaining or increasing the level of population. Mobility at lower social levels was evidently also high if the considerable turnover of population from one tax collection to the next is a good indicator. In 1570 only half of the 2300 registered poor in Norwich were locally born, and if the young children are removed the percentage rises markedly.

The larger town could not survive without migration which was essential to maintain its numbers. The stimulus to individuals to move usually divided into betterment migration and subsistence migration. The benefits of the first which encompasses the movement of apprentices and others expecting improved employment prospects seems clear; the benefits of the second which includes people who were little more than vagrants, includes the prospect of work even if unskilled, food in times of famine, and charities.

The geographical origins of apprentices can occasionally be established from freemen's rolls but the poor avoided registration. What evidence there is suggests that the routes which English migrants took to the city were often well worn and they went very often to districts where they might find friends or kinsmen or where they had commercial connections. Immigrants did not necessarily come as strangers to the town, and find support networks when they arrived or forge them in the neighbour-hoods in which they settled, or sometimes in the gilds where they had a strong hold. Those who came as apprentices came to a settled place in the society. They did not necessarily stay. There is substantial evidence of the out-migration of skilled artisans especially when they had finished their apprenticeships, and the tendency of skilled workmen to move to places where there was demand for their skills.

Analysis of apprenticeship records in Bristol show that in the 1530s over 70 per cent came from outside the city. Between 1625 and 35 the percentage had dropped to just under two thirds but it still reflects the extent to which the city was not self-generating. Two thirds of those taking the freedom each year had been apprentices and nearly 16 per cent more were admitted by marriage.[8] Most apprentices came from the county – in Norwich 70 per cent came from Norfolk and another 11 from Suffolk. Although most were described as sons of husbandmen, the number of gentlemen's sons was rising steadily. Prolific gentlemen of the highest rank like the Knightleys of Fawsley did not hesitate to apprentice younger sons or marry their younger daughters to London merchants even though their eldest sons might marry the daughters of dukes, and serve as cupbearers to the king.

Sources of migrants in Ireland were somewhat different. A town like Galway according to Oliver St John 'rarely admit any new English to have freedom or education among them and never any of the Irish'.[9] The ethnic composition of many towns can be ascertained from the 1659 census and shows marked variations. In the small towns in Ulster there were more settlers than natives in the towns but in Munster there were more than six Irish to every settler and Connacht and Leinster fall in between.

Those who came as refugees from religious persecution had a more difficult time. Most came to towns with enough of their like to be assured of a church of their own – even if, as at Canterbury, they were assigned a part of another church as a meeting place. While the refugees were often predominantly trained in the same craft, such as textiles in sixteenth-century Canterbury or silk weaving, they were not confined to this. The refugees in Bristol in the late seventeenth century included sailors, fishermen, salters, and farmers as well as wealthy merchants and textile workers.

The ties which bound people together in a town were thus both complex and variable. One aspect which is often overlooked is the landlord/tenant relationship. Most people rented their dwelling place and thus had a relationship with a wealthier individual. Where the town elite also owned much of the property, they had considerable leverage over those who were their tenants. Pound states that 40 per cent of the poor in Norwich lived in property which belonged to the aldermen although they, in their official capacity, were discouraging the inward migration of such people.[10]

The cost of housing varied from town to town. In the capitals rents for the more prestigious houses were up to £60–80 p.a. by 1700. In the poorest areas a house might cost £20 to rent and given that journeymen might only earn that in a year over and above board, there was a great tendency to rent rooms out to help balance the budget. A first-floor room in a prestigious street could bring in up to £20 a year.

Household and Family

Some aspects of the family can be established from parish registers. The average age of people of different rank at marriage, the number of children and the percentage of those who survived, length of marriage and the percentage of remarriages are reasonably well known. Families, however, did not always live together for long periods. Apart from the inevitable absences of those like sailors, whose trade took them away, children were apprenticed out or put into service at an early age while more distant relatives might come to share in a household. The form households took is manifold and the process of change over time complex. A household might comprise a single person, a married couple without children or servants, parents and children (simple families), extended families (families with grandparents, aunts and uncles, cousins) or families with resident servants.

Urban theorists postulate that there was a difference between town and country in terms of a 'complex' household structure and significant regional differences. In fact, the evidence seems to suggest that urban households in Britain between 1500 and 1700 were less complex than the national average, with fewer having residential kin. Shurer has found no evidence of geographical differences except those that can be explained by occupational variation.[11] Establishing the facts can be difficult. Apparently composite households are sometimes still familial – an aunt fostering orphaned nephews or mother and widowed daughter. In general, however, the town household and family has proved statistically very similar to that of the general population. The very wealthy household in the town was offset as in the country by the one-person household. The typical family size was 4.25 to 4.5 and the percentage of extended families no higher than overall. The percentage of households headed by a woman may have been slightly larger and the number of children per household was significantly lower, their place taken by the rather more frequent presence of a servant. In London, Bristol and Edinburgh the percentage of households with servants is positively related to wealth and the percentage with children negatively related. The average number of hearths in the larger towns, compared to the countryside, however, does suggest that wealth was beginning to be concentrated in the town.

Women in Urban Society

Women's ability to work independently may have been deteriorating in this period. Medieval historians have found evidence to suggest that a shortage of skilled labour in the fifteenth century had enabled women to obtain recognition in their own right. In the sixteenth century, so far as can be seen, the pressure was to limit their freedom of action. The extent to which the woman was permitted to work independently outside the household where she might be wife, daughter or servant is a vexed question, not helped by the probability that regulations varied, and were enforced or ignored depending on the cycles of prosperity and recession. Women's employment patterns and roles tended to be less regulated and more casual than those of men, affected by the average age of marriage and the attitude of the authorities. In the sixteenth-century town, authorities aimed at a hierarchy of individuals with a person responsible for every urban dweller, and preferred women and young people to be acknowledged servants in a household, either in domestic work or other forms of labour. In their attempts to police drunkenness and disorder Chester and Manchester prohibited women from keeping taverns or even from working in taverns unless they were the wife or daughter of the owner, although ale wives continued in other towns such as Gloucester, Hereford, Nottingham and Coventry. At the same time it appears that women not only worked in fish curing in the ports but that a few went as salters with the fleets to Newfoundland.[12]

In many towns the balance of the sexes was unfavourable to women who significantly outnumbered men. Nevertheless, the age of women at first marriage was significantly younger in the town. Women thus often found themselves working with and for their husbands. Their apparent standing, however, was to some extent deceptive. It was often they who managed the family social contacts, inaugurating and arranging the family personal and business relationships.

The Urban Social Experience

Historians may analyse the structures of urban life both in terms of statics and dynamics but analysis does not in itself provide a sense of the experience of that life at the various levels of society and in the very different circumstances of the great capitals or the small semi-rural towns. The lived experience probably took for granted the systemic structure of society. The factors which preoccupied inhabitants were the bread-and-butter issues of life – the cost of housing, supplies of food and water, education for children, care for the elderly and infirm, provision of entertainment at one end of the scale and spiritual comfort and guidance at the other. Getting a living is poorly understood. The idea that the work of craftsmen and petty traders was regular and well controlled is less and less plausible. Studies of the role of the second-hand market, especially in clothing, and the pawnbroker, demonstrate the hand-to-mouth life of many whose family economy was evidently both fragmented and piecemeal.

Penetrating the private sphere of the household presents even more insuperable difficulties. It probably did not precisely match the formal structures of authority and power elaborated in the law and church doctrine. Household management, usually in the woman's hands, was carried on in circumstances which differed totally from those of the present day. It required different skills and clearly varied much more significantly between the better-off and the poor who might have no hearth on which to cook their food. The houses of the comfortably off were better provided with beds, tables, chairs, crockery and cutlery. As the century progressed the distinctions grew more marked. In 1500 furnishings even amongst the wealthy were generally sparse, trestle tables and benches and stools dominating inventories. As time went on frame tables, chairs, carpets and feather beds became more common. At the same time, differences between the capitals and provinces were increasing.

Organising water supplies when few houses had taps or wells was onerous but a source of social interaction. Food supplies involved different problems of preservation and cooking, when household ovens were rare and refrigeration impossible. Clothing had to be hand-sewn. Professional health-care was so limited, precarious and expensive that the housewife's recipe books were as full of herbal remedies for major and minor ailments as they were for other domestic needs. In the larger households the life of the domestics rushing up and down stairs with water and coal, cleaning and washing and drying manually can occasionally be glimpsed in a diary like Pepys'. Many stayed only a short time in any one family. Despite the large number of domestics, in a town like Edinburgh only a minority of families had a live-in servant and those which did had only one. The wife would therefore rarely be leisured.

Evidence of diet, however, suggests that households not in the category of the destitute poor were probably adequately fed, although our ignorance of health problems such as intestinal parasites should restrain us from assuming that a reasonable diet resulted in adequate nourishment. The three meals were breakfast, supper and dinner and the ordinary menu might include beer, milk, bread, porridge, cheese, cake, meats, cabbage, carrots, turnips, beans and peas. Apples and pears were common fruits but better-off households ate more exotic fruits and cherries and plums seasonally.

Social and personal identity were partly established by clothing, hair care and jewellery. Interest in this was not simply individual, there was also a strong element of social control. Although the sumptuary laws were routinely breached, class distinctions in dress were maintained by occupational needs (often effectively a uniform) and price controls. Cheap woollens were the hallmark of the poor, formal silk robes a requirement of aldermen and their wives. Wills and inventories suggest that the ordinary citizen had little more than working clothes and Sunday best but recent work on theft of clothing illuminates both the relatively high cost and therefore value of clothes and underlines the importance of the bride's trousseau. When a fustian coat would be more than a labourer's wages for a fortnight, and a cloth suit would absorb three or four months income, they were not frequently replaced. How clean they were kept is an unanswerable question although the market for soap was growing.

It is possible to recreate aspects of the life of the wealthier citizens as they went about their daily business. They were not necessarily law abiding and some of their feuds and their motivation and attitude to life have found permanent record in legal cases. The life of humbler and poorer folk is harder to penetrate. In general they appear only when their behaviour has attracted the unfavourable attention of the authorities and then the presentation of events, restructured to fit legal categories, needs careful treatment if it is to reveal very much. Underdown sees some of the residents of Dorchester as a 'defeated underclass' whose leisure hours were filled with casual parties, dropping in on friends and enjoyment of the semi-illegal pleasures of dancing and carousing which might end in tippling matches. These were the people who played games deemed illegal like nine holes and skittles, who sought to continue the Maypole and the Midsummer bonfire, and who were predominantly those charged with domestic violence. For a community of under 3000 the 250 average annual number of cases in the Dorchester offenders' book in the mid-1630s, suggests a high level of alienation from the norms being imposed.[13] There are occasional indications of a sense of partiality in the social controls, a glazier complaining that the prosecutions were 'persecuting poor men not rich' while one woman felt the minister was a hypocrite acting for his own profit. At the same time, Underdown perceives a lively youth culture, a sophisticated use of ridicule and a fairly standard sense of a moral economy which required a fair distribution of food in famine years.

The drop in average life expectancy from 37.4 in Elizabethan times to 32.3 in the seventeenth century, suggests that the conditions of life were if anything worsening, particularly for the poor. Historians who attempt to count the poor find they have problems of identification. Recently, the early consensus that they represented at least a fifth and sometimes a third of all people has been revised as there has been an increasing recognition that not all those exempt from such taxes as the hearth tax were necessarily poor by contemporary standards. Some were able to leave wills giving a few goods to their families and friends, others contributed to local poor rates.[14] The poor in need of relief were under 10 per cent of the population. This of course is not the whole story. The occasional survey like that at Norwich in 1570 shows that in many families both husband and wife and often the children were working but were so badly paid that they were still unable to make ends meet. When there were depressions in a major industry, the level of distress rose rapidly.

The extent to which the poor were able to participate in the educational facilities provided in many towns, and so better themselves, is hard to establish, although where records survive, 'free' or scholarship places do not seem to have reached the lowest echelons. Schooling was an important way of training the next generation in accepted ways of discipline, internalising the division of hours for work and hours for play and holidays, and creating bonds of friendship and association. The licensed custom of schoolboys barring the door against the master and holding revels on certain days was a form of managing tensions not confined to juveniles. As the period progressed, differences between the education of the gentry and merchants were becoming blurred so that cultural assumptions were shared. The urban poor, however, were often able to read, although the men scored significantly better than the women.

Experiences of urban life undoubtedly varied. London's size made it unique, but towns like Dublin, Edinburgh, York, Bristol and Norwich, all of them compared by contemporaries to London, offered a range of experiences different from those common in the small towns whose population numbered no more than a thousand. What attracted people to the growing towns has not been carefully investigated. Success and power in a large town required a high level of wealth. It offered the prospect of higher income to specialists and greater business opportunities. The interplay between specialists living in close proximity produced high-quality goods at lower prices. The availability of professional entertainment and charity may also have attracted some. On the other hand, the relative amount of power or influence which a modestly prosperous ordinary craftsman might have in a small town could make it more attractive to one whose ambitions were realistic; the prospect of his children surviving and the comparative purchasing power of his income might also be greater.

The distribution and display of wealth seems related to the size and variety of the upper echelons of urban society: government officials, lawyers, attorneys, notaries, clerics, church officials, doctors, merchants and town officials. The numbers of uncontrolled non-respectable people were presumably larger in the big towns, and social tensions were sometimes exacerbated where there were sizeable and partially ghettoised alien communities or 'birds of passage' such as long-term, resident 'foreign' merchants who served as a focus for the discontent of the powerless.

Conclusion

The growing complexity of urban society in the larger towns, with a resultant cross-cutting of social relationships was helping to create a more fluid community. At the same time the poor who had once lived cheek by jowl with their betters were increasingly relegated to the less salubrious areas with fewer utilities. This would fit the criteria of some urban theorists about the prerequisites for urbanisation. It cannot, however, be carried too far. In 1700 most towns were still small and fairly undifferentiated and had few of the gentry or professional residents who were forming the basis of consumer demand in some of the larger ports and county towns. The variety of social life in the cities was not replicated everywhere, certainly indicating the appearance of a pyramid, perhaps of a hierarchy of towns.

3

TOWNS AND RELIGIOUS CHANGE

People in the sixteenth and seventeenth centuries were grappling with beliefs about the nature of this world and the existence of a life after death, the purpose of human life and the requirements of a Creator. This was a universal phenomenon but the effects of wide communal interactions in towns gave it a particular momentum. The Christian church from its establishment was always town-based. The very language of the religion was urban as it spoke of the city of God and the building of a new Jerusalem or warned that 'here is no abiding city'. A city was distinguished from a mere town simply on the basis of the presence of a cathedral and a cathedral often took up at least 10 per cent of the urban space. Towns were a key focus for religious instruction. Stow wrote that 'the doctrine of God is more fitly deliuered and the discipline thereof more aptly to bee executed, in peopled townes then abroad, by reason of the facilitie of common and often assembling'.[1]

Religion was also seen as the binding force of community identity. In many towns the authorities helped with the rebuilding of churches. The great feasts like Corpus Christi were the dates on which the towns before the Reformation held their pageants and presented plays, usually with religious themes. The Host was borne under a canopy, the bible was carried, banners representing the different gilds were displayed, hymns were sung, and townspeople dressed to represent the twelve apostles and other prominent biblical figures. Obedience to God was the cornerstone on which all lesser obedience, including obedience to town authorities, was erected.

Church Structure and the Towns

The church, however, had its own power structure and authority over the people in many matters which are now either private or secular, and town authorities would often resent its jurisdiction over aspects of their inhabitants' lives. Church courts heard moral cases, determined the legality of marriages and bastardy, judged cases of slander and debt and proved wills. Although they were held in the monarch's name, they did not accept royal interference. Archdeacons held their courts in the aisle of the church, and such courts were the most common way in which ordinary people were morally disciplined. It was therefore a potential competitor for control of the community although usually church and secular power provided mutual support. Conflict between town and ecclesiastical courts was best avoided. When it occurred it threatened to undermine all law and order. In Glasgow, John Shaw, Alexander Stuart and Thomas Law, bailies of the burgh, and other citizens, were excommunicated by the church commissaries for making and recording in their books certain statutes 'against the jurisdiction of Holy Mother Church', prohibiting any citizen from summoning another citizen before a spiritual judge if the matter could be completely decided before the bailies in the court house of Glasgow, a direct threat to religious rule.[2]

At the same time, a good deal of social welfare was provided by charitable gilds organised inside the church structure. Education was also largely in the hands of the church. Most towns had religious gilds, most dedicated to St George or to Corpus Christi or the Trinity. They were a means whereby local landowners and women could be associated with merchants and wealthy craftsmen in social activities. In Leicester, Trinity Gild had been established by Sir Richard Sacheverell and his wife Lady Hungerford, and held four gatherings a year for a meal and other festivities as well as ensuring the ceremonial burial of members in the church of St Mary's. The social function of the gild is reflected in the common requirements that the whole fraternity should attend the funeral of any brother, his wife, child or apprentice and that provision should be made of a hearse cloth or funeral pall for the purpose.[3] Whether or not their real role was secular rather than social or religious, and a means by which the burgess as a group could hold real property, there can be no doubt that many such gilds were very wealthy and an important instrument for social management. In Worcester the Trinity Gild was responsible for the elementary school, the almshouses, repair of the city wall and the bridge.[4] Their dissolution in Edward VI's reign was a major threat to urban well-being. Many gilds, foreseeing the development, had transferred the property away; others were able to buy it back from the Crown. Lincoln, for example, obtained the gild property for the relief of the city.[5]

The coming of the Reformation had a massive impact on towns. Since the friaries were uniformly situated in the county towns and many towns also housed the more important monasteries, their dissolution made a considerable difference even where the town did not, as at Battle, lose not only its major consumer but also its source of loans and charitable assistance. The destruction not only of the monasteries but also of the gilds and chantries was a blow both to town resources and organisation. Charitable activities and in some places covert forms of government had to be replaced. Towns sought to acquire the sites and land of friaries and monasteries at a favourable price or as a gift so that some of the amenities might be continued.

The increasing role of the laity in religion resulted in the town authorities achieving considerable practical control of the established church in their district. Over the years they either obtained the advowson of the churches, which enabled them to nominate the minister, or established salaried lectureships as an alternative. They came to see themselves as active participants in the maintenance of a godly life, however that was defined.

Resistance to the Reformation

The role of towns in disseminating religious ideas had always been considerable. The underground survival of Lollard heresy before the Reformation was for the most part in the larger towns where illicit practices were less likely to be noticeable. Some towns, particularly in the clothing areas, Tewkesbury for example, seem to have been early and continuing centres of non-conformity. The ideas and books of the Reformation originally came in through the ports, usually illegally. In places like Rye there were early divisions in the town between those who supported the existing structures and practices and those who favoured change.[6] The speed with which the reformed religion spread had much to do with the willingness of urban authorities to implement changes. Where there was tacit local resistance the changes could be merely superficial. In some cases it is hard to judge. The flat (and unconsciously humorous) entry in Dartmouth's town accounts in 1554, 'Paid for blutting out the ten commandments two shillings' tells us only that they obeyed an edict.[7]

In some towns there was apparently little residual adherence to the old ways while in the north of England there was a general reluctance to abandon familiar ways and the old religious Mystery cycles were performed with the approval of the town authorities well into Elizabeth's reign. Where, as at York, there was a covert attachment to the old forms of religion on the part of many of the clergy and town officials, it could take many years for changes to be thoroughly implemented. The recusancy laws were as far as possible ignored. In York it took great pressure from the dean to persuade the authorities to abandon the Creed play, much longer for the Corpus Christi plays and a direct prohibition from the ecclesiastical commission to end the 'York Ryding' which had traditionally heralded the Christmas period. The city in 1580 turned down a request for money for a preacher, changing their minds the following year with obvious reluctance. Not until the beginning of James I's reign do the authorities appear wholly reconciled and the poor appear to have responded by ceasing to attend churches whose interiors had been restructured to centre on pulpit and communion table.[8]

Growing Religious Powers of the Towns

Elsewhere, more willing authorities found themselves hampered by lack of resources. Private Acts such as that for Ipswich in 13 Elizabeth, which enabled the town to levy rates in parishes to support ministers and repair churches, were necessary to fill the gaps in responsibility left by the Dissolution of the monasteries, but also increased the town authorities' control. Town lecturers or preachers were appointed and paid an excellent salary by the authorities but usually could be dismissed with six months' notice which gave the town control over the doctrine preached. Accusations against such preachers for preaching (or not preaching) the new doctrine became more frequent. Preachers supported by the towns might none the less fall foul of the central government. In towns committed to preaching, it was possible to pass bye-laws requiring people to attend at least once a week. At Leicester in 1562, one member of each household had to attend a sermon every Wednesday and Friday from 7–8 a.m.[9] Towns with puritan leanings might implement regulations to ensure that the Sabbath was kept holy. At Norwich in 1570 it was decided that the gates should be shut from Saturday night to Monday morning and that on a Sunday there should be no feasts or wedding dinners.[10]

Certain towns in Wales, however, particularly Monmouth, the nearest town to the Jesuit college at the Cwm until it was destroyed in 1679, remained shelters for the recusants. The valley remained a stronghold of Catholicism and the close ties between country and town suggest that Monmouth had traditionalist leanings particularly as the Catholic Earl of Worcester increased his land holdings in the borough and so his political influence.[11] Elsewhere Protestantism was encouraged by the translation of the bible and service books into Welsh but it was not until the 1630s that puritan preaching in the major towns began to stimulate enthusiasm for reform amongst humbler people. This was not necessarily shared by the better-off who conspired to drive one charismatic preacher, Walter Cradock, from his curacy in Wrexham. Despite this Wrexham became a centre for unorthodox religious opinion and practice. The middling sort of people in many of the towns all round the coast became anti-clerical enthusiasts, attenders of sermons, and supporters of separatist principles.

The role of Irish towns in maintaining the old religion is perhaps not sufficiently stressed.[12] Their foreign contacts had not produced any early leaning towards heterodoxy, and there was an upswing in the building of churches just before the Reformation in Cork, Limerick and Galway due to the impact of the Observant friars on religious practice. Reformation from the centre was difficult in such remote and autonomous communities, that had easy access to the continent by sea, and while a personal visit from the governor might produce a gesture the protestant bishops' attempts to evangelise in these places largely failed. In 1567 Sidney making formal visits to the towns as governor was met at each by bishops and clergy wearing vestments designed to underline their commitment to their traditional religious beliefs. Priests were maintained in the cities throughout the sixteenth century and rich and poor openly attended mass. The religious disaffection was equally striking in Dublin where in 1603 an estimated 70 per cent of the population were Catholics.

The reassessment of the process whereby a Reformed Calvinist kirk was established in Scotland shows a similarly nuanced picture. It identifies some of the Scottish towns as the focus of overt or covert religious resistance. Aberdeen, for example, was religiously traditional for over a century despite various programs designed to convert the people to protestantism.[13] In 1559 they wanted neutrality between the Lords of the Congregation and the queen mother. On 4 January 1559 an assault on the religious houses of the burgh by a reforming mob from Angus and the Mearns, organised by David Mar, the dean of gild, when the provost was away, failed.[14] In 1560 when magnates in the area turned against the queen mother, Aberdeen found it prudent to co-operate (but as little as possible) in order to retain control over events in Aberdeen. The developments were a severe and unwelcome shock to the various communities that composed the burgh of Aberdeen and there was a discreet rearguard action for a decade; survival of popular Catholic beliefs and practices in Catholic households and gild. Catholic services could still be attended and there was a Catholic university in King's College until 1569. For some time even when the clergy refused to conform they were still paid. Monks stayed in their monasteries and received pensions from the council.[15] Catholic holidays, especially Christmas, continued to be observed and there were attempts to continue the Corpus Christi processions, Mayday and pageants. When the Catholic earls, Huntly and Errol, were allowed back into the country in 1595 there was much rejoicing; wine spices and sugar almonds were provided for a public banquet at the Market Cross. As late as 1608 Aberdeen created a grave scandal by sending two avowed papists to the General Assembly at Linlithgow.[16] There were fears of a Catholic uprising in the area around Aberdeen in 1626 and thereafter popery grew within the diocese of Aberdeen and Murrey.

The course of the Reformation in Ayr shows a more conformable urban reaction. Although it showed no early enthusiasm for change it did not overtly resist orders from Edinburgh in 1543 authorising the reading of the Scripture in English, and when Friar John Routh caused a riot by preaching against the innovation they confined him to the tollbooth and successfully prevented the master of Montgomery from rescuing him. Their ambiguity shows in the money they laid out for him and the hogshead of wine they continued to send the Grey Friars until the 1560s. They continued the holy days procession through the streets and the 'annual plays when the douce bailies played at Robin Hood and Little John in company with the Frenchmen hired for the occasion' until ordered to stop. In 1558, however, they paid for a minister and for twelve months the distinguished Christopher Goodman preached to them until he was translated to St Andrews. They were not, it seems, unduly concerned when no replacement could be obtained and a reader had to fill the gap. Paying ministers was an additional expense and although they had acquired the old church dues totalling just over £80 they were hard to collect and rising costs obliged them to tax. In the sixteenth century they were content with moderate ministers but in the early seventeenth, John Knox's son-in-law, John Welch, evangelised the area until James banished him.[17]

Religion provided one of the gravest challenges to secular control. The acrimony over the appointment of Robert Montgomery as Archbishop of Glasgow in 1580 provides a textbook example of town authorities' involvement in ecclesiastical disputes. In May 1582 the archbishop and presbytery were at odds over preaching in the cathedral. When Montgomery proposed to preach the next Sunday the presbytery met to deal with him but while they were deliberating the provost with the bailies and some citizens entered, prohibited them from proceeding and cited them to appear before the privy council. When the ministers refused, the magistrates forcibly seized the moderator, beat him and confined him in the tollbooth. The college students took up the cause and excluded the archbishop from the church, enabling their principal to preach on the text 'He that enters not by the door but by the window is a thief and a robber', and criticise the archbishop's simoniacal entry and the levity he had shown in all his proceedings. Fighting ensued and a serious tumult was apprehended, so the magistrates by tuck of drum and peal of bells called in the citizens to support them. Despite the king's early support for Montgomery, the town, with the help of their local patron, the Duke of Lennox, carried the day.[18] This typifies how, after the Reformation in Scotland local secular authorities gradually extended their control over ecclesiastical matters until the kirk sessions were effectively the moral arm of the town, despite the monarch's attempts to control the kirk directly.

Ultimately, by the early seventeenth century, in every kingdom, increasing urban control over the manner and content of religious presentation enabled the secular power to establish the dominant legitimate ideology. Towns which had free schools also had an excellent opportunity of influencing the religious attitudes of both town and surrounding countryside. It was not always easy for them to find schoolmasters whose teaching suited the town's inclinations, however, especially when the salaries were too low. The frequency with which religious books are mentioned in wills suggests strong religious interest. While the richer townsfolk were more likely to own them, the poor sometimes had bibles, prayer books and psalters which they could presumably read and which reflects the religious aspirations of the wider community.[19]

In Ireland, although the Ulster plantations were introducing protestantism, this urban hegemony favoured catholicism in Munster. Many of the migrants who came from Britain to the southern parts of Ireland were evidently recusants looking for more sympathetic surroundings. The government could not limit activity to Protestants and the fact that Walter Coppinger, who was a Catholic, was involved in the problems over ownership of Baltimore worried it considerably.[20]

Effects of Religion on Town Life

Religious enthusiasm could thus be one of the key elements in shaping the life of an urban community. When Dorset's county town, Dorchester, in many ways a typical community of about 2000, was largely destroyed by fire in 1613, its authorities tried to build it as a New Jerusalem in line with the preaching of its minister John White. The spiritual and emotional impact of the disaster even though there was only one death, was enough to persuade the more powerful families of the need to recognise that 'here is no abiding city' and to lead the poor and ignorant to godly ways. Forty years of godly struggle which had included the migration of many to the promise of a more religious society in America, faded in Dorchester as it did in so many cities after the experiences of the Civil Wars.[21]

English and Scottish town authorities thus saw themselves as a legitimate partner in local religious management before the Civil War and resented and resisted interference from the centre. While ardent puritans used the mayor's court to police the moral behaviour of residents, religion in towns became involved with secular aspirations and politics. In many places this came to a head in opposition to Laud's programme. While the Scottish reaction to the imposition of Laud's programme was explosive, town authorities in England were also perfectly prepared, if they felt strongly, to make their opposition to his alterations plain. In Worcester the corporation in 1637 refused to attend the cathedral services.[22] In Norwich, when the new bishop Wren, a Laudian supporter, attacked the puritans, suspending recalcitrant lecturers and requiring the magistrates to attend a service and sermon in the cathedral the aldermen petitioned the king and 500 residents emigrated. Later when orders came from parliament to destroy images and bury prayer books it was two of the town authorities who led townspeople to carry out the instructions in the cathedral.[23]

Uniformity was never a reality. Everywhere there were already small groups not only of Catholics but also of more radical forms of protestantism. The equality preached by such sects, which reduced the ministerial role to little more than guidance, led to the assertion of equality in other areas. The radicalisation of some urban communities spread from opposition to Laud to support for a more democratic polity.[24] The Civil Wars unleashed a variety of different Protestant persuasions all of whom hoped for recognition. Long standing creeds like those of the Baptists were joined by an increasing number of more radical millenarian sects such as the Quakers and the Muggletonians.

The authorities found themselves not merely struggling to establish or maintain protestantism, but facing the difficulties of growing non-conformity. This was not simply an English problem. Religion in Wales was shifting quite rapidly. Despite repression by the royalists the Baptist movement spread, mainly in the towns. By 1652 there were 261 Baptists mostly from small Welsh towns and four Calvinist churches in Hay-on-Wye, Llantrisant, Carmarthen and Abergavenny.[25] There were soon also Quakers whose preaching and debating caused riots particularly as they allowed women to preach. Alice Birkett was stripped and stoned in Llandaff for her pains.[26] Fox had promoted the emergence of radical sects in Wales by his well-known tour in which he concentrated on the most obvious Welsh towns including Cardiff, Swansea, Wrexham and Haverfordwest. While he got a hostile reception in some places like Lampeter, in others some of the thousands who came to hear him were converted and founded small communities which emerged in the towns when meeting houses were allowed to be licensed forty years later.

Bristol during and after the Civil War also found itself facing the enthusiasms generated by the Quakers and such individuals as Fox and Naylor. In the Restoration period many towns found that non-conformity could not be suppressed. In some cases, there may have been little motivation to do so amongst the urban officials since some even refused the religious tests themselves. For example, at Dartmouth, which later became a centre of non-conformity, the mayor and eight borough masters lost their positions and two ministers were ejected after the Act of Uniformity 1662.[27]

Many towns retreated from any attempt to enforce adherence to the established church. Central government concern over the growth of urban toleration of non-conformity appears in the Five Mile Act of 1665 which was particularly directed at non-conformists in towns. Urban co-operation in maintaining religious uniformity was crucial. The extent to which towns vigorously enforced the Acts and the degree of success they had in suppressing unorthodox services is, however, difficult to quantify. Clearly where there was a magistrate whole-heartedly committed to eradicating politically unacceptable views he would enjoy a virtually free rein and the result might well be a purge in one town although individuals might simply move to less rigid areas. Those not willing to risk the penalties of overt dissent might in any case become occasional conformers. Only a percentage were ever prosecuted. In some Devon towns, including Tiverton, Honiton and Cullompton, 1177 have been identified but only 468 were prosecuted in the county courts. Whether others were pursued in the town courts is impossible to tell.[28]

There are signs that the reasons for the eventual concessions to the non-conformists came from an increasing leaning of potential urban officials towards dissent. After the Act of Indulgence when dissenting meeting houses were registered, particularly in Wales, these were in the towns, and often belonged to members of the borough council and people who had been mayors. Church membership was still a formal requirement for government office, but credentials were not always rigorously checked.

Church architecture and internal arrangement reflected all these changes in religious practice and also the social hierarchy and political power both in the town and the region. As Protestantism was established so were the layout and arrangements altered. Before the Reformation the altars of the gilds were the focus of gild identity and piety and the churches also included the tombs of the lords and of some mayors. Aberdeen's church of St Nicholas had thirty altars and sixteen chaplains and was a burial place for the local lairds like the Leslies and the Irvines. The altars were removed at the Reformation, and the pulpit raised to the position of eminence. The physical act of opposition to Laud was prevention of the restoration of the altar to a place of eminence.

Even the seating in the churches followed hierarchical principles. In some places it is possible to follow the progress of individuals from the humble back pews to the front as they moved from apprentice to mayor. At the same time, the religious commitments even of less successful people saw them well up in the church. The positions at the front were reserved for the town officials and visiting dignitaries such as assize judges. On high holidays the corporation in its robes processed to their reserved seats for the service. They also attended the quarterly sermons of the common preacher on pain of a fine. Non-attendance at church was also a gesture of resistance to the existing authorities. Attendance at unauthorised open air meetings was an indication of significant social divisions in urban society and the potential for an alternative focus for urban life.

Conclusion

Towns had always been places where dissidents could find concealment. From the moment when the Reformation undermined a traditional consensus, religion had become a divisive issue and neither the church nor the town authorities were able to impose uniformity. By the end of the seventeenth century there was little general will even to attempt to do so. Whatever the law required there was a creeping willingness to tolerate alternative creeds provided they were discreet and their members decently behaved. Membership of the established church had political significance but a decreasing social role.

4

URBAN WEALTH, TOWNSMEN'S WEALTH

How people made their living, the work they did, the goods they produced or circulated and the technological and regulatory conditions under which they did so has shaped life throughout history. A differentiation of economic function is usually seen as the critical aspect which divides a town from a village even though most towns had an agricultural element, and many townsmen either to avoid regulations or in simple search of labour or resources carried out part of their business in the country. It is often claimed that amongst the distinguishing characteristics of a town are distinctive ways of organising work. Bringing people together in a restricted physical environment with a group of others with related specialities is thought to encourage a shift from the possession of general skills to a greater specialisation which improved the quality of the end product. This was what made town production better, but generally more expensive, than rural work. The prosperity of a town or its inhabitants, which is not necessarily the same thing, depended on urban services attracting customers.

Towns have sometimes been seen both by contemporaries and by historians not as a source of wealth but as its destroyer. The town, that is to say, was not productive because its inhabitants were predominantly administrators, clergy, lawyers, military men and the like who consumed but did not produce. The accusation

46

of being a parasite was levelled at London in the sixteenth century. The response was the commonplace image of the stomach distributing nourishment where it was most needed. Urban wealth ultimately depended on the overall prosperity of the country. As markets towns were the conduit which carried the country's product from one area to another and overseas, they were therefore constrained by the state of the economy. Towns necessarily shared in the kingdom's times of depression and should have equally shared the times of abundance. Shifts in international trade, continental or civil war affected the towns first. Colonialism offered a new source of profit.

English prosperity was dominated by cloth manufacture. The country also exported tin, some lead and coal, but it was the cloth trade which dominated her international fortunes and supported a significant percentage (perhaps as much as 10 per cent) of Britain's total population. A collapse in demand rapidly caused misery and destitution both in the towns and across a wide swathe of the country. Town fortunes, however, did not precisely reflect general economic trends. Usually measured in monetary terms, their prosperity is hard to evaluate.

Definitions of Wealth

Perceptions of wealth are ambiguous. Forms of 'stored obligations', that is money, exist in most communities but take very different forms. Between realisable assets (horses, camels, cows) and artificial social constructs (cowry shells, pieces of paper) lies a range of social perceptions of wealth from gold to fine clothes and comfortable living style. Mere evidence of trading and manufacturing activity does not give an accurate indication of wealth. The merchant juggling the greatest amount of business may already be effectively bankrupt. Preachers discouraging an overly eager interest in the affairs of this world, spoke in biblical terms of the amassing of goods, rather than abstract wealth.

Evidence of increasing material comfort is one way of identifying wealth which has both economic and social interest, but a simple list does not identify better built houses and improved sanitation, the quality of clothing or furniture. Average English urban families, however, apparently acquired few extra furnishings in the sixteenth century. In Worcester, apart from window glazing, Dyer considers that there is evidence of greater wealth only amongst the rich.[1] Increasing population put pressure on resources. Although preachers might point to God's providence in providing for every mouth a pair of hands, society was doing well to keep pace with modest individual needs. By the late seventeenth century, with a downturn in population growth, individual wealth seems to have increased. The numbers of affluent individuals who could afford both culture and consumption stimulated a remodelling of towns and town services.[2]

Another measure of wealth is the investment in fixed capital which towns represent. Between John Leland's itinerary in the 1530s and Celia Fiennes' and Defoe's around 1700, improvement had clearly taken place. The rentable value of town burgages in many towns rose. The cost of providing infrastructure and public amenities and building town houses can only be estimated but scattered figures for buildings and repairs after disaster give some benchmarks. After the fire in Dorchester in 1613, the overall capital losses were estimated at £80 000 or about £40 per capita, when a labourer might be lucky to earn £10 a year.[3] Town authorities invested in physical capital to make their settlement as attractive as possible to business. Quays were built at places like Dartmouth and Whitehaven either by the towns or private individuals. Cranes and warehouses, lighthouses and buoys were erected to make the port services better than those of competitors. Great royal shipyards, which covered twenty or more acres with docks, graving yards, rope walks and covered sail-lofts and similar private yards, required massive outlay. Despite the periodic destruction brought about by war or fire the fixed capital of the larger towns in all kingdoms appears to have substantially increased between 1500 and 1700. Not only extensive shipyards, but large-scale breweries, potteries, glassworks and foundries were beginning to grow up alongside impressive new public buildings. Physical capital, moreover, was only the most visible aspect of the capitalisation of trading and commercial facilities.

Merchant Wealth, Urban Poverty

Not all towns had sufficient income to build and maintain new infrastructure. Wealth assessed for central taxation was not necessarily equally available to the town. Town finances were not necessarily a direct reflection of the community's wealth or poverty. While some towns had rich bequests and the right to levy local tolls on goods, others had few independent resources. The sources of town income in the sixteenth century were not routinely 'rates' but such things as property, local customs, tolls, the rents of market stalls and perhaps the fines in the town courts. Most boroughs had some real estate. Some ports had local customs duties, and tolls. Town income thus varied considerably. Bristol, for example, had large resources while Leicester with a third of Bristol's population had under a sixth of its resources. Towns like Salisbury might be in financial difficulties, either temporary or long-term, because they had large numbers of poorer residents who needed assistance. At the same time some had resident gentry, merchants and tradesmen who enjoyed considerable wealth and prosperity.

The interaction between these two things is complex and self-reinforcing. Merchants would not stay in cities which could not take steps to take advantage of opportunities and make the necessary facilities available. Exeter merchants in the 1520s were moving to London because the services were better. Cities could not raise funds if their wealthiest residents would not co-operate. Interests overlapped but did not necessarily or precisely coincide. Part of the politics of self-government was the process of reaching a compromise. The alternative in Ireland was usually for a prominent landlord to act as patron. After the Civil War when ideas about taxation had been revised, rates became a more regular source of income.

The effectiveness of town councils in promoting their town's well-being depended on a complex set of variables relating to location, competition and the nature of the town's main function. Some could make a big difference. Bath exploited the mania for spas and invested in the 'leisure business'. Careful management of its social image and sizeable expenditure on providing good physical conditions paid off. In the seventeenth century it already congratulated itself on being 'in terms of social importance the second city of the realm'.[4]

All prosperous corporations were ultimately successful in persuading or obliging their residents to contribute to undertakings of general public benefit and increased their income. Bristol between 1556–7 and 1627–8 nearly trebled its income.[5] Norwich receipts multiplied tenfold by 1675.[6] Major Scottish burghs also saw their revenues improve. Glasgow's income trebled by 1700. The minnows at the bottom of the system, however, had to rely on generous patrons for such prestigious acquisitions as a new tollbooth.

Markets

Trade was the common feature of towns and the usual basis of their prosperity. In 1500 it was heavily regulated everywhere. Economic historians blame this regulation for urban difficulties in the sixteenth and early seventeenth century. They see it as a symptom of the inward-looking medieval town society which had to give way to an outward-looking free-market participation in international trade before economic growth could occur. Such a criticism applies to all kingdoms but may not be wholly justified.

Sixteenth-century people believed regulation was essential. The market economy was dominated by traditional assumptions of social responsibility and the notional 'just' price. Where food was concerned the popular sense of moral behaviour was likely to descend into riots if outrageous prices were demanded. This was a constraint on the free market in grain and other essential goods everywhere. In England, the price of bread and ale was set by JPs throughout the country in accordance with the ruling market price for grain. In Scotland, the town authorities did the same, occasionally provoking resistance from the bakers who claimed to be unable to make a living. In many town markets, the first hour of the sale of grain and some other foodstuffs were restricted to small-scale purchasers at 'reasonable' prices. In famine years there might be compulsory purchases and prohibition of overseas trade in foodstuffs. The reverse of this was the ability to hold down wages and limit expenditure on poor relief without inciting riots while keeping export goods competitive. Bigger towns like London and Norwich purchased corn which they used as a stock. Such regulations may have been inevitable in a period when famine was still a real threat once a decade on average.

The idea of an overriding communal good affected many aspects of the sixteenth- and seventeenth-century domestic market. The model was an economy with finite resources which had to be fairly shared. One aspect of its regulation was that all goods should physically pass through a real market place. All freemen should have the right to a share of goods brought to the market if they so wished. Prohibition of purchase outside the market was another aspect of this. It intentionally impeded bulk purchases of material before there had been an opportunity for locals to buy.

Gild regulations were aimed at quality control of goods for sale. The object of maintaining the reputation of particular products was not inconsistent with some of the aims of a free market. Many of the restrictions on free sale, however, were not directly controlled by the towns or for their benefit. Regulation of overseas trade was likely to involve non-market considerations particularly where defence was concerned. In the late fifteenth century an English statute required that foreign merchants bring in a percentage of bow staves in each cargo, for example. The export of heavy ordnance was forbidden under Elizabeth. In war years government priorities led to sudden prohibitions on ships sailing to particular overseas countries or carrying particular goods without a licence. Volume and trade and prices were all affected and, in the short term, underlying economic strength or weakness might be disguised.

Regulation was the justification for monopoly. The London merchants who benefited from the limitation of trade to companies authorised to trade to the Levant or the East Indies emphasised the need to maintain a stable price for goods by controlling the flow of goods on to the market. A regular trade was the most desirable trade. The practice of interloping – unauthorised merchants undertaking a single voyage as a short-term, profit-making venture – was condemned because these free riders had not contributed to the long-term costs of sustaining the market.

Regulations certainly distorted the market, but in the long run did not control it. Any shift from a restricted market to a more impersonal price-driven trade between 1500 and 1700 must not be exaggerated. The whole history of the highly regulatory customs and excise administration in the eighteenth century suggests that while a trend may exist the demarcation cannot be either clear or distinct.

The Urban Condition in the Sixteenth Century

Most urban historians argue that towns were in decline in England in 1500. Whether this is also true of the other kingdoms is less clear. While the overall internal structure of the towns in each kingdom had considerable similarities their economic circumstances differed. Ireland, Wales and Scotland were comparatively sparsely inhabited in 1500, had a limited number of craftsmen and depended on exporting raw materials. On average the towns were smaller and had a more restricted role.

In 1500 English towns were less populated than they had been in 1300. Whether this signifies decline has been disputed. Bridbury and Hadwin argue that their relative share of the kingdom's wealth had risen perhaps from as little as 4.4 per cent to as much as 10.9 per cent.[7] The pessimistic school, headed by Paul Slack and Peter Clark, claim that the majority of towns, apart from London, suffered from a protracted period of difficulties from well before 1500 to 1660. Phythian Adams sees a recovery starting in 1570. Clark and Slack, however, see a 'tidal wave' of problems from 1580 to 1604 which, after only a brief intermission, began again in the 1620s. Those who support this crisis scenario divide over the explanation. Clark lists commercial depression, military costs, and refugees; Slack primarily blames social maladjustment exacerbating town costs for poor relief when price inflation was reducing the spending power of town resources. To this he adds external interference and the 'cultural vacuum' left by the Reformation. Historians of particular towns, however, stress the elements of vitality implying that the effects of a restructuring of the urban hierarchy, producing as it did both winners and losers, produces an anecdotal impression of difficulties which is misleading.

Since cloth was England's major export, nearly doubling between 1480 and 1510, and rising another 75 per cent between 1530 and 1550, remaining stable under Elizabeth, it is surprising that most towns apparently did not share in any prosperity it generated. There are two principal reasons given for this – the growing dominance of London and a move of some cloth manufacturing to the countryside. The merchant adventurers had a monopoly on cloth export, increasingly shipping in protected convoys from London which, at its peak in the 1550s, handled 93 per cent of recorded exports. The clothiers preferred to organise production in communities which lacked gild regulations, so that places like Halifax and Leeds grew, as did the industrial villages in Gloucestershire, producing cheaper products of poorer quality which would sell at lower prices to a wider market, while towns like York, Lincoln, Beverley, Winchester and Stamford suffered.

Urban loss of the cloth industry, however, was not necessarily permanent. Colchester was only one of the towns which made a successful transition to the 'new draperies'.[8] When the poor in Norwich, possibly the largest provincial town, were surveyed in 1570 most were employed in woollen trades. Whatever the continuing demand for rural manufactured products the towns by the mid-sixteenth century were in a position to compete on price and full-time craftspeople were more able to meet an increasing demand for a wider range and quality of goods. The very largest towns could increasingly supply better specialists and a varied division of labour. Town production could be more quickly redirected to meet market trends. Urban merchants maintained an effective dominance over rural outwork and towns like York, although no longer a manufacturing centre, profited from its trade.

Town fortunes certainly fluctuated. The experiences of different areas, moreover, were dissimilar, varying with the particular international markets served. London and the eastern ports were badly affected by the fall of Antwerp in 1576, the south-western ports by wars with Spain. On the east coast, Hull suffered typical reverses in the course of a long-term upward trend. One of the main ports trading to north-eastern Europe, its wool trade had disappeared and its volume of overseas shipping dropped. In the 1530s the Hanse abandoned the town. By 1550, however, the town's fortunes were improving and for the rest of the century the number and tonnage of ships based at Hull increased. Coastwise trade to an extent replaced some of its foreign activities. It exported lead from Derbyshire but its main role was as an importer of raw materials for making linen and sailcloth.[9] The other major eastern ports had similar experiences.

South-western ports were in the long term advantaged by the new relative position of the Atlantic which Bristol had been exploring for some time. They were to benefit from the colonisation both of Ireland and America. In 1500, they mainly traded to Spain and Portugal in cloth and imported wine, dried fruits, oil and salt. Most built small craft. While cloth exports from the major ports dropped to a third by 1555–60, most being handled by and for London merchants, new forms of cloth revived the industry in the countryside and smaller inland towns and a new structure linked them to Bristol and Exeter as the main handling centres, benefiting both parties. While the traditional market towns either declined or grew only slowly, cloth-making centres like Painswick and Wotton-under-Edge more than quadrupled in size between 1500 and 1700, well outstripping general population growth.[10]

General trade also started recovering. By the 1550s Bristol merchants began to handle different commodities. Mixed cargoes for Portugal and Spain and the Mediterranean, including lead and tin from the Mendips, iron and coal from the forest of Dean, and fish, were substituted for cloth. Mixed import cargoes were even more profitable. Most ports prospered from the fisheries. Specialities developed in the types of preserving and curing for which a town was famous. There were inevitably problems. The industry had to follow the shifting shoals of herring and pilchards or perish, even if it required long voyages. Political conflicts could also affect the fleets. In the 1570s the Danes demanded to license those who set up workplaces on the beaches. This disrupted the Dartmouth cod fishing and eventually led the town to shift its interests to Newfoundland. Large-scale cod-fishing there led to sizeable fishing fleets of 50–80 vessels in Bristol, Dartmouth, Barnstaple, Plymouth and Exeter by the 1580s, and to an increasingly capitalised business which offered employment to between 1000 and 2000 people.[11] If necessary, armed ships protected the fishing boats.

The trade recovery was threatened by war with Spain after 1585. How damaging this was has been differently estimated. The privateering which replaced regular trade produced prize goods and the search for new markets and the discovery of new goods to trade may have stimulated new endeavours. When a privateer from Barnstaple could bring in a prize in 1591 containing four chests of gold, civet and elephants' teeth, it is not surprising that greed, more politely called entrepreneurial ambition, should be stirred in local hearts.

Industry certainly did not have to be urban and the 43 per cent of Stroudwater men who claimed in 1608 to be employed in cloth-making lived in very large villages not towns. Nevertheless, as the sixteenth century progressed, manufacturing once again became a basis of urban expansion. Towns which had once had no speciality or which had depended on cloth were diversifying into alternative manufactured goods. Although Worcester was still a major cloth-making town with 50 per cent of its merchants in the business it also started to make glass and brass pots, nails and paper.

Industries which started as rural activities, principally metal-working, became urban as transport costs, wage relativities, horizontal and vertical integration favoured its concentration. Small towns serving inaccessible mining communities originally retailed basic necessities. A large-scale enduring metal-working community, however, needed more sophisticated urban services and so towns developed away from obvious trade routes. In a town like Sheffield there were advantages in having a range of makers of different but related tools working in close proximity. They formed a reliable market for the producers of the raw materials, and a reliable source for the merchants wanting to deal in the end-product. The disadvantages of dealing with the disposal of rubbish from the workshops were less acute than the benefits of a system which guaranteed a regular supply of fixed quality raw materials and the output of a range of goods of varying quality. For long-distance trade, standardisation was a benefit. Midlands industrial settlements slowly developed full urban characteristics, sometimes using raw materials produced as far away as Ireland.

The modest fortunes of the small Welsh towns followed a similar pattern. Of the ten largest towns seven were ports and the other three were trading centres – Brecon, Denbigh and Wrexham. The most prosperous towns, apart from Wrexham, were the 24 coastal towns of English foundation which engaged in maritime trade. The fluctuations of their fortunes may be in counterpoint to the English since, with the support of the local lords, they resisted effective incorporation in the English customs system after the act of Union and became a place for evading payment of customs by unloading and transshipping goods. Cardiff in the 1570s was notorious for its connivance with pirates.[12]

Fish, corn, cereals and coal were exported to France or Ireland and Scotland or coastwise to Gloucester, Bristol and Tewkesbury. Ports which had had no ships of their own gradually acquired them between the 1560s and 1580s. Swansea had a strong local shipbuilding tradition and most of the 37 ships which regularly sailed between Swansea and Mumbles are thought to have been locally built. Overseas trade, however, was dominated by English and French merchants; resident merchants were mainly involved in a coastal trade which was growing slowly . They sent out coal, alum, slate, butter, barley, wheat and malt and took in timber, salt fish, tallow, cloth and wool.[13]

In a few Welsh towns manufacturing became important. Carmarthen, whose hinterland provided good winter pasture, became the centre of a sizeable woollen industry producing primarily friezes and cottons. Wrexham was a centre for leather goods and iron work. A high proportion of townsmen were still also farmers. In a small but comparatively prosperous Welsh town like Cowbridge, cattle were driven daily to pasture and a bye-law stipulated that they should not be milked in the town street. Cardiff had fields in which corn was grown and a moor from which hay was obtained. The wills of Swansea townspeople include farming implements. Such self-sufficiency preserved their inhabitants from the more drastic swings of fortunes which affected those wholly dependent on cloth, but also precluded the profits of specialisation. Small-scale crafts were to be found in most towns, but few specialisations although Haverfordwest had a reputation for leather goods, with gilds of glovers, felt-makers, hatters, cordwainers and shoemakers. They primarily supplied the surrounding countryside with goods and services including entertainments from cockfighting to puppet shows. Like their English counterparts, if less obviously, they were increasing the range of the commodities they could offer for sale including such items as spectacles and razors.

In the sixteenth century most of Ireland's few towns were ports in the south-east with fewer than a thousand people. Gaelic society was structured around war not trade but ports were necessary for staple exports such as grain, wool, fish, tallow, timber, salt, salt beef, herring and salmon, hides, with a lesser amount of manufactured goods such as coverlets and mantles and 'cotton' and, as the century progressed, linen cloth and yarn. There was therefore a fairly steady demand for basic urban service. Even so, periods of depression in the countryside might slow trade, affecting the towns and creating tensions from which trouble could develop. As the century progressed Wexford, Youghal and Waterford prospered from increasing trade in timber; Cork, despite the antagonism of neighbours and pirates, prospered because it was the obvious outlet for south-eastern trade. Trade with England at least quadrupled and the long-established trade with the continent also grew.[14] Although Dublin was becoming the largest centre for trade we should not under-estimate the wealth and prosperity of the nineteen other ports, although Galway and Sligo declined.

Industry, on the other hand, grew slowly. Ireland did not have extensive craft skills or a large enough population to make it profitable. Attempts by governors like Henry Sidney to promote manufacturing in the 'loyal' towns usually backfired. After 1580 a general upturn in urban fortunes was accompanied by the plantation of new towns in Munster with some prosperous small settlements developing but, despite advertising for artisans, industry remained backward.

A steady domestic market for metal work, building and clothing, provided employment in many Scottish towns which served the domestic market. The few large towns, primarily on the east coast and the Firth of Forth were also involved in the export trade. They exported hides, skins, wool, coarse cloth, plaiding, knitted hose and fish. In return they imported timber, iron, flax, hemp, pitch, tar, wine, fine cloths and spices. In good years they exported grain but in poor ones they needed to import large quantities so that the country's economy was on a perpetual knife edge. Manufacturing processes were relatively backwards, cloth and linen were coarse, mainly rural in origin and comparatively unprofitable. Trade was exclusively in the hands of the merchant gild, and royal burghs and exports went to staple towns in Europe. The number of ships was not large, in the mid-sixteenth century the fleet to Veere containing only 17 ships. More ships – 50 to 100 – went to Scandinavia each year to exchange linen and grain for timber.[15] The fortunes of the principal participants – the east coast burghs, especially Edinburgh, Aberdeen, Dundee, – fluctuated with European demand. They supplemented their regular trade, however, with very effective piracy. The period as a whole was relatively prosperous and the towns grew to meet the needs, some in the 'long' sixteenth century doubling their population.

Seventeenth-century Changes

Political disruption of urban life in the seventeenth century was as great as it had ever been in the sixteenth. In the 1620s the Thirty Years War disrupted trade to Spain and France and encouraged privateering and piracy which caused heavy losses to many towns especially in the south and west. Overseas trade rose again in the 1630s but in 1639–40 there was another recession. In the 1640s and 50s towns throughout Britain were turned upside down by the effects of war and taxation. The urban prosperity of the Restoration was disturbed by periodic political and military turmoil, and halted for a time in the early 1690s, particularly in Ireland, when business slumped as a result of war, drought and European recession. Shifts in the relative position of particular towns were also affected by changing overseas trading regions. Most towns, however, were increasingly able to counteract the worst of these outside influences.

By 1600, regional English ports had regained 25 per cent of the export trade and were doing more business in absolute terms than before. Diversification reduced the vulnerability of the ports to a downturn in a particular trade. Different trades like cloth and fish often rose and fell at different times so that one could offset the effect of the other. One trade which grew sharply before 1640 in the western ports was the importation of wine. This rose from under 10 000 tons to 20 000 by the 1620s and nearly 50 000 in 1639. While two-thirds went to London the total amounts unloaded in Bristol and Exeter grew significantly, and Southampton and Hull also participated.[16]

The later seventeenth century saw a considerable increase in coastal trade and in inland traffic. The number of merchant ships was rising and despite fluctuations continued to grow throughout the seventeenth century. The stimulus of the cross-Atlantic trade was being realised by the 1590s. In the 1620s and 30s Hull's Baltic trade was affected by the Thirty Years War but Hull found alternative markets and in the Restoration period its volume of trade once more began to rise sharply. By 1700 it was poised to concentrate all the sea-borne local trade in its hands.

Trade was both diversifying and expanding. English shipbuilding confirms this. After a period in the sixteenth and early seventeenth century when it found it hard to compete with the Dutch it was now becoming highly efficient and its output was growing. Most ports had at least repair facilities and centres for fitting out and victualling. Shipyards multiplied. The Thames estuary was lined with such yards and they were to be found all along the Essex coast.

Industry was also again concentrating in the towns. Towns like Crediton, Cullompton, Tiverton and Exeter in the twenty years before the Civil War became the centres for the new industry in serges; Torrington and Barnstaple centres for the manufacture of baize; Taunton, Wellington and Chad for 'Taunton cottons'. Birmingham and Manchester also began their rapid upward growth.

The growth of trade with colonies in America and the West Indies in the seventeenth century also led to new industries such as tobacco-curing and sugar-refining in many of the ports and increased demand for manufactured implements for colonial sale. Bristol found that brass and pewter goods, a range of specialist metal industries including bell-founding, glass-making and later soap-making, helped fill the gap that the cloth industry had left.[17] The major business in fish which involved not only catching but also salting and curing the catch expanded in both Welsh and south-western ports. Specialists who dealt in nothing but fish dominated a complex trade. Towns in Ireland, Wales and Cornwall and Devon all brought fish to Redcliffe which supplied the whole of the inland West Midlands.

Internal domestic trade is harder to quantify, but lesser East Anglian market towns were recovering by the late sixteenth century. By the seventeenth, many had their own particular market specialty. Diss, North Walsham, Thetford and Swaffham were known for corn, Attleborough for cattle and sheep, and particular towns were centres for worsted or linen. The regular congregating of large numbers of people led doctors, surgeons and apothecaries to establish themselves. The snowballing effect led to their becoming well-favoured country towns, with substantial middle-rank residents living in comfortable houses. Changing transport and communications patterns could assist a town to grow. Thus Lechlade, at the head of the navigable part of the Thames, after a period of decline in the sixteenth century when its wool merchants' houses sat empty, grew with the development of road and river transport in the seventeenth century.

After a shaky start, even towns whose main function was administrative recovered. They prospered as centres of consumption for those who came to attend courts and render accounts. The dominant bureaucracy, whether lay or clerical, was likely to be moderately prosperous and provide a steady demand. This development started in the late sixteenth century but is particularly marked in the Restoration period when the wealth of the gentry and the 'middling sort' increased.

Ireland's urban transformation was dramatic. New towns multiplied and old ones expanded. As the century progressed, growing population and increasing commercialisation changed the shape of the economy and those new towns which succeeded provided the focus. Belfast and the other towns of the Ulster settlement, small as they were, provided a point of penetration for the reshaping of the country.

Growth was primarily the result of a change in the organisation of rural production. A rise in the volume of exports resulted in substantial growth in the ports which handled them, despite the often primitive shipping. The refocusing of Irish trade on England and away from the continent saw a change in the pattern and volume of trade. Much of the trade was carried in English ships, but ports grew with demand for mariners and unskilled labourers, both men and women, who loaded and unloaded the cargoes.

Ireland was also able to share in the colonisation and plantation of North America. New breeds of sheep and cattle led to increasing demand for live Irish animals until the English laws in 1663 and 1667 put an end to this. Butter, cheese and salt beef for the colonies and the navy replaced it. There were important fluctuations – the timber trade boomed in the 1630s and 40s and then died away as the forests were logged out. The fickle herring and pilchard deserted Irish waters reducing fish exports at the same time. The civil wars resulted in nearly two decades of depression. The Irish economy did not start recovering until the late 1660s and suffered another set-back with the Williamite wars in 1689–91. Nevertheless exports rose sharply over the period, towns grew concurrently and the country's wealth increased to the point where there was consumer demand for imports of luxury goods such as tobacco.[18]

The extension of government control also helped the prosperity of the smaller towns. A town like Sligo had declined in the sixteenth century, especially when the herring shoals disappeared in the 1590s. In the seventeenth century it became the centre of English administration and a garrison town. Migrants, mainly

Scots, established the usual trades and it became a comfortable 'county town'.[19]

Few towns in Ireland except Dublin and Kilkenny had much manufacturing before 1660, but later Cork, Waterford and Belfast grew as industrial producers of glass, salt, leather and sugar using mainly imported raw material;[20] English migrants in Conakilty and Tallow promoted textile industries; French refugees helped develop the silk industry in Dublin. The domestic Irish market slowly expanded under this stimulus. The rebuilding of Dublin and the expansion of its leisure facilities suggests that material wealth was substantially increasing although apart from Dublin most towns were poor. A great deal of this growth was, from the beginning, controlled from London. Irish ports had never traded much with one another and by the Restoration the limited local banking and credit facilities reinforced the direct link to London.

In the early seventeenth century the volume of Scottish trade in linen, coal and salt rose. The west coast ports began to expand with increasing trade to Ireland in herrings, coal and brandy. A network of market centres and smaller towns was developing in the lowlands. After the end of the long sixteenth century, however, Scottish towns had far more troubles than their English counterparts. European wars had a more serious impact on Scottish than on English towns. The collapse of trade with the Dutch in the middle of the century led to a crisis for the east coast towns. Recurrent bad harvests, English tariff policy, especially in the 1630s, and the steady migration of Scots from the kingdom constrained growth. In the early 1650s the economy virtually collapsed and recovery was delayed by a trade war with England in the 1660s. The devastation of the countryside carried burghs like Dundee and Aberdeen with it. Wars in the 1690s once again disrupted east coast trade and depressed the ports. The west coast ports and Glasgow, however, were profiting from illicit trade in tobacco and other colonial exports.

Most towns in 1691 were less populous and prosperous than they had been in 1639, which is the antithesis of the English, Welsh or Irish experience. Amongst the few exceptions are some of the inland towns. Crieff, a borough of regality in Scotland, is an excellent example of a successful inland tryst or cattle market of the sort which Lynch sees as expanding in the seventeenth century.

Merchant Practices

One reason for developing prosperity was increasing mercantile professional ability. In 1500, British merchants lacked the skills which made the Italians so effective. Businesses were small and transitory, risks were if possible avoided and there was comparatively little specialisation, even merchant adventurers dealing in a range of imported goods. The closure of the traditional markets like Antwerp, pushed reluctant English merchants into a more entrepreneurial attitude. In the 1560s they started interloping in the prohibited Spanish and Portuguese American markets; in the 1570s they pushed into the Mediterranean; in the 1580s they began hesitantly to consider colonisation and in the 1590s and 1600s they traded directly to the East. All of this required more sophisticated business practices: sources of credit, insurance, and ultimately banking facilities. The merchants who did best were those London merchants who started with adequate capital, but when a lucky 'adventure' (trading voyage) could offer a profit of 400 per cent many poorer people became involved. Not all were in business. The chartered companies raised their money by offering shares to sleeping partners and many better-off politicians and landowners became shareholders, developing a community of interest between property holders of different sorts which was increasingly important in politics and social life by the end of the seventeenth century. As trading patterns became more complex, the bigger merchants specialised in particular commodities and markets, profiting from both insider knowledge and a large market share. Government finances moved towards the Dutch model in which long-term loans from the business community were critical for balancing the budget. The establishment of the Bank of England in 1694 served both mercantile, financial and government ends by providing a means for harnessing money, credit and the incipient stock market.

Dublin was not in a position to provide a rival service and, with the bulk of Irish exports passing through England, became a financial satellite whose merchants operated as conduits for services emanating in London. Edinburgh was also unable to compete on a global level despite the same close links of merchant and landowner. Her merchants were neither numerous nor wealthy enough to provide large-scale credit and merchant money was typically put into wadsetting (loans to lairds secured on their estates) which gave the safest return rather than trade ventures or industry. While merchant risk-taking expanded in Scotland in the early seventeenth century, overseas trade until 1700 remained in the hands of a comparatively few merchants who did not specialise, most being both exporters and importers of all kinds of goods who would also turn their hands to credit and loan activities if they offered a profit.[21] Although in 1600 Aberdeen had about 70 overseas merchants specialising in one commodity, their habit of avoiding partnerships, and limited credit and banking facilities, constrained their business.[22] Absence of specialisation tended to disadvantage them and Scotland was slowly drawn into the wider orbit of financial services supplied by London.

Changes in wholesale business were matched by changes in successful retail practices in the more important towns. Shops ceased to be a front room open to the street where the shutter was lowered to form a counter and most work was 'bespoke' as the craftsman kept a very limited stock. The newer more sophisticated system which spread out from London towards the end of the seventeenth century provided the client with comfort and the possibility of trying the wares before they were purchased. This further differentiated levels in the hierarchy as merchants in the smaller market towns continued to use workshops.

The Distribution of Wealth Amongst Town-dwellers

The wealthiest inhabitants of many English and Welsh towns were not the merchants but the nobles, gentlemen or senior clergy who resided there. What passed for wealth in one town, moreover, was insignificant in another. Wills and inventories show that occupation for occupation, Londoners were wealthier than their provincial counterparts, although merchants from Bristol, Exeter and Norwich impressed even Londoners with their state. Smaller towns occasionally had a particularly wealthy individual but most were limited by the opportunities the town afforded.

If lists of freemen, tax records and apprenticeship records are used to provide a rough estimate of the wealth of different occupational groups it becomes clear that variations between the kingdoms relate mainly to size and function and there are marked similarities between towns with the same size and function. A regular pattern of crafts observable in most towns serves as a template against which specialisation can be measured. Butchers and bakers, tailors and cobblers were the first to appear in any moderately sizeable concentration of population.

Up to twenty occupations are found in smaller towns, forty to a hundred in larger. Occupations found in most towns include the victualling trades: bakers, brewers, maltsters, millers, butchers, fishmongers, innkeepers and alehouse keepers; clothing trades like drapers, weavers, tailors, tanners (leather workers) and cobblers; building trades like carpenters, and perhaps masons, and plumbers; providers of light like candle makers and wax chandlers; generalist metal workers like blacksmiths, coopers (barrel makers) and clerks.

More specialist trades found mainly in larger towns include more specialist ironworkers, builders (tilers and glaziers) and shoemakers; utensil-makers like potters and pewterers; specialist woodworkers like joiners; weapons-makers like bowyers, and fletchers; saddlers as well as mercers; cordwainers; vintners; and in ports, fishermen, rope-makers, shipwrights and sail-makers.

Others found only in the largest towns or specialist towns include booksellers and printers; gun founders; gold and silversmiths; button-makers, hatters and cappers; glovers and hose knitters, tuckers and felt-makers; cutlers and dyers; and shipbuilders. While most trades can be found throughout the period, some, overtaken by technology like the fletchers, gradually declined, while others like glaziers grew.

The smallest towns had specialists in at least twenty trades, and as a rough rule of thumb, the more trades, the larger and more prosperous a town was likely to be. A growing town like Swansea in Wales had as varied a list of occupations as most English towns. Agriculture was a common occupation in the smaller towns but its relative significance tended to dwindle, the larger any particular town became. While typical small market towns would have craftsmen who worked for the immediate neighbourhood and residents whose agricultural concerns were at least equal to their craft interests and who provided a direct link between town and countryside, in larger towns only a few stock owners producing milk, butter and cheese are found.

The numbers of separate trades noted in the bigger towns was rising sharply in the seventeenth century – Norwich had over two hundred by 1700, which suggests a growing specialisation.

Most historians group crafts under more general headings either by types of activity or by type of product, in order to make comparisons and distinguish the main function of the town from subsidiary ones. Seven general types of activity are used: gentry; professional; military and civil officials; merchant; manufacturing and processing; servants; manual, farming and sea. Several of these activities, however, do not produce goods so that a division by product relates only to three or four, if servants are included. The type of product can be summarised as clothing, food and drink, distribution, building, textiles, household, leather, personal services, metal workers, and miscellaneous.

If at least 15 to 20 per cent of trades are usually in the food, drink and clothing sectors, concentrations in particular areas then become obvious. In the early 1520s Norwich, Coventry and Worcester, for instance, all had over 30 per cent in textiles in 1524 which suggests a major specialisation. In Scotland, 30 per cent of Musselburgh's population, 42 per cent of Paisley's and 20 per cent of Perth's were in textiles. This distinguishes them from Aberdeen and Greenock where 21 per cent and 37 per cent respectively were engaged in cooperage. As Irish towns grew and many of the plantation towns were inhabited by significant if not overwhelming numbers of English and Scottish migrants, they started to show the same patterns of occupations, although in smaller towns there was a doubling up of occupations.

The balance between master craftsmen, merchants, retailers and labourers also varied. In the 1524 subsidy 38 per cent in York of people named were paid wages, 40 per cent in Norwich and 46 per cent in Exeter. Welsh town dwellers were relatively poor. In 1543 in Cardiff and Swansea about 40 per cent were taxed on £1–2 and under 10 per cent on £21 although Swansea was markedly poorer than Cardiff.

Most Scottish urban wealth at this time was in the hands of the merchants. Perth was unusual in having her wealth more widely spread with some very wealthy craftsmen. In a merchant town like Aberdeen only 28 per cent were engaged in manufacturing while in Dalkeith and Perth the percentage of 59 and 63 per cent respectively shows a greater dependence on craft.[23] Distribution of wealth thus varied between towns with different functions. Some lacked a significant commercial group, others an agricultural group, while carriers were concentrated in major ports and market towns.

These occupational names may not accurately represent reality. Jobs changed over the course of time; women without formal qualifications worked for fathers and husbands. The growth of specialities within occupations, which was increasing particularly after 1650, can often only be established by collecting job descriptions from miscellaneous sources and may have started well before their first appearance. The forty new trades which appeared in the Norwich freemens' register between 1601 and 1675 suggest a high rate of development in the period.

These general groupings, if disaggregated, show the relative wealth which went with particular occupations and changes in their rank order over time. In most cases the evidence, such as it is, shows a marked pyramidal distribution. The poor, always the largest group, usually made up anything between one-third and three-quarters of the total. Wealth was concentrated in certain professions. A much higher percentage of merchants were likely to pay tax and to pay it at the highest levels. Cloth workers and leather workers were much less likely to pay and, if they did, to pay at the lowest level. Metal workers were even poorer. To some extent this was reflected in the premiums masters demanded for taking apprentices and so wealthy parents were more able to put their children where wealth might be expected, although being a merchant was a hazardous profession with so many potential disasters beyond the individual's control that many once wealthy merchants ended their days impoverished. Apprenticeship lists over time, show a shift from declining trades to burgeoning new ones, illustrating the process of change.

Conclusion

All the evidence points to a considerable change in the sources both of urban wealth and of townspeople's wealth in all the kingdoms between 1500 and 1700. Towns were developing more regular reliable sources of income from which to meet the growing demands for expenditure on improved facilities. In England, Wales and Ireland this seems to go with improved living standards for all except perhaps the very poor. Merchants, in addition to the older staples, carried different goods to new markets and brought back a wider range of goods, some unheard of in 1500. England, which had started ahead, remained ahead. The birth pangs of change caused a crisis in most English provincial towns, although the timing and duration of that crisis differed from town to town. As a result, some towns declined but most survived at a modestly prosperous level while a few like Birmingham grew from nothing into one of the major towns in the country.

The effects of the development between 1500 and 1700 of an international trading network stretching from China to the New World stimulated both production and demand. This in turn made for long-term capital, and improved transmission of information made banks, postal services, common carriers and newspapers essential to all. A slow improvement in the domestic technological base saw the appearance of new products to meet increasingly specialised consumer demand. Better transport helped carry a wider range and volume of goods to all parts of the country to the profit of the towns and those who lived in them. The urban dimension of the economic process meant that an unfulfilled need which promised a profit was rapidly met by the development of a new craft or service, adding to the diversity of occupational structure. Towns, that is to say, were critical to the development of the economy.

5

CONTROLLING TOWNS; TOWN SELF-GOVERNMENT

Self-government is at the heart of town identity. The nature of that government is a critical part of what gives a town its particular identity in terms of the extent of the authority, who had the power to make decisions and what was the main purpose to which they put their power. These factors are critical to understanding the role of a town. The form of such government was changing between 1500 and 1700. The appearance of a highly independent oligarchy in larger boroughs had been identified as one of the 'most notable features' of English urban history in the period. It was the independence of the town elite and their ability to carry their town with them which made them a force to be reckoned with in politics and, during the Civil War, in many towns the problem was that the natural elite were unwilling to serve in such a capacity.[1]

Oligarchies were self-perpetuating but not necessarily impermeable. They were more likely to be linked by marriage than by blood in most English towns. In some Irish towns like Cork and Galway, however, the dominance of certain surnames is much more stable. In Scotland the merchants were likely to leave administration to the lairds who established quasi-hereditary rights to the office of provost. In any case the slow replacement of one family by another meant that the idea of the 'natural' leader was maintained.

The Nature of a Freeman

In theory the freeman, and what he could and should do, was the basis of town life and men living in the town should be freemen. The exclusive rights of a freeman inside the town was what enabled the authorities to impose common practices in the interest of the whole community. The freeman had responsibilities to the community. His commitment to it could not be diluted. He was forbidden to take the livery of a lord or gentleman; he swore not to take his fellows to law outside the town, and if he disobeyed he could be disenfranchised or fined. By 1500, however, not all male residents were freemen. Many towns already limited the numbers they would admit, condemning many to wait for the privilege, and in practice, fewer and fewer people were prepared or able to pay the costs of taking the freedom. At least half passed their lives in the town simply as residents.

The advantages of being a freeman as the period progressed and town government became more oligarchic, had less and less to do with self-government. The advantages freedom conferred came to depend on the form of your business. Exemption from tolls and such charges throughout England could be a considerable saving to those who travelled from market to market and fair to fair on business, carrying with them the evidence of their citizenship. As the pre-emptive right of the town to buy the whole of a cargo of a ship (a town bargain) fell into disuse the freeman's right to a share at the agreed price became less valuable. Such rights lost their attraction.

The Acceptability of Oligarchic Power

The central government preferred power to be focused in a few hands and to hold them responsible for controlling those under them. When the sympathies of the ordinary people resulted in disobedience, town privileges were threatened, a penalty which gave the oligarchy some leverage with the middling sort. Oligarchs, however, needed some favour and credit with ordinary people if they were to be effective in times of crisis.

Avoiding evidence of opposition and maintaining the appearance of consensus was important to the town's autonomy. Risings which the towns were unable to control were liable to result in a loss of privileges and fines. Evidence that there was widespread and continuous anti-authoritarian resentment of the oligarchy by the poorer sort throughout the period is hard to find although the poor might assemble at election time to see what influence they could exert. In the seventeenth century there were anti-oligarchical agitations at Newcastle, Maldon, High Wycombe, Woodstock, Nottingham, Norwich and Colchester, but townspeople in many towns, especially perhaps in the older Irish towns, were more notorious for following their mayor than opposing him. In England conflict over municipal arrangements seems the exception rather than the rule, although certain of the larger cities, for example, York, saw fairly frequent violence at the mayoral elections in the first quarter of the sixteenth century until the franchise was limited.[2]

Town life was not free from strife but this usually took place within an accepted structure of inequality. Violence was, however, quite frequently directed at the nearest authorities by both men and women. In Carrickfergus between 1569 and 1640 all but one of nineteen recorded accusations of violence involved the town authorities.[3] This was not necessarily politically oriented or directed in a simple fashion by the resentment of the poor for the rich. More often it was the outcome of contention between different groups in the same trade struggling to increase their own share of a business as for example between shearmen and tuckers or between two businesses over a limited resource such as a power supply. Riots against machinery which threatened livelihood were not a common feature of town protests until the late seventeenth century when in the East End there were riots against the Dutch loom led by the weavers, which involved breaking into premises and destroying the looms. Riots over religious matters were more likely. Divisions here bore no certain relationship to social status or rank but could divide a community from top to bottom on factional lines. It was the women who protested, with violence, in some places in England at the dissolution of their local religious houses.

The image of consensus as the norm may be deceptive. In Norwich where elections in the sixteenth and early seventeenth century were usually so peaceful as to deserve the description of stately ritual, the Civil War saw the appearance of a rift which split the community and engendered serious riots and disaffection.[4] Divisions within towns frequently seem to represent factional interests whether economic, social or religious or a combination of both which split the elite rather than splitting elite from ordinary citizens.

One reason for seeking consensus was the fear of an appeal to the monarch and the possibility of unpopular royal intervention. Such intervention was not always effective. In Wales where there seem to have been rather more frequent factional disputes than in England the mayoral contests in Monmouth in 1519 led to an appeal to the king and council of the Duchy of Lancaster for a change to the electorate to bring to an end the 'great riots, affrays and unlawful assemblies', but it had little effect.[5]

In Scotland where there were numerous disputes in the sixteenth century there was a similar fear of royal intervention. Some may have been occupation-based with the crafts demanding a role in government. Parliamentary intervention in 1555 to place all craftsmen in burghs under the provost, bailies and council was overturned by Mary of Guise. On the other hand religious divisions are equally likely.[6] Such tensions recurred from time to time. In 1583 Glasgow was threatened with an affray between merchants and craftsmen. In 1606 the deputy bailie Matthew Stuart and the town fought over the town 'freedom'. Consistent, widespread opposition to town authority, however, is no more evident here than in England.

The Role of a Charter

These powers of self-government were not wholly dependent on possessing a charter. The bigger towns generally had one, but the rights awarded were not uniform. David Sacks writing about England and Wales believes that a borough charter is a critical element in a town's autonomous existence, the moment which 'transforms the market settlement into a fully fledged urban community'. The incorporation was the 'crowning moment' of constitutional development.[7] Robert Tittler, on the other hand, thinks that it was largely a matter of prestige in the sixteenth century.

While it was clearly not essential, it was useful. A charter did two things. It set up secure rights to hold a range of courts and it awarded the freemen of the town certain privileges, typically exemption from toll, and most other levies for all their wares and merchandise throughout the kingdom. The variations could be considerable: charters were not uniform, they could be and frequently were amended. Throughout the period such emendations generally restricted access to the freedom and participation in election, on the alleged grounds of the unruly nature of the commonalty and their lack of contribution to the common purse. People who could not contribute to the expenses should not contribute to decisions over expenditure.

The crown, though, had no real wish to assume a permanent direct role in urban management. Indeed, the monarch saw advantages in increasing a town's privileges in order at the same time to increase its responsibilities. Charters were granted throughout the period to new boroughs in both England, Wales and Ireland in return for loyalty. When loyalty was suspect, however, the crown used *Quo Warranto* proceedings to challenge traditional rights and to resume them. *Quo warranto* proceedings were a favourite royal device for altering the basis of relationship between central and local government. In the 1620s they were used in Ireland, in the 1630s against Bristol, which was obliged to abandon its claim to absolute independence from the court of admiralty.

The differences between a town with a charter and one without varies with the particular aspect of urban affairs in question. Market towns had market courts. A charter did not exempt town inhabitants from all liability to obey the summons of other crown courts. On the other hand incorporation enabled a borough to sue and be sued like an individual in the courts and this, while not an everyday occurrence, could be vital to the maintenance of rights important for the well-being of the community. A corporate existence made it easier for a town to take retaliatory or even aggressive action against its rivals. Towns thus used the royal courts to get a resolution, hopefully in their favour. For the same reason, ports sought and sometimes managed to obtain the admiralty jurisdiction which allowed them to hear sea-causes, a very important consideration for sea-going merchants.

The relationship between political independence and economic prosperity is not, however, self-evident. Towns which were theoretically entirely dependent could enjoy greater material well-being than those that were self-governing. Wrexham, for instance, perhaps denied a charter because its population was predominantly Welsh, flourished without any municipal organisation beyond manorial courts because of its strategic importance and its role in regional Welsh trade and industry. It had a shire hall called the common hall and Hall of Pleas with a grand chamber used for the great and quarter sessions. When this was dilapidated, it was the county which raised the money for its repair.[8]

The sixteenth and seventeenth centuries saw continuing changes in the extent and nature of town self-government. Town authorities took what steps they could to supplement the basic powers their town charter gave them by additional powers which freed the town from the intrusion of central government or other authorities. The more successful of them obtained incorporation in the sixteenth century. York, Bristol, Newcastle upon Tyne, Hull, Norwich, Lincoln, Arundel and a handful of others had by 1603 the rare privilege of county status which entitled them to more extensive legal authority and complete protection from interference from the county sheriff. Towns excluded the county authorities from serving ordinary writs or arresting people in the town.

Most towns which had no royal charter were simple market towns on the estate of a subject who had no wish to divest him or herself of the benefits which the town could produce. They were therefore governed through the ordinary apparatus of the manor. Such an individual might grant some self-government through a charter or more rarely ask the monarch to confer additional rights. Not all such towns were small. Bury St Edmund's, which belonged to the abbey, was one of the largest and wealthiest in England. In this period, moreover, it was often new or fast-growing towns like Sheffield, owned by private individuals, which were the fastest growing and it has been argued that this was in part due to the absence of gild regulation.

There were disadvantages to living in such a town. The interests of the lord might not coincide with those of the inhabitants. The functions of constables, conservators and justices would be exercised by bailiffs appointed by the lord against whom the inhabitants had few avenues of appeal. The relationship of such towns with their lords could be tense. Wells, which had made efforts to obtain independence from the bishop throughout the Middle Ages, only succeeded in 1589 when episcopal finances were at a low ebb. Before that the bishops had asserted as much control as was prudent without driving the burgesses away. A town like Stow-on-the-Wold was able throughout the sixteenth century to behave as if it were self-governing and when in 1605 a change of lord threatened interference it maintained a legal struggle for a quarter of a century.[9]

Welsh and Irish towns came under the same rules as English towns but Scottish towns were somewhat different. They fell into three clear categories, although their level of political, social or economic importance is not necessarily determined by that category. Royal burghs which the monarch had established on his domain not only had self-government but also valuable privileges which only the monarch could confer – a monopoly of foreign and domestic trade and a monopoly over their hinterland. These were several times reconfirmed by parliament in the sixteenth century. Their rights were more likely to be uniform than those of English towns.

Burghs of barony had charters from the great baronial families or ecclesiastics that imitated royal grants as far as they could. They had self-government and numbers of them were established from the fifteenth century with a weekly market, annual fair and crafts designed to meet strict local demands for goods and services. Burghs of regality were held from lords in the same way but with additional rights. Towns rarely appeared without some formal legal status. The royal burghs were by definition members of the Convention of Royal Burghs but the burghs of barony or regality might also join when they became liable to contribute to royal taxation. This greater legal clarity probably made less difference in practice than would at first seem likely.

The Town Authorities

In English, Welsh and Irish chartered towns the oligarchy were formally selected by and from the townsmen although the appointed office of steward could still be significant. The principal honourable officials were unpaid. The honorary officials might be changed and augmented, and positions might be amalgamated or divided as the town's needs altered but they almost invariably included the mayor and aldermen, although in a few chartered towns like Kingston upon Thames and Worcester, the main officials were two unpaid bailiffs. There was a small group, often 'the twelve', or in larger towns 'the twenty-four' who were aldermen frequently chosen for life, and a larger 'lower house' – the forty-eight (or twenty-four) – and in some places an assembly of freemen who participated to different degrees in decision-making. The town finances were usually supervised by one or more chamberlains although in a larger town there might be a number of officers. The often complicated process of electing aldermen made it in many places what it was overtly in some, a self-replacing system whereby the existing aldermen determined who should join them. In towns without charters the principal officials were commonly long-term salaried bailiffs primarily responsible to whoever was the landlord, although in some places the townsmen had won the right to select the bailiffs for themselves from amongst their fellows.

The Scottish position, where the principal officer was the provost, often a local lord, had slightly different divisions of power from the English. Perth, for instance, was governed by a provost, four bailies and a council of twelve. This was an elite, self-perpetuating body, where each Michaelmas the outgoing council chose the new one and then old and new, together with the deacons of the incorporated crafts, elected a provost and four bailies to serve as magistrates for the coming year.

Innumerable studies have shown that those selected for the dignity of town office were overwhelmingly the wealthiest in the town. Studies of the *cursus honorum* in various towns show that men first held office by their early thirties and had reached the top by their mid to late forties. The total number of individuals in the course of a century who were aldermen in any given town was not necessarily very large. In York in the sixteenth century there were 106. By 1550, 58 served on average 12.5 years and from 1551–1600 48 served 18 years.[10] This position did not change significantly in the seventeenth century.

Occupying a position of rank within a town could be costly, involving personal expense and in exceptional circumstances even ruin. Service was therefore widely seen as an appropriate contribution to be expected from those who could afford it. It implied a legalised fusion of power and property. Some historians have discerned a 'flight from office' in the late Middle Ages which has been equated with an urban crisis, although there were still places where there was competition for the honour. Town bye-laws usually provided for a substantial fine for those who refused, which could become a major source of town finances.

The disadvantages of being a mayor could be considerable. Mayors who followed their own consciences, however popular they may have been with their fellow citizens, were increasingly likely to be stripped of their powers by the central government as it slowly extended its ability to enforce its wishes. On numerous occasions where mayors asserted town privileges against the politically powerful they found themselves in gaol for their pains, and not always reimbursed by the town. Mayors could be the focus for personal resentment – most towns had special fines for those who assaulted the town officers precisely because they were likely to be targets of violence. Sometimes more complicated civil attacks could ruin the mayor. Other hazards included the octopus-like tentacles of the requirements of accounting in the Exchequer.

The oligarchy, then, had an unrivalled opportunity to preserve its own interests. When York, Chester and Exeter limited the right to trade abroad to those who were solely merchants it favoured the group from which the oligarchy was drawn and curtailed the possibility of craftsmen slowly transferring to merchant status. Excluding traders from the market unless they took the town freedom hampered country traders who did not contribute to town rates. The confusion of public and private sometimes also led to corruption as the mayor, chamberlains or aldermen took advantage of their position to manipulate town property or rights in their own favour.

Town Procedures

However they were chosen, and with whatever reluctance they accepted, mayor and aldermen were the monarch's officers, bound by royal law. In all major decisions the mayor was to take the advice of the city's council, usually the aldermen, who were the 'brothers' of the mayor, and of an inner body of advisers for day to day business. General policy issues touching on important matters, for example, problems of mercantile or marine law, particularly in relation to methods of raising credit, like bills of adventure, would also go to the twenty-four or forty-eight.

In the town the mayor had various hats he could wear. He was normally a JP and clerk of the market, which gave him authority to set prices unless the royal court was in the vicinity when the markets fell within the 'verge' and control of the markets passed to the king's clerk of the market. These powers did not entirely prevent outside interference. Towns, if they could, liked to get the extended powers which enabled them to hear cases normally reserved for the Crown, to impose punishments normally reserved for quarter sessions or assizes and to exercise admiralty jurisdiction. Responsibility for maintaining order was the mayor's but inhabitants were expected to come at his summons to help put down affrays and help maintain the king's peace.

The unpaid officials were supplemented by as many paid officials as the town could afford. Senior in dignity was the recorder, the professional legal officer, often someone who went on to a major post in the central courts. Next was the town clerk who also required legal skills – sometimes the position was sold to its occupant who made his living from the fees. Towns which had royal pleas also had at least one coroner. Most towns had a considerable list of less dignified paid officials from constables to ale tasters, clerks of the market, haywards, gaolers, cooks and chaplains, bellmen and others. The wealthier the town the wider the range. Most were men, but where there were poor houses or bridewells women might be employed as overseers of the women's work.

Town government followed a certain pattern in most towns. Some towns had what amount to manuals to guide the 'amateurs' who undertook the work and guides to the precedents which controlled the town's practices. How and where the groups who were supposed to make policy met and how such meetings were notified was slowly formalised. In most larger towns by the mid-sixteenth century there was a regular weekly meeting which was announced by a specific signal such as the blowing of a trumpet. Rules of procedure were gradually developed. The major towns came to set down rules and penalties for giving notice of meetings, the reading of minutes, the number required for a quorum, failure to attend or leaving early. Regulations governed the manner and order in which members were to speak and the number of times they could do so on a single issue and whether unanimity was required.[11]

The role of the gilds in urban management has been down-played in most towns but should not be ignored as craft gilds and companies which regulated trade practices existed in most towns. Membership of a gild was evidently desirable, and where towns had only a few gilds they might take in craftsmen from vaguely associated – or in some cases quite unassociated – areas. Their main use seems to have been in organising such things as tax assessments for the corporation. Although members may have had an annual feast and felt an obligation to contribute to their colleagues' funerals there is little evidence of any other role. Membership tied an artisan to a largely artificial framework so far as limitations on what he could do were concerned.[12]

Town Responsibilities

The responsibilities which were thus undertaken by town officials were complex and the interests of central and local government sometimes mismatched. The primary object of town government was to enable the community to enjoy the maximum well-being and that meant the best infrastructure that they could afford.

A community's survival eventually depended on food and water, housing and defence. The daily business of town government revolved around the management and maintenance of essential services. Towns' defences have already been referred to and in many towns absorbed a significant percentage of town income. Analysis of a town's expenditure shows the changing face of its problems as it lurched from crisis to crisis. The disruption of war years can be seen in extraordinary military expenses. Dislocation due to plague was costly in other years. Intermittent expenses such as legal costs, payments to commissioners for attending parliaments and conventions, state and local celebrations, gifts of wine to distinguished visitors and help to the needy and distressed may in any one year overbalance the budget, delaying the performance of common jobs such as repairing roads and bridges, shoring up the harbour bulwark, repointing the tollbooth, mending the town clock and paying employees.

One of the trickiest issues and one which caused the most trouble was the management of the measures and prices of bread and ale. There was a clear relationship between the idea of fixed wage levels and the price of bread. A shortfall in food supplies was the most likely event to trigger a rising or a organised mob taking the law into its own hands and forcibly distributing grain it had seized at 'fair' prices. To ensure that the town price was seen to be fair the council normally prevented anyone in the trade from sitting as part of the jury which settled such matters. If large gatherings were expected, special precautions were taken to ensure that prices did not rise to take advantage of the position. Precautions were also taken to ensure that the poor could buy in small quantities at a reasonable price, frequently by allocating the first market hour to such purchases.

The strict regulation of bread, meat and ale inevitably caused friction and occasionally conflict when the bakers, butchers and brewers thought that their profit margins had been cut too fine. Occasionally they went on strike, refusing to work at their trade, but the central government did not look favourably on this and they were usually obliged to bake and brew even when the basic ingredients were scarce and no profit could be made. If conditions grew too difficult the central government itself took a hand to prevent hoarding. The larger towns like Norwich and Bristol eventually followed London's lead in managing their own corn market and buying sufficient stocks for distribution at regulated prices.[13] Other towns did so in crisis times, buying corn for resale to the poor at lower prices and levying the rich to provide the subsidy. Towns were also usually responsible for regulating the itinerant bakers who went out into the countryside with their loaves for sale. Inns, taverns and ale houses in which food and drink was served needed to be licensed and to obey the bye-laws.

Water supply, sewerage and cleanliness took another important slice of town revenue. Wells and springs, even outside the town boundaries, were diligently protected. An abundant or even adequate water supply was a natural blessing. Towns without it were likely to face considerable expenditure. Northampton had water brought by conduit by the late Middle Ages and was constantly enlarging and improving and overhauling its supply, although in drought years there were still problems. Chester had similar arrangements after 1575. The concept was to bring the water to a central cistern from which it could be drawn. The practice was emulated by other towns as and when they could afford it. London, where a company of water carriers had drawn water from the Thames for sale, eventually allowed private enterprise to solve the growing problem by bringing water from the Lea.

Paved streets and drainage were important. In towns on steep hillsides like Newcastle, the paving might be designed to give horses purchase. Causeways or paved packhorse routes outside the towns were desirable. Towns situated on rivers usually had bridges to maintain. The town authorities also jealously guarded the town fields which, although they did not supply all the town's food, were an essential buffer.

In ports, improvement of quays and piers, river dredging and marker buoys could make the difference between survival as a community and disappearance. Control over the harbour was therefore essential. When, as at Dartmouth, the river was part of the Earldom of Cornwall, the authorities sought to be appointed as the 'water bailiffs' who collected dues and regulated offences to avoid conflict of interest and were able to hold the office, with only two breaks from 1508 to the mid-nineteenth century. By the sixteenth century Aberdeen had sufficient authority to fix its own dues on ships and goods and provide protection and beacons. Ports routinely made rules about harbour safety. Regulations were reiterated, doubtless often fruitlessly, against dumping in the channels of ballast or rubbish. Where access to the port and its quays was tricky, as it so often was, towns regulated the pilotage.

Disaster Management

Prevention or containment of epidemic diseases was a continuing problem. The slow spread of rigid quarantine rules across the country from the capitals to the greater towns and eventually to the smaller more isolated places can be mapped. In Scotland, Edinburgh enforced such rules by 1530 and Aberdeen followed suit. In Ayr by 1544, at the tidings of the epidemic's approach, the streets were cleaned, the ports guarded by a special watch, strangers were required to have a certificate of health issued by the authorities of their own town; sickness was to be brought to the magistrates' attention; those with the plague were to be isolated on the 'foule mure', a stretch of waste ground forming part of the burrowfield, in hastily erected wooden booths and looked after by the 'foul clengers' and their infected goods and gear boiled up in large cauldrons. Those who tried unsuccessfully to escape were burned with a hot iron on the cheek. Infected houses were disinfected by water and fire; ships were quarantined. The costs to the town were very great – half of the 'Common Good' in a year.[14] In England, the practice had reached Worcester by 1593[15] and was dramatically introduced at the persuasion of the minister at Eyam in 1663.

Tempest, fire and flood were further looming disasters. Taking preventative steps to prevent or control fires was a major headache for the authorities. They endeavoured to regulate building materials to outlaw the most easily flammable, to isolate bake-houses, check chimneys and chimney sweeps and they arranged for ladders and buckets and hooks to be available usually as a requirement from a group of citizens, but often to little effect. Major fires destroyed large parts of Tiverton, Nantwich, Northampton and Dorchester. Tewkesbury near the confluence of the Severn and Avon had a recurrent flood problem.

Welfare and Education

The towns were also deeply involved in the care of the poor, the orphaned and the sick. Poor relief could be costly and the costs escalated dramatically at moments of crisis such as famine or plague when the numbers of dependent widows and orphans were likely to rise suddenly. A temporary crisis could see as many as 20 per cent of the inhabitants receiving relief but stringent means testing usually kept the average percentage below 2, although there were many others who were in need of assistance. Commonly, towns preferred to use mechanisms which provided cheap food, rather than direct subsidy. Swansea regularly bought up to a third of all the goods brought to the town hall for resale to the poor. The introduction of workhouses towards the end of the sixteenth century marks a turning point in which sympathy for the out-of-work turned to criticism of the lazy and attempts to extract labour which would pay for their maintenance. Even children, the elderly and infirm were not wholly exempt from this attitude. The special court of orphans which existed in some towns was only for those with an inheritance to be cared for.

The spiritual and intellectual development of the young, however, served an important function in supplying the next generation of citizens. Towns sometimes had loan funds available to assist young journeymen who wanted to set up in business for themselves, or a fund to provide poor young girls with a dowry. They often had a grammar or a free school and they increasingly interfered with what had been the church's prerogative of controlling schools. Where the Reformation had resulted in the confiscation of the property which had supported the school, they attempted to reestablish it from lands or bequests under their control. They not only appointed these grammar schoolmasters but increasingly sought to control the syllabus and license other schoolteachers despite problems in finding able and competent men.

We can get an insight into what was provided in a typical town school from the surviving school regulations for Monmouth. The number of scholars was limited to 100 with two masters, probably adequate for the size of the town. The day started at 7 a.m. with prayers, dinner was at 11 a.m. and school resumed from 1.30 to 5 except on Thursdays. Annual holidays were Christmas, Easter and Whitsun. Scripture played a prominent part in the curriculum but the six levels were primarily concerned to learn to understand, read, write, and pen English, Latin and Greek.[16] The masters did their best to make the grind more palatable by using sentences – vulgari – which related to their pupils' experiences.

In the later Middle Ages towns had normally provided for some forms of entertainment. Waits or minstrels were routinely paid and towns might own musical instruments. Until strict Protestantism took hold towns also encouraged the production of plays and pageants. In Aberdeen at Candlemas, for example, craftsmen presented a play, *The Three Kings of Cologne.* Ipswich routinely levied money from the portmen, the twenty-four and freemen to pay artificers for staging the Corpus Christi plays and to those who made and looked after costumes and ornaments. Spreading Protestant austerity after 1570 meant that town licensing of wandering players was refused or hedged with restrictions.

Authorities later struggled against morris dancing and maypoles as heathen activities. Sport, however, was supported in some towns. Glasgow paid for six footballs on Shrove Tuesday. Golf was seen as recreational and permissible in many Scottish towns and racing was even allowed in some.[17] In the seventeenth century cockpits were built in towns patronised by the gentry. Bear baiting was popular. On the other hand, towns in all the kingdoms regulated what were called unlawful games (usually various forms of gambling).

Management of all these activities was a form of social control, sometimes using the carrot and other times the stick, but in all things pursuing a long-term policy. Pageants and plays could be a means of persuasion; bye-laws that regulated the times at which people could drink in ale houses and the length of time they could spend there used penalties. Religious and economic motives reinforced a patriarchal sense of social propriety. Numerous towns, for example, were taking steps to restrict the opportunities open to single women and to control their behaviour. Bye-laws prohibited feasting at churchings (the ceremony celebrating a woman's return to church after giving birth) permitting only a simple 'mess of meat' for gossips and midwives.

Financing Town Government

Funding all this activity was often a problem. Towns in 1500 had a variety of sources of income but they were rarely sufficient. Although levies for particular purposes were becoming more frequent and rates in the seventeenth century became the main source of revenue, towns in the sixteenth century depended on such things as property, local customs, tolls, the rents of market stalls and perhaps the fines in the town courts, local customs duties and the like. In Ireland in the sixteenth century the big ports like Cork had royal customs duties as well. Scottish towns had a similar mixture of resources.

Town income thus varied considerably but everywhere needed to be increased if advantage was to be taken of potential opportunities. A great deal of effort was spent on attracting business, ensuring that merchants found it profitable to operate in their town rather than a neighbouring town. Towns improved their facilities in ways calculated to attract merchants and used their powers to provide the services which would ease business. Additional markets and fairs, for example, could be a significant economic boost to the town, and the swift justice which the market or fair court offered was an attraction to traders. Regulating, recording and preserving business transactions was a jealously guarded right because, if a town had a reputation for probity and fairness, merchants would be more anxious to trade there.

Retention of the assizes and other administrative functions were worth fighting for, because they brought in the gentry and prosperous rural people for significant periods and while they were there they spent money. The benefits of immediate and final local decision-making in administrative and judicial matters were unquestionably a factor in the willingness of individuals, particularly transitory merchants, to do business in a locality. A particular town's power to manoeuvre may have been limited. Southampton, badly affected by the monopolies of the Levant company, was not very successful.[18] The extent to which towns could achieve improvements to their position often depended directly upon their existing resources.

A new charter, or even a confirmation of an old one, required a series of payments to the bureaucrats and possibly even larger *douceurs* to those who promoted it. Even presenting a private bill to parliament involved fees to the clerks and if it was to be heard in time, measures to ensure it was high in the pile of bills and sympathetically received. The monarch's assent was even more problematic. Too great a display of wealth would certainly be remembered at more inconvenient moments, too little would not achieve results. Lawsuits were costly and not always successful.

In many cases, the private resources of the officials became involved in the process, since the direct resources of the town frequently bore no relationship to the wealth of its citizens. Most towns, however, benefited considerably from the fees attached to admissions to citizenship and would sometimes open the freedom to a certain number in order to raise sums for particular purposes. Thus in 1582, when Shrewsbury wanted to pay for a preacher, it raised £400 by admitting 80 new freemen and in 1583 it admitted 20 more to pay for its new charter.[19] Other towns found themselves borrowing to meet specific needs such as a corn supply for the poor, expecting to recoup the money and repay the loan when the goods were retailed.

Bequests were therefore very welcome and were well publicised sometimes for centuries. At Rochester in 1579, Richard Watts esquire, a town resident, left money to provide lodging for one night for six poor travellers who also received four pence to help them on their way. On the main route to the capital from the continent this was a helpful charity, and nearly two centuries later another Richard Watts, as mayor, erected a monument in the cathedral commemorating it.

Such actions were useful in encouraging others and one may suspect much quiet preparation preceded the charitable bequests of the wealthy. Towns probably preferred gifts which relieved them of inevitable expenditure like the repair of bridges rather than complicated provisions like those of the mid-sixteenth-century London mayor and alderman Thomas White, which were to provide capital loans for promising but impoverished young journeymen in several provincial towns, although over the years creative accounting enabled Coventry to milk the rising proceeds of that endowment.

Reducing expenditure was also popular. Pleas of poverty in the face of royal demands were common. Although the ports urged the government to supply navy vessels to patrol the coasts against pirates they sought to minimise levies to pay for them. This is not surprising as they usually faced heavy expenditure to maintain the harbour and access from silting to which the central government made no contribution.

There was a general tendency to present work which had a public face as the private responsibility of the citizen. Thus private acts of parliament required householders to keep the streets in front of their houses paved. Bye-laws required them to keep the streets clean and in some places to provide lanterns and candles during certain hours in the evening so that the streets would be lit. When the free labour of the citizens was pushed to its limits, however, levies had to be resorted to, especially in plague years when extra cleanliness was desirable.

Law Enforcement

Towns were inevitably places where disputes resulted in conflict so that one defining physical characteristic of a town was a gaol and it was the authorities' job to make sure the gaol was secure, particularly since the common law rules about the escape of those imprisoned on civil charges made those responsible liable for considerable damages. Boroughs typically had authority over both civil and at least lesser criminal actions. The nature of this authority was what most distinguished a borough from a town without a royal charter and gave at least some advantage to the borough town. The borough courts' records were vital to trading activities. The courts usually met at least weekly, while the manorial courts held in non-incorporated towns normally met only thrice yearly, or at most once every three weeks. There would be a court associated with the market but limited to cases arising in the market time.

In handling matters from the routine affairs of nuisance, vagrancy, apprenticeships and defective weights, to complex mercantile disputes, real and movable property and debts, contracts and breaches of agreement, the authorities needed integrated legal powers. Admiralty jurisdiction was essential to enable ports to hear cases which might prejudice the common good such as those relating to fish garths or to wrecks sunk in the channels to the impediment of the ships and fishing boats using the harbour as well as cases for breach of contract or negligence which had a marine component and problems with pilots or fishing matters. Scottish towns had similar judicial arrangements and similar potential limitations on their powers. In Ayr the claims of other tribunals had to be admitted although burghal jurisdiction could be extended by a royal commission of justiciary.

The mayor's duty of enforcing law and maintaining order was not confined to borough inhabitants, which was particularly hard on towns which were regular transit points for travellers or visiting sailors. Soldiers were a particular problem as it was never wholly clear whether a case belonged to the town or to the army provost-marshal. Towns where soldiers were regularly embarked such as Dover or Rye, Bristol or Chester, developed their own defensive techniques including the visible erection of gallows to remind the soldiers of authority. Bye-laws usually stipulated that visitors to the town leave their weapons at their inn or hostelry before going out into the town.

Conclusion

Town self-government was never absolute. At every period it was subject to interference both by the local gentry and by central government. Towns knew which side their bread was buttered. Even fully fledged chartered towns often owed their prosperity to the support and encouragement of a local patron who provided the political leverage which produced useful concessions from the central government and very often the capital necessary to realise the projects. Frequently it was only external funding of the construction of a critical piece of infrastructure, such as a pier, which determined which settlement would prosper. Towns which attempted to challenge the power of the local lord were likely to find themselves backing down.

Relations with royal officials could be more fraught because royal favour was expensive to obtain and not always reliable. Co-operation and mutual trust between town officials, shire authorities, ecclesiastical courts, admiralty and the Councils was ideal but not always achieved. Central government expected town support and obedience. The extent to which towns avoided obeying or answering may have varied but intransigent contumacy would bring punishment. The crown expected the oligarchy to suppress local riots and resistance including food riots, religious riots, political riots and charges of corruption and favouritism.

Town autonomy became increasingly notional as central government increased its resources and reduced its tolerance of disobedience. Even in the sixteenth century the Scottish crown was beginning to override its burghs, and as the seventeenth century progressed the Stuarts also interfered more and more in town appointments. The relationship was changing in other ways, however. The power that the oligarchs possessed was strengthened by the regular meetings of parliament which permitted towns to develop common strategies and which could be used to protect their interest.

6

THE CAPITALS

A capital does not have to be the largest city in the state. It does not have to be the wealthiest, or the cultural centre. The single necessary criteria for a capital is apparently that it be the administrative centre of a state. Edinburgh only became the capital of Scotland when the Stuarts removed from Perth after the assassination of James I in 1437. Royal government was carried on from Westminster and London city authorities took pains to exclude royal visits to the city except on formal ceremonial occasions. The monarch had no residence in the city; important meetings were usually held at Blackfriars. The close proximity of Westminster to London, however, gave the city all the advantages of the capital without some of its inconveniences and it had been the premier city since the Normans. Dublin's position as late as the 1630s has been described as 'less the capital of a kingdom, as was its constitutional position, than the centre of a colony'.[1] Wales had four regional centres of administration, no one of which was more important than another, for before the English conquest Wales had never acknowledged a single centre and there was no advantage to the English monarchs in creating one.

Growth of the Capitals

As the period progressed the three capitals became increasingly

91

dominant. Each came to house a growing percentage of the total population of the kingdom. All grew at a faster rate than the general population, and were at least double the size of their nearest urban rivals. This can be measured both in terms of physical change and the provision of services as well as by the complex occupational and social structure which they sustained. In 1500 all three cities were walled, defensive areas with comparatively little suburban growth. By 1700 they had outgrown their walls, and suburbs sprawled in several directions, so that they deserved the title of metropolis, which confuses the issue of the area covered in any estimate. Was 'London' just the city within the walls, or the area 'within and without', the 25 wards, or 113 or 122–3 parishes, the 'city and suburbs' or 'London and Westminster'.[2] Edinburgh likewise may be the city within the walls, or the extended area which includes the separate borough of regality of Canongate, and Bristo.

Dublin in 1500 was the smallest. As a city of probably 4000 people, although significantly larger than Limerick, Waterford or Cork, it was still smaller than a number of English provincial towns. After 1600 it experienced the most rapid exponential growth in the period. In 1682 the population was counted as 64 483, nearly six times the size of its nearest rivals and by 1728 it had reached 146 675. Its growing wealth was reflected in its dramatic rebuilding.

Edinburgh was growing more slowly and it was significantly less wealthy than London. By 1560 it had a population within the walls of c.12 000 and including the Canongate 15–18 000; probably not even twice the size of Aberdeen and no larger than the biggest of England's provincial cities. By 1592 the city within had only grown to 15 000 and by 1650 to perhaps 20 000, still no larger than Norwich. By the 1690s greater Edinburgh which included North and South Leith had reached 40–47 000, 2.5 times the size of Glasgow which was a real competitor for the dominant mercantile role. Its residents, however, may have been less wealthy than they had been at the beginning of the century.

London far outstripped them both. From 1500 when there may have been 50 000 residents within and without, it had grown by 1600 to about 250 000. By 1700 the built-up area extended far beyond the centre with its 120 000 residents and this metropolitan area counted around 500 000 people, seven times larger than Dublin and twenty times larger than the nearest English town. It was the largest city in Europe and possibly the fourth largest in the world. Perhaps four times larger than the next largest English city in 1500, its wealthiest merchants were already far wealthier than the merchants in the smaller cities and towns. Their wealth surpassed that of many of the gentry and nobility and the London oligarchy funded both monarch and empire.

The moments of greatest growth, however, did not coincide with periods of general demographic growth. The period after 1580 when general growth was slowing saw rapid growth in London. The period after 1650 when general population was probably falling was again a period of growth in London and Dublin.

Topographical Structure

Rebuilding in all three cities had imposed a new image of order upon the public face of the city, a social landscape which reflected the diminishing importance of walls and the increasing importance of public buildings, including great churches. London ceased to conform to the older social pattern whereby the wealthy lived in 'a central straggling core' of parishes while the poor lived nearer the walls. As houses near the big arterial routes became less attractive, the rich began to live in segregated areas away from the worst pollution. On the other hand, the growth of the dock areas and the shipbuilding yards below London Bridge, was creating an area of shipwrights and sailors which had few very wealthy residents. Nearby villages specialising in particular crafts were drawn into the metropolitan orbit. The West End was beginning to grow as the area in which polite society had houses occupied at least in what was becoming known as 'the Season'.

At the beginning of the sixteenth-century Edinburgh still had open spaces and yards. By the end of the sixteenth century these were built over, the housing in the wynds was going upwards and the water supply was giving cause for concern. The centre was still the home of professional and merchant, however. Canongate housed manufacturing while North and South Leith and West Kirk were poor.

Dublin in the sixteenth century was poorly built. Stanihurst's claim that Dublin excelled 'in gorgeous buildings, in the multitude of people, in martiall chivalrie, in obedience and loyaltie, in the abundance of wealth, in largeness of hospitalitie, in maneres and civilitie' is more a testament to his rhetorical skills than of the real facts. Clocks were a sufficient novelty when they were introduced in 1560 to be the subject of derivative verse. The cathedral itself in the early seventeenth century was so dilapidated that lotteries to raise money for repairs were permitted. In 1630, that indefatigable traveller Sir William Brereton noted the expansion of buildings to new areas, but it was after the Restoration that most growth occurred. New bridges were erected, suburbs were developed, a great deal of the central buildings were rebuilt in a classical style and the corporation built an impressive new Thosel which was to be a meeting place not only for the council but also for merchants and gilds.

City/Crown Relationships

The internal government of a capital city involves difficulties greater than those of an ordinary town. The advantages which accrue from the business central government brings to the city are partially offset by the additional demands. The competing needs of the central government, and the ramifications of the decisions the city fathers make as a local institution on the interests of central government in matters from the policing of the streets, the management of leisure activities and the water supply, make external interference a high probability.

Unlike Paris, however, which was never able wholly to shed royal direction, the three British capitals were all formally self-governing. All three cities were very conscious of their identity and standing, which they demonstrated through a variety of ceremonial acts, similar to those in smaller towns but carried out with far more pomp and drama. Marking their territory was one face of authority, the other was the symbolism of legitimation, the source of the signs of authority with which the city's officials might surround themselves which showed their ultimate responsibility to the monarch. The city mace, a sword, a collar and a cap of maintenance were all signs of loyalty.

Claims that London's government was quite separate from the central government are exaggerated. Certainly they were proud of their autonomy and strove to maintain it. Obvious royal intervention in the choice of mayor was certainly rare, but influence was another matter and mutual advantage made the relationship more subtle. The capital's relationship to the Crown was exceptional and complicated. It was reflected in the public ceremonies which surrounded their formal and informal meetings. It was expressed in quarrels over jurisdictional competence between city and royal officials. It was influenced by the city's military capacity. It underlay the monarch's efforts to intervene in city troubles.

The greatest threat to autonomy came if the city authorities lost internal control. In London when the crowd overpowered the forces of the lord mayor and the other city magistrates and compelled them to have the gaols opened and the prisoners released during the 1517 'evil May day' riots, Surrey and his father Norfolk entered the city by force on the king's behalf, captured the ringleaders and quelled the trouble. When in September there was the threat of a further outbreak the city authorities were anxious to handle it themselves and produced 3000 city householders in battle array.

London thereafter paid careful attention to its own defences. In 1549 it had its watch and trained bands on alert to deal with any spread of the country risings. In 1554 the city stood to arms as the first uprising that century to reach its walls approached. London continued to be a source of troops for royal armies down to the Civil War. Even after the Restoration many citizens had arms.[3] The Civil Wars led to a much greater level of central government interference with the army in London. The factional politics of the city at the time were complex, but no one could fail to notice that on two occasions in 1647 and 1649 when the city refused to obey a parliamentary order the lord mayor himself and several aldermen were sent to the Tower.

Royal demands after the Restoration were greater but the influence of the political parties in the city had increased on the same scale. Serving the monarch was one thing, admitting his interference in internal politics another. Preventing it demanded that the authorities maintain control over the increasingly anonymous crowd. Londoners were the representatives of the kingdom in many public displays. It was the London crowd which turned out for royal coronations and funerals and London officials who marched in the processions. The role of the London crowd in politics was increasingly unpredictable as the seventeenth century progressed. The anti-popery marches which began in 1673–80 brought a renewed threat of violence. There was increasingly a risk of rioting amongst the anonymous poor. City politics required the maintenance of control.

London was usually remote from battles, but both Dublin and Edinburgh faced direct threats especially in the sixteenth century. The Dublin authorities, while mindful of the respect due their autonomy, were closely associated with the central government which was based in the city. This was the capital without a resident monarch, where the role of lord deputy could be transferred from one faction to another or to a complete outsider. It was nonetheless the capital of a kingdom which felt itself able to crown a king – Lambert Simnel in Christchurch Cathedral, with all due pomp and ceremony. It was also a capital under constant external threat. Where London faced an army once in a century, Dublin faced one on average once a decade in the sixteenth century. Capital of a kingdom that was never wholly obedient, the city which protected the royal bureaucrats and councillors was the locus of considerable street battles between supporters of rival political factions fighting for control of the machinery and authority of government and in the process damaging the buildings. The mayor and corporation were held responsible and were once obliged to do penance for the sacrilege by walking naked but for their shirts in the Corpus Christi processions carrying lighted candles.

Although by Elizabeth's reign it had effectively become a garrison town, Dublin's militia continued to be an important element in its own defence. The mustering of the town troops four times a year before the mayor was no mere ceremony. The military gild of St George had 120 mounted archers, 40 horses, 40 pages and 500 crack troops. Every merchant was required to have a jake-bow, armour and sword of his own and those belonging to other crafts a bow and arrows and a sword.[4] The central government enabled it to buy gunpowder. On a number of occasions it was able without assistance to march out and defeat its threatening native neighbours on its own as well as serving under the governors or deputies. This military preparedness made potential risings, like the attempt in 1581 to overthrow the government and take the castle, particularly dangerous. Nevertheless, the city fathers maintained their right to try the offenders who were Dublin freemen.[5] In 1586 it was estimated that there were 1200 men armed with weapons in the city whose residents still only numbered several thousand. Dublin's role in the Civil War was critical to the campaigns. First held for Charles in 1646, its outworks were strengthened but it surrendered to parliamentary forces in 1647. Dissatisfaction with the crushing taxes parliament imposed led to the army revolt in Dublin in 1660 and a local desire to see Dublin as a true capital, not subject to taxation by the English parliament without the Irish parliament's consent. In the 1688 revolution its role was equally significant.

Relations between Edinburgh's government and royal government in the sixteenth century were more ambivalent. Balancing local and national roles was a delicate matter. Control of Edinburgh was critical in the political feuding that dominated central government in sixteenth-century Scotland. Interference by monarch or governor in Edinburgh politics was common. Unlike London, but like Dublin, it housed the royal administration and national political struggles took place in its streets. The city authorities might assert their privileged status, but monarch or governor often intervened in the choice of provost and a city official like Sir Adam Otterburn, seven times provost, was also a lord of sessions and a member of the royal council.

The city's self-confidence in its 'auld privilegis' was great enough to allow it to challenge the royal government itself but not with total success. When the city's concern over trading rights at Leith became involved with state politics, the city barred the gates to Arran and elected a different provost. The King's Council thereupon gaoled Edinburgh's councillors and ordered them to beg Arran's pardon. The City authorities refused and the matter was ultimately compromised.[6]

Edinburgh's citizens were also well armed and able to take military action in their own defence. When English armies came over the border in force, Edinburgh was a key military position to be taken and the city authorities often had to attempt to defend themselves or make their own peace terms. They were obliged to surrender to Hertford in 1547 when he ravaged southern Scotland. The city failed to achieve a separate agreement, however, and was burned. Lynch sees central government intervention in city affairs as becoming more blatant and frequent as the sixteenth century progressed. In 1571–2 as the civil war reached its climax, the city was under siege; the merchants were divided into factions and those who did not go into exile found themselves powerless to prevent Grange from entering the city, strengthening its fortifications and directing its policies.[7] In the seventeenth century the relationship changed as the monarch no longer resided there, and the city's attitude to the Scottish council underwent various shifts, while it found it prudent to employ a lobbyist at the court in London.

City Government

The structure of the capitals' self-government was similar to that in other major cities but the outcome could be very different. In London, which was both city and county long before 1500, the city had its own law courts and regulated its own affairs. The role of the freemen and common council was increasingly subordinate. The elite who ruled were the aldermen, elected by the wards. These were the wealthiest merchants on whom the ruinously expensive costs of office were imposed as well as the duty to be foremost in setting the example of lending to the monarch or making charitable provision for the poor. From 1523 to 1672, however, many wealthy men sought to avoid the office, even going to the lengths of preferring imprisonment for refusal.[8]

The lords of Dublin who were managing a small and local region in 1500 were both wealthy and powerful. The gilds in the city, both the merchant gild and the craft gilds such as tailors, weavers and brewers with their public halls were all part of a system of personal management. Originally in the hands of bailiffs, the structure was remodelled in English style at various points, the last in 1548 when it became, like London, both city and county, with a mayor and aldermen, sheriffs and commons, although this made little difference to the origins and social standing of the individuals who dominated city politics.

Edinburgh's government below the level of provost was also dominated by the merchants. The influence of the crafts in the city was always subordinate to that of the merchant gild, which monopolised external trade and which, until 1583 when craft representation on the council became mandatory, provided the members of the town Council. In the second half of the sixteenth century the gildry was opened to craft masters who did not soil their own hands, involving only six or seven of the 14 incorporated crafts. If one excludes the lawyers, who were debarred from service except as town clerks, the town council was mainly run by the small group of the very wealthy who also invested in schemes concerning credit. [9]

Law and Order in the City

The convenient availability of central courts reduced the control of the city courts. Londoners used whichever suited them, and the chief baron of the Exchequer sat in the Guildhall most afternoons in term time for their convenience. This alternative in civil matters made the maintenance of obedience possibly more difficult but there was a comparative absence of unrest in London in the sixteenth century despite the rapid growth in its size, periodic inflation and unemployment. Despite the wide gap between rich and poor, its social instability and strife have been exaggerated.

The livery companies may have been the mediators who reconciled the two. The pivot of overlapping and linked circles, they tied the institutional structure together giving the rulers a direct form of communication to the humbler Londoners. They were able regularly to tax their members, even the poorest, to raise money for royal loans, they judicially resolved internal conflict and made welfare provisions, providing a real means of resolving crises and of maintaining order. The possibility of social mobility, however remote, also helped legitimate the power of those above.[10]

The livery companies had a similar role in the Edinburgh hierarchy of control and manipulation, while the establishment of new gilds in Dublin in the late seventeenth century suggests that they were equally essential there. In all three cities therefore the increasingly complex social hierarchy which directly resulted from their multifaceted economic and social functions was held together by institutions which provided a personal, vertical link from top to bottom.

Local Government

The logistics of managing very large entities are different in kind from those of managing smaller ones. All three cities, moreover, were plagued with problems which arose from a metropolitan area which extended beyond the boundaries of their authority. A water supply, which in a small town might be met from a small number of wells, required reservoirs and aqueducts. Sewage polluted the local streams and rivers. A regular watch or city guard at night, and constables to apprehend wrongdoers at all times had to replace the citizen's turn. Managing the city's grain supply extended beyond regulating the market to the acquisition and disbursing of a city stock. Controlling the city vagrant who found hidey-holes in the warrens of semi-derelict, back-lane housing, slid in and out of the separate jurisdictions of the liberties and scraped a living from dishonest as well as honest means, was harder in a crowded city street than in a small market town. Provision for the poor who flocked to the city more in hope than expectation of sustenance was more complicated than in a town where they were settled and identified. London's comparative anonymity exacerbated these social problems. The numerous foundlings recovered from the streets are just one example of this.

Disasters such as famine, plague and fires, of which all three capitals had their share, not only spread faster in crowded and insanitary urban conditions, but were a threat to all the places to and from which goods and people passed. Worse, perhaps, the removal of the site of government disrupted business. Edinburgh's plague in 1530 found the city council imposing draconian rules on its citizens and punishing breaches with death or banishment. Dublin's plague in 1575 killed 3000 people and it was said 'grass grew in the streets'. London saw the central courts adjourn to Hertford, St Albans or more rarely Oxford, on numerous occasions.

Financial Resources

All three cities for most of the period suffered from a chronic shortage of financial resources. London had rental properties but they were insufficient for ordinary, let alone extraordinary expenses, and the city came to rely on the fines from those refusing office for many of its needs. They also borrowed at interest from the Orphans' court and other funds. Major expenses like the rebuilding after the Fire in 1666 saw it teetering on the verge of bankruptcy. Dublin and Edinburgh were equally poor and dependent on the property they owned and neither had any means of regular borrowing from its wealthy members, although Edinburgh frequently borrowed on an ad hoc basis and was able to buy up land in the Canongate and elsewhere. Dublin in the sixteenth century found that craftsmen and merchants retired to the countryside to avoid paying the cess and it was not until the 1650s that the city corporation, debt-ridden as a result of its support of the king, was willing to promote building projects.

Edinburgh and Dublin, however, were still small enough for most of the period to rely on traditional management practices. Both had a limited number of paid employees and relied on regulations enforcing self-help on residents for much of the work. Although its mayor was clerk of the markets, and had admiralty jurisdiction over much of the adjacent coast, Dublin had many of the characteristics of a fairly small town. Disputes over fisheries in the Liffey, problems over such nuisances as dunghills, swine wandering the streets, pig sties and similar issues dominated the city council thinking for much of the period.[11]

By the mid-seventeenth century, Edinburgh was growing large enough to require a reorganisation of its administrative structure. In the 1640s and 1650s the original divisions of town into quarters were replaced by six parishes in the inner town and more in the outer with the subsequent building of new parish churches. By 1674 the city council were tackling the water problem by bringing supplies from outside the town, attempting to enforce a building code and provide public lighting. Planned housing, promoted by tax concessions, was being constructed.[12]

London from the outset was too large for an unpaid system and it had a sizeable number of city employees whose job it was to oversee the behaviour of the residents and their adherence to various rules. Its problems were infinitely greater in 1500 than either Edinburgh's or Dublin's. They remained greater in 1700. Much of the day-to-day business was delegated to the wards where it was managed by the alderman with a body of assistants, but many problems could not be confined within ward boundaries. Management of the markets, of the hospitals, of the bridge, were all in the hands of specialists.

Solutions to major supply problems were increasingly found in privatisation schemes. Water carriers drawing water from the polluted Thames were replaced by a scheme to bring it by aqueduct from the Lea, which required the co-operation of the central government. The buckets and brooms, ladders and hooks of the traditional fire-service were still kept in the churches, but after the Great Fire, insurance companies began to keep their own engines for extinguishing fires in property they had covered.

The city officers had only limited authority in key areas and little control over some of the aspects of trade and industry which determined the city's prosperity. With so much of the country's trade passing through London, its relations with the royal customs officers and the admiralty were crucial and inevitably the source of disputes. When city entrepreneurs were able to 'farm' some of these positions, however, they did this in their own interests and not in those of the city. London had long ceased to be a city held together by common interests.

All three capitals took their responsibilities for the care of the sick and orphans very seriously. Although the building of hospitals was often left to private benefactors, they were conscious of the prestige attached to the possession of such facilities. When Dublin started on its rebuilding in the 1670s and 1680s the Royal Hospital was one of its glories. In Edinburgh welfare provision remained in the hands of the kirk treasurer.

Religion

Comparative anonymity made large cities places in which religious heresy could flourish and spread. Control over secret meetings was likely to be ineffective. Imposing uniformity was likely to be difficult. People could go from parish to parish to find services to suit them, whatever the regulations. Division in belief raised the possibilities of riot or even massacre. This was the point at which the local and the national met with greatest force. Even enforcing public agreement on aldermen could not be easily achieved at moments of religious discord. The ordinary people in the capitals did not hesitate to make their attitudes felt. When there was the possibility of a restoration of catholicism in Britain under the later Stuarts, the London crowds, by now thoroughly Protestant, demonstrated with anti-papal pageants which drew on complex fears of sexuality and dirt.

Formal church structure was dissimilar. Neither Edinburgh nor London was home to an archbishopric, and Dublin was not the premier archbishopric in Ireland before the Reformation. The bishop of London did not live in the city, which gave a special importance to the role of the dean of St Pauls. The bishopric was notoriously plagued with financial and administrative problems and, despite the ecclesiastical courts and the gaol in the city, the established church had little control over the people or patronage of the city benefices. The laity, through the vestries, were able to take effective control.

103

While London had a plethora of small city parishes, often with only a few hundred parishioners and in the gift of a variety of religious and lay patrons, Dublin had few parishes and Edinburgh, originally only one church. Increasing population led to subdivision of parishes in both Edinburgh and Dublin in the seventeenth century. Seven new parishes in Edinburgh and six outside were still too few for the growing number of potential parishioners. Dublin saw both subdivision and demolition of church buildings in the established church, as well as the building of meeting houses for sects and for Catholics.

The importance of the capital made its religious attitudes of critical importance. Dublin does not seem to have been affected by Protestant ideas from the continent before the Reformation and the imposition of the English Reformation in Ireland did not find a ready acceptance. It seems to have been accepted whole-heartedly only by those dependent for their employment on the central government. The city council was divided between Catholic and Protestant. Before 1612 men who held the mayoralty were quite likely to be Catholics, and until 1641 Catholics might still be on the corporation council or occasionally sheriffs.[13] In the early seventeenth century Dubliners were still for the most part Catholics. The Jesuits who were promoting the Counter-Reformation were openly known and although James had insisted on steps to exclude Catholics from office, Strafford was prepared to negotiate with them for assistance in the war against Scotland. Although migration from England after the restoration brought in more Protestants so that by 1700 Dublin was a largely Protestant city, in 1689 services in the Dublin churches used Catholic rites.

Edinburgh does not seem to have been initially any more dissatisfied with the old forms of religion than Dublin. The power of the craft gilds in their religious aspect derived from their appointment of chaplains to serve their own altars in the churches and they were profoundly unhappy with the destruction of altars which Knox inspired. In the 1560s Lynch describes the Reformation as a 'stop–go affair shot through with ambiguities and compromises'.[14] The Protestants were in a minority in the 1560s, and only Protestant royal government and pressure from the kirk sessions eventually brought most of the inhabitants to a Protestant frame of mind. The secular urban authorities then dominated the overt kirk structure because the church was dependent on them for its resources.

London had been more receptive than either to new ideas before 1530 but for a long time it was a microcosm of the nation, sheltering at the same time older Lollards, people who had early taken up the new Protestant ideas and those still committed to traditional ideas and practices.[15] This made its management particularly tricky as particular parishes might shelter individuals of very divergent views. Riots over religion were a very real possibility and uniformity was never achieved. While individual parishes might promote puritan lectureships others lagged behind good Protestant practice. The parish churches were dominated by their vestries, usually composed of the wealthiest parishioners who were also the main source of clerical funds as the problems of collecting urban tithes became more acute. The existence of private chapels in and about the city belonging to the various resident aliens such as the ambassadors and foreign merchant enclaves made effective policing of dissidence impossible, although the management of the required Easter communion and similar events gave some control over religious behaviour.

The Social Function of the Capital

One of the problems which always faced the resident freemen in any capital was the number of important people who maintained a residence in the city without being free or often eligible to be free. In London before the Dissolution many long-established religious bodies had 'Inns' some of which were liberties while the great aristocrats had houses either inside or just outside the walls. The Dissolution provided a unique opportunity for lawyers, gentry and others to obtain a footing in the city by acquiring a share of the ex-monastic houses. The city was thus full of influential, more or less long-term residents who did not participate in city government, and some of whom were an important part of central government. They worshipped in their local parish church alongside city people; they had their pews allocated according to their status; they became colleagues, friends and relatives.

Added to this, more and more country gentlemen and country merchants were visiting the capital on legal business. The amount of business handled by the law courts at Westminster quadrupled. The advantage of access to the court when it was at Greenwich or Westminster added to the attraction. Families like the Thynnes of Longleat expected someone to be in London during the legal terms virtually every year, wheeling and dealing between the law and royal concessions to expand their interests.

All of this resulted in a highly flexible integration of those of different callings and fruitful interaction between capital and country. By the Restoration, London business ventures involved bureaucrats and lawyers, wealthy clergy and physicians, the politicians as well as the money-managers, who turned the government's never-ending need for advances and loans into a new form of business.

Dublin on a far smaller scale had a similar role. It was throughout the period inhabited by important local gentry families who had townhouses as well as country houses. This led to early integration. A prolific family like the Grattons had members in all areas of the establishment. While the eldest son was a JP who lived on his patrimony, his six brothers included a physician, merchant, free-school master and three clerics.[16] This business involvement was, if anything, even more dominant at least by the second half of the seventeenth century in Edinburgh. The informal integration of the individuals who represented the different bases of power in the realm, land, capital and religion as power shifted from a focus on the crown to more oligarchic forms of government had significant implications for their dominance throughout the nation.

Centres of Culture and Leisure Pursuits

The capitals in this period were becoming centres for leisure and cultural activities which were more specialised and sophisticated than those available elsewhere, as well as the more common entertainments of cockfighting, bull- and bear-baiting. The development created problems as well as possibilities for the capital, as theatre was so attractive and so dangerous a source of ideas and criticisms that both central government and city authorities were involved in efforts to licence and control it. The capitals were also involved in managing the new and dangerously anonymous craft of the printer, whose cheap broadsides, pictorial for the illiterate, could circulate at considerable speed. They attacked the problem by increasingly distinguishing between permissible upper-class entertainments and the suspect amusements of the poor. The spread of books to the wider literate public was part of a process in which leisure started to become a more widespread industry, with music rooms and public ballrooms, art galleries and museums, clubs for gentlemen and societies to promote and debate new ideas. Leisure and culture were altering to meet the upper-class demand for forms of entertainment which distinguished 'polite' society from the masses, simplifying control of the lower classes.

Dublin only slowly followed London's lead. At the outset, there were plays and players in ecclesiastical dramas like the gild plays on the feasts of Corpus Christi and St George, although it was better known for its tippling rooms, but with no certain printer of its own, books had to be imported and sophisticated public leisure activities were limited. It was not until Wentworth's arrival that a real 'royal court' was developed; attempts were made to put drama on a regular basis and other opportunities for display and amusement to attract the Irish nobility introduced. This had some success, and despite the setbacks of the civil wars, Dublin's role as a cultural centre grew rapidly both in sporting, musical and literary directions. Printers multiplied so that the small literary circle had the means of seeing their works spread throughout the kingdom. The Dublin Philosophical Society (1683) was copied from the London Royal Society. Edinburgh's encouragement of cultural life was more restricted, not developing until the 1670s and 80s, when intellectual and professional pursuits received some royal encouragement.

Education, however, was not a major service of the capital.

London's educational role was surprisingly restricted, although the Inns of Court provided legal education and it had some well-known schools. Edinburgh's high school and college provided education for the gentry. In contrast, Dublin was able to offer tertiary education after 1591 when Trinity college was founded.

Wealth and Position

By 1700, position in all three capitals was determined by social status and wealth and more of both was needed than anywhere else in the kingdom. In London there was a clear hierarchy in the business sphere extending from the 600–1000 wholesale overseas merchants through the modest retailers and the small masters to the journeymen and the unskilled labourers. Wealth begat wealth and those who started with capital were those most likely to succeed. Various analyses of different sources demonstrate that to embark on a prestigious trade without some backing was a very risky venture. Even with capital a thorough knowledge of the market was required and most started by specialising in a particular area, only diversifying as success made additional capital available. Trade was not the only route to wealth. Builders, cloth finishers, distillers and even a bodice-maker ended with assets of over £10 000 but initial capital was essential.

Poor men could not contemplate a London apprenticeship, particularly in the more exclusive businesses. London apprentices might be rowdy adolescents but they were drawn from an elite, two-thirds of whom were drawn from the capital or the southeastern counties. Arranging an apprenticeship was as important as arranging a marriage and like marriage was usually managed by friends or professional intermediaries.[17]

Women, despite the restrictions from which they suffered, had means of supporting themselves and could attempt to do so. Although only a few widows and single women lived well they did not have to be chaperoned. Some women, usually the wives of freemen, could practise their own trades. It was expected that a woman would learn her husband's trade if she did not know it already. A typical business for a woman was running a tavern or chophouse, selling food and drink, or some aspect of the clothing business, either at the manufacturing or millinery end.

Edinburgh was following a different path. The growing number of professionals such as lawyers and physicians, clerics and teachers, who made the city their home, were beginning markedly to influence its policies. Whereas in 1500 her merchants had dominated foreign trade, after the 1640s the proportion of merchants in the population was decreasing sharply while the professional element was increasing. The level of wealth achieved by even the top echelon in Edinburgh was in no way comparable to London. Only 18 per cent in 1690 were assessed at over £5000. Whereas the average number of hearths in London was 5.5, in Edinburgh it was 2.9. They were comfortable but not ostentatious. Middle ranks found middle echelon jobs. Significantly, the burgess by the seventeenth century admitted lawyers, acknowledging a shift in the basis of the city's prosperity and together with the merchants they overweighed the craft burgess in all aspects of city life. Edinburgh's hierarchy in 1690 was headed by 3.5 per cent gentry, 6.7 per cent professional, 5.3 per cent merchants, 22 per cent craft and manufacturing, 0.9 per cent military and civic officials, 10.7 per cent manual workers, farmers and seamen with 50 per cent servants at the bottom. Not all professionals were wealthy. The ministers of religion and schoolteachers often paid tax at the lowest level. Craftsmen were also predominantly in the lowest two bands. The few wealthy craftsmen were goldsmiths or in trades that catered to the luxury end of the market.

Eighty-seven per cent of Edinburgh's c.8000 apprentices between 1583 and 1699 came from a 50-mile radius of the city, a more restricted pool than London's and less variegated than Dublin's. Apprentices were quite numerous but in many trades like that of surgeon only approximately a third completed their training or passed the exams. Less than 25 per cent ever became burgess although this varied from trade to trade. In the general population, women significantly outnumbered men, many of them servants.

Dublin's social structure was closer to London's than Edinburgh's. Unlike Edinburgh it was increasing and consolidating its dominance of foreign trade and industry and merchants remained the most prominent of its social groups, although the professionals, state officials, resident gentry and intellectuals were highly influential.

Economic Function

London's growing dominance in the sixteenth century appears to have depended on the reciprocal stimulus which concentration of functions in the same area produced. Its key trading position was reinforced by an increasingly wide variety of specialist industries made possibly by the focusing of demand in a single place. Its growth was achieved in the sixteenth century by successful competition with its less well-placed provincial rivals in the cloth trade. In 1600, 75 per cent of its exports was cloth primarily sent to the Low Countries and Eastern Europe. The first half of the seventeenth century saw this trade slump to half its previous volume and value. That London continued to grow and prosper resulted from its merchants' ability to open up new markets for different goods in the Levant, India and the Americas, and to benefit from a continuing healthy demand for imports.[18] As the centre around which credit, banking and share trafficking developed in the seventeenth century it made access to capital easier for those close at hand and this helped to make it at the same time an important manufacturing city with a wide range of products and a level of specialist skills which were not easily matched.

As well as the usual retailing trade in food and drink, London was developing large-scale brewing. Legislation early discouraged inns and taverns in the city from brewing their own beer because of the problems of fuel. Demand for the services of inns and ale houses by the increasing numbers of visitors meant that demand for grain and beer was massive and by 1700 there were 150–200 'great' inns and innumerable lesser establishments. Thirty thousand people may have been engaged in catering and entertainment.

At the same time London had available a low-wage sector, mainly women and children, who could be easily exploited.[19] As it became an urban conglomerate, the people spilled over into suburbs, particularly in the East End, which were impossible for the London authorities to control. Wages were kept low by the pressure of newcomers desperate for work. Numbers in Stepney and Whitechapel grew to 20 000 by 1600 and 90 000 by 1700. The total population in the suburbs by the later seventeenth century was about 330 000.[20]

One of the trades which developed in the seventeenth century, especially in the areas around Spitalfields with the arrival of religious refugees, was the silk industry – it was claimed that in 1700 there were 10 000 looms in Spitalfields alone. London's dominance of the cloth-exporting trade made it the centre for much of the cloth-finishing industries and its role as social capital made it a centre for the manufacture of clothing. Leather-working trades, metal trades, brewing, glassware and pottery, soap-making, tobacco-refining and sugar factories were also widespread. In the parish of St Botolph's, which numbered around 10 000 people, 11 per cent were involved in textiles, and 11 per cent in metal working, 6 per cent of them in the production of armaments including gunpowder mills.[21]

London's dominance promoted shipbuilding in the Thames and Medway. Yards capable of building and outfitting naval ships or the big East Indiamen had wet and dry docks, mast ponds, rope walks, sail lofts and were likely to employ hundreds of men in innumerable different crafts. Portsmouth, which had been the main royal shipyard in the fifteenth century, lost ground to Deptford and Woolwich and by the end of the sixteenth century Chatham was developing. While technically outside London, these yards were within range of the capital. Its market for ships by the mid-seventeenth century was drawing on shipbuilding yards in Essex and Suffolk, encouraging growth in places like Woodbridge. In 1646 ten parliamentary ships were being built in provincial yards downriver from the Thames estuary.[22]

The expansion of the population resulted in an expansion of building and the building trades, especially after the Fire in 1666 when 9000 houses alone were built. Innovations in some industries were resulting in new forms of purpose-built structures – complexes of warehouses and workshops. All of this helped to stimulate the development of credit facilities. The Royal Exchange became the centre for all-important business decisions. The different traders each had their different meeting place at which bargains might be concluded. Middlemen or brokers had their specialities which facilitated the process whereby buyer and seller could identify one another. Blackwall Hall was the venue for all cloth trade, often carried out by sample and by commission. London merchants as the seventeenth century progressed also carried the goods they imported to fairs all over the country for resale, and at others bought or ordered goods and settled accounts. The development of a large-scale money market drew people from all over the country. London has for good reason been seen as the engine of growth for the country. It was the pump which circulated all the lifeblood of the economy through the realm, drawing it in and sending it out again.

Dublin's economic role in 1500 was largely limited to its own immediate hinterland. Its inland trade was always a very important part of its business and it suffered considerable disruption if there was trouble in Leinster or Munster. Quite a proportion of the wealthier population must have been the royal officers of the exchequer, chancery and law courts, together with the churchmen who worked in the city, the customs officers and others in royal employ including the soldiers who for want of barracks were billeted on the people. Its merchant community was still quite small and much of its trade was managed by foreigners, and carried in foreign ships. The gild of merchants did its best to alter this by periodically claiming infringement of their monopoly which resulted in a serious dispute in the 1530s with the London traders.

Dublin at this stage was not the commercial focus for the whole of Ireland, which was still divided into largely autonomous regions. In the later sixteenth century it even appeared to be losing trade to Drogheda which had a better harbour. Careful management of petitions to London helped revive its trade. Its commercial infrastructure was also improving, largely through the granting of privileges to individuals in return for their work in upgrading, extending and building quays, marking channels and keeping the channel clear of refuse. Trade with Chester, Liverpool and Bristol was vigorous. There was in the early seventeenth century only one printer but later in the century there were several, all in Castle Street. Industrial activity was increasing although trade was still mainly in raw materials. Apart from its many brewers, it had a cloth-making industry which was said to keep 40 men at work and shipbuilding on the south bank of the Liffey was increasing. Both sailing ships and galleys were reputedly constructed. Galleys were cheaper and quicker to build and brought a good return.[23]

By the mid-seventeenth century Dublin was beginning to emulate London's role. The burst in growth seems to have come from migrants from England especially Chester. Between 1672 and 1687 there were estimated to be 35 000 migrants from England.[24] The arrival of Protestant refugees from France after the revocation of the edict of Nantes also gave a major boost to the silk industry. It also saw the development of intensive industrial settlement in the area called the liberties.[25] There were also Dutch and German migrants. Demand for luxury goods shows an increased power of consumption, presumably arising from the growth of commercial agriculture. Dublin developed commercial and banking facilities and began to dominate the export trade. It exported wool, cloth, linen and yarn and imported most luxuries, ousting Galway from its wine trade monopoly.[26] It also inhibited the growth of lesser ports as far away as Sligo which failed to develop a hinterland wide enough to draw in more than local trade.[27] It suffered a major set-back while under virtual siege in the early 1640s when the merchants' gild of Holy Trinity was near bankruptcy, but recovered by the 1660s and strengthened in the 1670s. New markets were built and large numbers of small specialised gilds were established to cover the new crafts. The corporation was offering incentives to attract new skilled settlers. Its convenient location for trade being channelled increasingly to England alone, combined with its administrative role and the credit services it could supply, made it the obvious conduit for the goods being produced in newly commercialised agricultural areas. These were beginning to include processed material such as salt beef in barrels and fine linens, resulting in a steady rise in the percentage of customs revenue collected in its port until it accounted for half of the Irish total.

The explanation for the growth into what in the early eighteenth century perhaps entitled Dublin to be considered the second city in the British Isles – even perhaps surpassing Edinburgh – seems to be its increasing integration into a developing single British economic network. The participation of at least the bigger merchants in a money transmission service which used bills of exchange to settle accounts across the three kingdoms, was providing Dublin with an edge over the other cities.

Edinburgh in contrast lost commercial ground towards 1700. In 1558 it had 747 merchants and 717 craftsmen but numbers grew only modestly if at all thereafter. There may have been no more than 6–700 merchants in 1700. Although it was consolidating its grip over all sectors of trade and credit at the expense of other towns until 1649, the Edinburgh money market horizons subsequently shrank.[28] Between 1600 and 1680 the burgess community was about 1800–2000, which represents 7 per cent of population and 30 per cent of households. Goods which came overland were mainly cloth, silk and clothing requirements. The foreign import trade was dominated by a few wealthy individuals, Robert and William Blackwood paying almost one-fifth of the customs at Edinburgh in 1690. Merchants continued to scatter their cargoes between different ships to spread the risk. Only the wealthy, probably 25 per cent of the total number of merchants, could safely afford the greater capital costs and the risk of foreign trade.

Edinburgh merchants continued to be comparative generalists, most dealing as wholesalers, trading in a multiplicity of goods and markets, acting as factors, moneylenders and bill brokers and probably thereby losing ground to the London specialists. The development of regular credit and exchange facilities was slow. The merchants took the opportunities they were offered and confronted the risks, but were unable to compete with London merchants who could specialise in a single area. Joint-stock ventures with inactive shareholders were developing. Professionals and gentry were willing to put their money into such schemes. Most Edinburgh investors in the Darien scheme were wealthy, not all were merchants, but its failure casts considerable light on the difficulties and shortcomings of the Scottish business structure. Scottish agriculture, moreover, was not as productive as English and was not benefiting from the surge which commercialisation had brought to Ireland, so that demand for imports and other consumer goods was constrained by the more limited available purse. High thinking and plain living were both a recommended virtue and a necessity.

The overall effects were masked by the many positive developments which occurred. By the late seventeenth century Edinburgh had a respectable number of large-scale industries including printing works and breweries, some run by widows. Between 1635 and 1699 textiles dropped from 7.8 per cent to 3.2 per cent and food and drink rose from 30.8 to 33.6 per cent, a sign that the city was providing a greater 'service' function. Like London and Dublin it experienced some loosening of restrictive bonds but the merchant company resisted this. Although membership of the merchant company was no longer essential for trading abroad and burgesses no longer had a monopoly of the right to manufacture in the town, the old gild mind-set continued.

Occupational Structure

The occupational structure of all three capitals was becoming more complex. The number of different named trades was increasing as specialisation made it desirable for an individual to proclaim particular rather than general skills. A breakdown of occupations into their functional base and their main activity gives some idea of London's main functions. About 60 per cent of occupations in 1700 were manufacturing based. However, if one divides occupations by activity as Beier does one ends with 40.4 per cent in production, 35.9 in exchange and 23 per cent 'other' which includes professionals. It is here that the problems of area become acute. The inner city housed the merchants and professionals; if one includes the outer suburbs where there were fewer, the percentage drops.

Edinburgh's balance was different. Throughout the later seventeenth century production accounted for about 44 per cent while 'exchange' dropped and 'other' including professionals, expanded from 21.5 to 35 per cent. Between 1664 and 1694 the percentage of those describing themselves as merchants halves from 32.9 to 18.7 while the 'professions' nearly doubles from 11.5 to 20.6. Clearly Edinburgh's professional group was more critical to the city than London's. Twenty-two per cent were engaged in manufacturing (34 per cent if the domestic servants are removed) – a significant proportion of the population.[29] It is hard to make comparisons solely on the basis of percentages, however. The similarities of the socio-economic structures of London and Edinburgh may be misleading if one ignores the structural changes which were transforming the face of London industry.

Edinburgh was a much smaller city with significantly fewer occupations – 180 compared to 721 in London – which include considerable numbers in luxury and service activities especially in areas like medicine and law. Advocates, and their clerks, the judiciary and other legal officials, goldsmiths and wigmakers, booksellers, fencing masters, musicians and virginal makers, surgeons, doctors of medicine, apothecaries, schoolmasters and schoolmistresses represent a large professional element. Lists of the top twenty Edinburgh occupations 1635–1699 show the rise of wigmakers, surgeons, candle makers, glovers and tobacconists as well as members of the legal profession. This suggests that while there may have been a substantial amount of manufacturing it was not the large-scale business that London housed. The craft evidence shows that bakers, shoemakers and weavers were poor and most craftsmen were only modestly prosperous, although those in the building trades were wealthier and wrights, especially shipwrights, did quite well. Those in the poorest crafts probably moonlighted to make ends meet.

Women had gradually lost the brewing business to men but they managed their husband's businesses as widows and occupations open to them included midwives, butter wives, fruit wives, seamstresses, and schoolmistresses. There were three women members of the Merchant Company and men were admitted in their wife's right. Women's problems were with increasing specialisation and professionalism. None the less the inward port books show 35 women apparently trading in their own right and renting properties in their own right.[30] Like London, where 25 per cent were in intermittent or casual domestic work, Edinburgh women's work was fragmented.

In the 1630s Dublin was seeing the rise of new trades in the luxury areas – tailors and silk dyers, plasterers and builders. Although the difficulties of the Civil Wars and Interregnum cut off this development, it recurred in the Restoration as numerous new craft gilds were established to accommodate the new developments. By the 1690s the numbers of trades were at least equal to those in Edinburgh.

All three capitals were thus a major focus for consumers. London had always been a centre from which more exotic goods were routinely ordered when a member of any family visited but by the second half of the seventeenth century a more sophisticated consumer consciousness was revolutionising the process of retail sale. Shops were being transformed from warehouses into places of comfort. Retail traders were increasingly not manufacturers or craftsmen but made their living from the variety of goods which could be examined and compared under one roof. Edinburgh followed London but probably more slowly with many merchants still trading from their warehouses.

Conclusion

One reason for the growing size of the capitals was that their 'region' expanded between 1500 and 1700 until it was virtually coterminous with the nation. Part of the explanation for this lies in the spin-off from an increasing centralisation of government. As more and more people had to visit the capital to answer for their role in government, to attend the law courts, to sit in parliament, they developed links with the resident merchants and professionals, were drawn into city schemes and projects and carried back city luxuries to the countryside. London merchants, by virtue of their improved information systems, their specialisation in one branch of the trade and their ability to co-operate with a government anxious to maintain its regulatory authority over foreign trade, were able increasingly to dominate. When new companies such as the East India company were established with new forms of trading practices the stock in the companies came to be held by gentry and aristocracy as well as merchants, but the merchants managed the business.

Growth in size was accompanied by an increasing permeability. The exclusiveness of the city had to a large extent disappeared as merchants established networks and agreements with merchants in other cities and towns both in Britain and abroad, which at least potentially disassociated the interests of the individual from those of the city. Investment in merchant ventures by non-merchants was becoming a commonplace – the lending of money to the government an increasingly routine part of city life.

All three capitals developed between 1500 and 1700 not only as administrative centres but as the financial hubs of the kingdom and also as major commercial and legal centres. In the sixteenth century London seems to have grown at the expense of the surrounding country towns, but by 1700 the demands that it made seem to have been providing a new and different stimulus to nearby towns which were beginning to provide it with useful services. At the same time both Dublin and Edinburgh were being drawn into a network focused on London.

7

THE PLACE OF THE TOWN IN THE KINGDOM

Towns were central both to government and to society. The Roman tradition saw towns as the main generator of culture and civilisation, centres of social intercourse and administration. Renaissance ideas in the late fifteenth century revived this concept. The educated, like Stow in his apology for London, said men were gathered into cities 'for honestie and vtilities sake, . . . first men by this nearenes of conuersation are withdrawn from barabarous feritie and force to a certaine mildnes of manners and to humanity and iustice: whereby they are contented to giue and take right, to and from their equals and inferiors and to heare and obey their heades and superiors'.[1]

Urban renewal using classical rules of proportion, uniformity and grandeur did not occur in England until the Restoration, but the structure of the earlier Tudor and Stuart town was nonetheless a formal representation of due order and hierarchy. It embodied classical ideas of government dividing public from private space. The concept immediately generated its antithesis – the innocent, natural society of the country – but the value of the town in government could not be denied. The role that towns played, however, was not constant and the relationship shifted with the period as a variable in the movement towards a modern centralised state.

Town and Royal Power

Towns were the medium through which authority and civilisation could be imposed. In Wales and Ireland where under Gaelic lordship towns had been insignificant, developing more around religious centres than governmental ones, the establishment of new towns went hand in hand with the extension of royal power. Raymond Gillespie has characterised this as the 'process of creating structures in which the everyday life of a colonial society could operate'.[2] Such towns were often inhabited by people of a different race and culture. Although some Welsh towns had Welsh antecedents, and continued to be inhabited mainly by the Welsh, of which Wrexham was probably the most important, most were associated with 'English' conquest, especially Caernarvon, Flint, Rhuddlan and Beaumaris.[3] Acts of the English parliament sought to prohibit the Welsh from becoming urban freemen. Early Irish settlements had also been essentially Anglo-Norman and most remained distinct from their Irish hinterland.

Central financial resources until the Restoration did not permit the Tudor or Stuart monarchs to employ a permanent standing army and its bureaucrats were too few to impose obedience to the law forcibly. For most of the period the co-operation of local bodies who accepted the arguments for due order was essential, especially since the congregation of many people inevitably gave rise to disputes and the need for immediate action in routine matters.

The Crown conceded urban self-government but insisted on ultimate control. The rhetoric of borough charters shows that monarchs gave privileges in return for assistance to groups of people who were willing to be amenable to royal direction. The Cinque Ports, for example, had their rights in return for the provision of a large part of the English monarch's shipping for war, if and when required. Dartmouth's charter stipulated that it supply two ships of war of 120 tons. A more usual arrangement was the one whereby the citizens of Carlisle for border service were made free of most local tolls and taxes for all their wares and merchandise throughout the kingdom.

A town given a charter by the monarch was an integral and necessary part of royal government and public authority. There was a distinct tension between the contradictory faces of town life: between its drive for autonomy and its responsibility to king and kingdom, but both were critical to the town's governmental function. The mace and in some cases the sword permitted to be carried before the mayor were royal symbols which bore the royal arms upon them. They were ceremonially surrendered whenever a monarch visited a town, to emphasise the relationship. In four royal cities in Ireland, Dublin, Waterford, Limerick and Cork the mayor also had a sword borne before him, sheathed in peace but naked in war. Oaths whose maintenance was a sacred obligation bound the officials and the first obligation was to the monarch and the maintenance of his or her laws.

Towns which did not have charters, often because the site of the settlement belonged to another landowner, although they were still largely enforcing the common law as modified by local custom, had a more tenuous involvement with government. In Scotland such burghs of regality had charters from their lords and if the burgh was also the centre of the lord's administration of his regality it was an important focus of local authority. Exception-ally, Glasgow which belonged to the bishop of Glasgow, was confirmed by William the Lion as a burgh with all the freedom and customs which any royal burgh in Scotland possessed and in 1450 the city and barony was elevated into a regality. The dual role was symbolised by the mace which had the royal arms on the upper end and the bishops' arms on the lower.[4]

Towns and the Law

Towns were thus a vital element in a system in which day-to-day authority was delegated to self-financing communities at all levels. What kept them in line was not force but a shared commitment to common received ideas expressed by religion in which the family was the basic building block, paternal authority its regulator and the model from which all higher authority drew its inspiration. This was, throughout the period, a double-edged sword. Conscience could lead the town authorities to lead local urban resistance to crown dictates. Town authorities could show political opposition. In 1661, for example, many of the Dumfries council absolutely refused the new oath.[5] Stow thought that this was an aspect of their function – that 'the assemblies of men in Cities and great Townes are a continuall bridle against tyranny'.[6]

The Crown, most of the time, especially in the earlier period, had to rely mainly on persuasion to keep towns obedient. If boroughs were not given both criminal and civil jurisdiction, at least in lesser matters, trade would have ground to a halt with disastrous consequences for central government as well as society. The borough courts' decision and their records were vital to trading activities. Every chartered borough had at least one 'court of record' so that deeds and decisions on real and movable property and debts, contracts and breaches of agreement once recorded would be unassailable evidence throughout the land.

The different courts in the borough used either common law, civil law or the law merchant. The law merchant was the most critical to the speedy and efficient resolution of business differences. In such courts disputes over partnerships, accounts, contracts and obligations could be resolved without the strict rules about admissible evidence and the opportunity for delays which often choked common law procedures. In ports maritime pleas were usually only adjournable from tide to tide if they involved strangers and in a fair court they were adjournable only from hour to hour. Written recognisances of debt called statutes staple were an important element in business practice and towns which had a court of staple could enrol them and enforce their execution. While Scotland used civil law, the town court function was much the same and deeds and contracts were registered in court books. Despite formal differences, the practices were familiar to any merchant who needed judgement.

In most towns the bench consisted of the mayor and a variable number of aldermen. As magistrates they were amateurs, less likely than the county gentry to have any legal training although usually familiar with the sort of problems which arose. For legal advice they had to rely on the town clerk who was usually legally trained or clerks of the court. This was a weakness as, increasingly in more important cases in the seventeenth century, individuals resorted to professional legal advisers who would seek to with-

draw cases to the central courts. In the larger ports it therefore became more common to insist that the Recorder be resident and sit with the mayor. Although the business of the central
courts was soaring and beginning to include much town litigation, the work of the town courts was also booming. Kings Lynn
Guildhall Court heard an average of 1000 cases a year in the
second half of the seventeenth century and it has been shown
that virtually every male resident from rich to poor made use of
it.[7]

Ports were usually able to obtain admiralty jurisdiction without
which they were powerless to hear civil or criminal cases and
enforce action on matters which might prejudice the common
good. This was one of the areas in which central government was
beginning to encroach on local in the period. Unless the grant
totally excluded admiralty intervention, there could still be conflicts as occurred in Bristol during Elizabeth's reign and which led
to the suspension of local admiralty jurisdiction for three years in
1582.[8] When Dartmouth was challenged by the vice-admiral of
Devon, its mayor, on more than one occasion, endured several
weeks in gaol rather than yield and the corporation successfully
fought legal cases over its authority in both sixteenth and
seventeenth centuries. The tension between the town and its
neighbour, the Carew family, who were usually vice-admirals,
was a significant aspect of local politics.[9]

Part of the problem was the perhaps unresolvable issue of
whether local needs had precedence over national interest in
matters of diplomacy, war and piracy. In the early seventeenth
century the central court of admiralty made a prolonged effort to
reduce the powers of various ports which held the jurisdiction.
The ports defended their rights bitterly and at length, but most
had eventually to concede at least a right of appeal to the central
court. In Scotland there was similar conflict over 'royal' jurisdiction between the admiral and seaports over authority within the
harbour and port and the rights to hold courts.

The aldermen as JPs had power of criminal jurisdiction although some crimes had to be referred to assizes. Lesser criminal
actions remained the town's province. Where the town had
sheriffs they held the court which dealt with petty offences.

The commonest crime was probably an affray which was usually punished by a fine which might vary in size depending on whether or not blood was shed and also on the place and time of the offence. Offences on market day or at the high cross attracted heavier penalties than at other places. Other punishments included the whip, the stocks (or cage) or for some, in the larger towns, confinement to an institution like London's Bridewell.

Only towns incorporated as counties heard the assize charges such as murder or witchcraft but the period saw numerous additional towns so incorporated. Some Scottish burghs also had this jurisdiction but Lynch says that the balance between royal law and burgh law was shifting in the sixteenth century. While towns fought to defend their privileges, the Crown increasingly overrode them.

Central and Local Government

The relationship between central and local government institutions was a constant source of tension. The privileges, grace and favour which the monarch had bestowed could be withdrawn, a fact that towns usually bore in mind. When towns refused to obey the monarch or their lawfully selected officials the public record of such disobedience usually refers to rebellion, a term which to our eyes may seem a gross exaggeration but which appropriately represents the threat to government. The town courts were not left to apply the law exactly as it suited them, however. Writs could call cases to higher courts if towns seemed to be abusing the law and statutes which they were supposed to uphold.

Central government policy, however, often favoured expanding the town's responsibilities even if it meant enhancing their legal position. Between 1530 and the end of the 1550s, possibly because the dissolution of the monasteries had disrupted the established channels of charity, the central government granted upgraded charters to forty odd boroughs. The form of government was oligarchic which suited the hierarchical sense of the rulers; the carrot was greater control over the militia and the quid pro quo the duty to regulate social and economic problems, that is, to manage the poor.

Establishing more direct control over town government required Crown power to appoint and remove officials. When the later Stuarts began to interfere in towns appointments it caused much consternation. While the various oaths by which officials affirmed their acceptance of the established church and royal prerogatives ensured some conformity to royal wishes, the Stuarts after 1660 sought absolute obedience. In 1662 the commissioners appointed by the Restoration parliament 'for the regulation of corporacions' struck off the town rolls those who were uncooperative. Subsequent attempts to enhance royal power by inserting into charters clauses which would give them power to promote some individuals and prohibit others were a major source of urban anxiety. Traditionally charters were confirmed by monarchs after their accession and modifications were rarely made to the contents without the town authorities' approval. It was part of the essence of self-government that the towns selected their own officers. There was determined opposition to Charles II and James II when they attempted to alter charters to introduce a royal power of review. The accommodation which was eventually achieved with William III reflected a shift of town attitude to the benefits of royal support. Annual meetings of parliament provided an alternative negotiating forum, so that while towns in Britain were still in the hands of local interests which included aristocracy, gentry and bourgeoisie, central and local power was more smoothly integrated.

Towns and Royal Taxation

Towns were essential to royal taxation both of land-based and of sea-borne resources. Customs were valuable, collected at specified port towns and the cooperation of town authorities important to effective collection. Protecting the land meant policing the sea and this also required the active participation of the local community. In looking to sea, monarchs might also seek to tax those who fished close to the shore-line, like the Spanish and

Biskayans who came to fish off Ireland or the Dutch who came for the herring fishing off Yarmouth. Here too, the cooperation of local towns was essential.

Both Scottish and English monarchs bestowed privileges on towns in return for income. In Scotland, the monarchs were heavily dependent on taxing the towns. This in turn gave the towns considerable leverage in other matters which affected their interests.

Monopolies granted incorporated bodies of merchants the sole rights to trade abroad in return for a structure easy to control and tax. The English Merchants of the Staple who dealt in wool through Calais and the Merchant Adventurers who dealt in cloth had their parallels in Scotland. By an act of 1466 only burgesses of Royal Burghs were allowed to go out of the realm to trade. The Scottish Staple can thus be seen as the Scottish nation organised for the purpose of foreign trade. The burghs had searchers of their own to enforce the rules. Edinburgh, which increasingly monopolised overseas trade, required all those who were to sail in a ship to appear at the tollbooth and be registered, and forbade the skipper to carry anyone not certified to him from the tollbooth. The towns, however, left decisions on where the Staple should be to the monarch or regent. The king enforced the monopoly and expected to name the conservator although if it came to a dispute both sides eventually felt the need to compromise.[10]

By 1600, the joint stock companies, like the East India company, had a monopoly which limited trading with particular markets to a small number of privileged individuals and gave those merchants the power to regulate trade. This inserted a new level of authority between town and monarch and freed the merchants from some urban controls. Those merchants involved who were also concerned with the lucrative farming of the customs, in return accepted impositions over and above the usual customs, a vital form of unparliamentary revenue in the early seventeenth century. In the Middle Ages and early sixteenth century, English monarchs had usually borrowed from powerful European merchant syndicates who in return had received privileges over customs. By the later sixteenth century they had to turn to their own merchant community whose increased ability and willingness to lend had to be fostered. By the Restoration, the role of the Whig city financiers was essential to the management of government business.

Towns and Defence

Defence of the realm was a key function in which towns were required to participate. It has generally been held that towns in Britain had much less influence than cities on the Continent and that their military role was never considerable but it may be circumstances rather than preparedness that gives this impression. Cities were required to police their walls. The duty of watch and ward was more strictly enforced in times of crisis but its neglect was a punishable offence. Admitting rebels to a town was a serious crime. Even admitting an enemy where resistance was clearly futile could be interpreted as treasonable.

While not all towns had walls, and in Scotland they were a late development, defences were necessary if a town was likely to need to resist a siege during the period. Unless a town site had natural protection town walls were essential to national defence both as refuges and as a source of troops. Even with walls a town could suffer continual destruction. The experience of Cashel in Ireland was by no means uncommon. The cathedral of Cashel, the seat of an archbishopric, a borough and market town, was burned in 1495 by the earl of Kildare, sometime royal deputy, who was at odds with the archbishop. In 1603 the town surrendered to Mountjoy to avoid destruction. In 1647 it was taken by storm and it narrowly avoided a similar fate in 1690. Town walls in the seventeenth century were not obsolete. New walls were built in the seventeenth century around Irish plantation towns.

Monarchs had long contributed to the maintenance of defences for towns in vulnerable locations, such as Carlisle, Berwick, Durham, the Welsh towns and towns along the south coast. The records of the king's works in the sixteenth century show that in strategic areas the monarch continued to contribute. The magnificent town walls of Berwick were constructed under Elizabeth before Mary Queen of Scots' fall decreased the Scottish threat.

Many towns in the sixteenth century upgraded and modernised their walls, and bought themselves guns. Repair work on the walls of many towns was an ongoing expense. The idea that English town authorities adopted a policy of benign neglect because the period from 1500 to 1640 saw little fighting on English soil is unjustified. The military preparedness of towns in England in this period has been underestimated. Coastal towns were always in need of protection against unheralded attacks by sea. French reports noted that Dartmouth was unwalled but it had an earth bastion with guns at the harbour entrance and a castle with 50 guards and 24 guns in excellent order.[11] Bristol occasionally reorganised its defences. The speed with which inland town defences were refurbished for the Civil Wars suggests that even there the decay was exaggerated.

Towns also manned their own defences. The town's role in defence was still both important and independent down to the end of the Civil War. Townsmen had weapons and knew how to use them. Bye-laws obliged men to exercise regularly at the butts so that they were competent archers and stipulated the armaments that individuals of various standing had to have. Certainly the militia could not match the professional soldier but that does not mean that its role was negligible. Northern towns particularly needed to be able to respond quickly to attack, perhaps before the monarch had even been notified of a threat. The garrisons in the castles at Carlisle and Berwick-on-Tweed were the main stiffening of local forces, which were thin on the ground.

As in the counties there were two types of military activity which might be required – service in the monarch's wars outside the kingdom, or local service. Towns were required to send small numbers of men to serve the king for twenty days or a month in his wars. They were also expected to contribute to voluntary gifts. Otherwise the town's principal role was self-defence. The militia was not obliged to serve in wars outside the kingdom and membership of the militia generally exempted individuals from being pressed for service elsewhere. Men of some substance therefore joined. The mayor often mustered the town militia separately from the county, and bigger towns like Worcester which did not have that privilege fought constantly with the shire authorities over its contributions.[12] A court of array to review men and arms was held annually in many towns. Such assemblies often attracted side-shows and a carnival atmosphere but their more serious aspects should not be underplayed.

Monarchs used town control of their own musters as both a carrot and a stick. Portsmouth was punished by denying its mayor a place in the commission for musters, Leicester rewarded with the grant that they should take place under their steward and no other. Encouraging town patriotism probably produced better results than obliterating town in county companies. Bristol in 1561 sent 20 uniformed gunners to the county musters, but once it obtained exemption became more lavish, investing in a pair of drums, and a dozen ells of fine silk for an ensign in the municipal colours of red, blue and yellow embellished with gold buttons and tassels. By 1570 the city was spending over £65 on equipping 160 soldiers with such items as breeches and coats with lace sleeves, iron corslets and handguns. The trained bands regularly engaged in gunnery practice.[13]

English towns were an invaluable source of ordinary troops for the Crown throughout the period. Southampton in 1610 mustered about 750 men out of a total of 6000 for Hampshire.[14] Newcastle provided 500 militia in 1639. As the newer weapons of pike and caliver came in, towns were more likely than the countryside to be able to provide their common soldiers with up-to-date equipment while the self-equipped might be well armed. In 1569 London supplied 4000 foot, 2000 carrying calivers, to the army against Scotland. The 1558 act confirmed town freedom from interference by commissioners but the towns' charter rights did nothing to secure them from the lords lieutenant.[15]

The ceremonial role of the urban trained bands underlines their strength. In 1559 the government, aided by the London livery companies, staged an impressive military demonstration for diplomats. London soldiers exercised with guns and pikes to the sound of drums, fifes and trumpets.[16] Bristol took care to show the strength of its trained bands in the celebrations arranged for the visits of both Elizabeth (1574) and Anne of Denmark (1613).[17] In the 1630s the city not only had three companies of foot but a voluntary company of 'the better sort' with their own artillery house where they held a big yearly feast for the local gentry.[18]

James I and VI abolished the Statute of Array, but the local militia continued and towns still preferred to be independent of the county. The dispatch of the militia away from the town or county was very unpopular, both because of the vulnerability it caused at the town and the disruption it caused town business. Towns were, however, vulnerable because of the numbers they could provide.

Concentration on land-forces overlooks the extent to which the ports undertook some of their own defence at sea. At Bristol in the 1610s the merchant venturers year after year fitted out three or more ships to patrol the Severn estuary. Other ports like Plymouth did the same. Dartmouth people were described as 'warlike and constantly at sea with vessels to attack the Spaniards and other enemies'. Waiting for the royal navy or even contributing to special expeditions was rarely adequate.

The military potential of the towns in Ireland was even more critical. All the royal towns had significant and well-trained militia. When Sir William Pelham visited Limerick in 1579 the mayor appeared before him with 1000 armed citizens. In 1584 the militia numbered 800. Cork's numbered 400 and Waterford's 600. Even allowing for exaggeration, given the supposed size of the towns the numbers suggest that every able adult male was expected to be available for militia service. This was not unreasonable. The towns were in the front line of insurgent attacks. In 1568 Lady St Leger was besieged in Cork by insurgents and was only relieved when Sir Henry Sidney arrived with English troops.

In Scotland the role of the urban militia in defending the city was significant both in the city's government and in its social hierarchy for much of the period. Its role in military matters had led the Scottish parliament in 1457 to forbid under the highest penalties the making of bands and leagues between towns and lords other than the king or the town's own lord. The act was renewed in 1491 and 1555. Towns were required to send contingents in arms to parliaments if requested to help keep the peace. Towns, a chief focus of military action in time of war, took their own precautions to avert destruction, not always successfully. The Scottish border towns were a bitter warning. Annan was burned twice, Hawick three times, Dumfries four times and many others including Jedburgh, Kelso, Irvine and Kirkcudbright at least once in the sixteenth century.[19] Holding towns made the difference between victory and defeat. In the Bishops' Wars in 1638–9 it was the fall of Edinburgh, Dumbarton, Dalkeith and Aberdeen that disrupted Charles' plans.

Military capability meant that larger towns also had the potential for independent political action particularly in times of war, civil war or insurrection. The Civil War involved towns in all four kingdoms in great stress and destruction. In every campaign, the fall of towns marked critical turning points. Towns made their own decisions about support for either party. Some were pragmatic or indifferent, others had religious convictions. Either way, they were of vital importance. Many of the county towns in each kingdom had the county weapons and ammunition repository as well as the town's. There was a sudden rush to repair or rebuild town defences. The medieval walls at places like Leicester were encircled by further more modern defences. Town forces had to participate in their own defence and in places like Plymouth and Gloucester their role was critical. A rising town like Birmingham which was supplying sword blades to the parliament could become a centre of attack. While many towns sought only to avoid destruction, Leicester held doggedly for the parliament, and during the royal siege women fought in the breach and as the garrison was driven back from street to street townspeople fired from their windows on the royal troops.

The daily experience of living with troops, whatever their political persuasion, generally resulted in friction even where sympathies had initially rested with the occupier. At Nottingham the townspeople were moved to fury and riot when the governor, Colonel Hutchinson, confined rebuilding of defences to the castle and removed the town's own guns to strengthen it. The gaoling of 14 senior officials made matters worse. The obligations of billeting soldiers caused miseries that outweighed the benefits of defence.[20]

Employment in areas which related to war industries did not compensate for the loss of employment in others. The general destruction and the death of the young and able men who were conscripted was devastating. Intentional punitive firing of towns like Wrexham and Oswestry added to the destruction of capital and depression of the economy. The misery was often exacerbated by visitations of plague as at Lichfield in 1645 and 1646 when 821 died.[21]

Towns, nevertheless, should not be seen simply as victims. Members of Parliament representing the English towns contributed to the decisions of the Long Parliament even if they did not always heed their constituents' wishes. London's position was critical and its defection was the worst blow Charles I received.

The experience of civil war may have discouraged urban authorities from overt resistance subsequently but the need for defence remained strong in coastal towns. The Dutch wars both under Cromwell and under Charles II were a serious threat to the channel ports and a lesser threat elsewhere. The establishment of a permanent army created new sources of difficulties as some towns became barrack towns with resident companies of professional troops while the urban militia faded into insignificance. Neither the Dutch nor the French wars resulted in a landing in England, and their urban impact was eventually more the result of the sea struggle for the West Indies, but defence remained an important consideration. Particularly in Ireland and Scotland after the ejection of the Stuarts in 1688 towns were once again involved in assault and destruction. Their citizens were by no means passive in these struggles. At the onset of the siege of Derry it was after all the young townsmen, the apprentice-boys, who shut the gates against Antrim's redshanks and the citizen army participated in the defence, only to find themselves eventually unpaid either for their services or the destruction of their property.[22]

The Importance of Particular Towns to the Crown

Some towns were more involved in royal power plays than others. Towns which were important to government control were treated rather differently from the majority of less critical centres. On the one hand they were favoured, on the other they were more tightly controlled. The political events which were focused in them were of national significance. Glasgow, the home base of the Lennoxes, did not enjoy the luxury of isolation. It was involved in every national contest. Glasgow castle was taken and retaken in 1515–6 in factional fighting during the minority of James V. In the 1543 struggle for control of Mary's government, Lennox and his men with all the townsmen and the churchmen unsuccessfully tried to defend the city. Throughout Mary's reign, control of Glasgow remained a crucial factional issue.

Carmarthen was similarly critical. The nearest thing to a Welsh capital it was the centre of south Wales and the home of Edmund Tudor and Rhys ap Thomas who was the chief lord in Wales. Its pre-eminent position in the area was recognised by the right to have the sword carried unsheathed when Britain was at war along with the silver oar of the Admiral.[23] When the elder Rhys died the town became the focus of a dispute over political power between his grandson and the Ferrers which extended beyond Rhys's execution and was promoted by the urban authorities. The outcome was a pitched battle in which the mayor used his authority to raise 300 men with bills and other weapons. Controlling Carmarthen was critical to Tudor plans for integrating Wales into a single kingdom with England and subsequent riots and bloodshed were carefully monitored by the central government.

In Ireland, outside the Pale, the royal towns, effectively autonomous, were the strategic key to monarchical power. Such cities had a strong sense of personal identity. In the sixteenth century, Galway, Cork and Limerick pursued their own policies. They had close trading contacts with Spain and France and were obvious landing places for continental troops in any war. They were therefore the centre of critical events in most of the national crises. Although their merchants were persistently suspected of trading arms to the rebels, they were pushed by self-interest and the mutual distrust of Old English and native Irish into ostentatious demonstrations of loyalty. It was exceptional when at

Killmalloch in 1583 the mayor and some inhabitants enabled the rebels to sack the town. Billeting of soldiers, however, strained loyalty. In 1599 Cork refused point-blank and in Limerick the town and garrison came to blows, the townsmen besieging the soldiers in a church. Nevertheless, only Kinsale went over to the rebels. The military importance of the sites meant that they often became the headquarters of English armies, while naval ships defended the sea access.

Towns and the Creation of the Nation State

The English and Scottish monarchs' creation of an effective national state in the sixteenth and seventeenth centuries required direct control of towns as centres from which to control the countryside. In 1500 such control was far from secure even in England. Extension of direct royal authority to local areas was not a simple matter of appointing officers of the central courts in adequate numbers and ensuring that they were honest, hardworking and loyal above all to the Crown. There were always more locals, with stronger personal interests and better local knowledge and contacts. The relationship between town officials and royal officials, such as customs officers, or church officials, especially in cathedral towns, could be tense and give rise to disputes over spheres of authority. Bristol in the second half of the sixteenth century regularly quarrelled with the customs officials over seizures of goods and turned a blind eye to recovery of goods by force, even when it resulted in a pitched battle. No matter how compelling the evidence, men were frequently acquitted.

National security also obliged the English monarch to bridle the old towns in Ireland. In the sixteenth century, costs dictated the use of the carrot rather than the stick. The Crown extended the privilege of English-style charters to a range of established towns hoping to reinforce their loyalty as they had military strength. Reducing the towns' independence was a slow process. Only at the end of the sixteenth century were effective steps taken to limit and subordinate towns in Munster.[24]

James I and VI in the aftermath of the failure of the rebellion of the earls was able to take more drastic steps. Open moves to promote their religious preferences on Elizabeth's death provided the occasion for the restriction of independence. Charles Blount, Lord Mountjoy, responded to Waterford's assertion of its privileges, that he would cut King John's charter with King James's sword and threatened to raze the town and throw salt on the ruins. When the citizens of Cork took arms and denied Sir Charles Wilmot entrance, the event was treated as a full-scale rising. Queen Fort in Cork was thereafter rebuilt as a citadel to ensure the town's cooperation. Local patriotism remained stronger than national throughout the seventeenth century. Blockaded by the insurgents, Cork townspeople were involved in two unsuccessful conspiracies to betray the city to the besiegers in 1644. In 1688–92 it was first ransacked by MacCarty and then by James II. The towns were kept garrisoned and their fortifications in repair well into the eighteenth century as part of Britain's defensive policy.

Creating New Towns

Towns, however difficult to control, were none the less essential to national policy. If they did not exist, they had to be created. The town network was by no means complete in any of the kingdoms. Numbers of new towns were established between 1500 and 1700. In England and Scotland they were predominantly spontaneous or private ventures. In Ireland they were government inspired. By 1700, there were few areas left without convenient access to a town.

Founding towns as a colonising process had begun in Wales in the late thirteenth century. An urban pattern of largely 'intrusive' settlements had been part of a process of conquest and assimilation. Welsh towns were generally walled and their citizens armed. In this way they could be mobilised in local factional disputes. Although they conformed to an overall government plan for reducing the country to obedience the non-planted towns were mostly reorganised native vills very similar to Dyer's 'unofficial' trade centres in the West Midlands.[25] They remained small and as their military rationale disappeared some decayed. Crown control in many Welsh towns by the sixteenth century had been largely superseded by local gentry influence.

Alongside policies to control the old Irish town, the government was looking to establish new ones. The Munster settlement produced a number of viable towns. They were haphazardly located and less regularly laid out than the government would have liked but the venture was successful due mainly to capital invested by speculators and landowners.

Under James the process continued. The government's blueprints were modified under pressure from essential private partners so that the original plan was only implemented in a minority of cases and the outcome was more limited than the government had hoped. Nevertheless, the establishment and later growth of small towns, mostly at sites which had long been recognised as strategic or where decayed settlements existed, was vital for government. Some of the Irish county towns were so tiny that contributions to buildings and repair had to be met by a levy on the county.[26] They were primarily military and administrative. Local landowners, however, valued them both as social and trading centres. They invested in the towns, received the revenues of markets and tolls, and encouraged development. Towns that grew generally had a good location for trade in a rural area with potential for commercial agriculture. Derry by 1612–15 already had twenty merchants wealthy enough to trade as far afield as Bordeaux, Dieppe, Bilbao and Rouen. Proximity to a harbour with access to the sea was an advantage. Failures were often associated with entrepreneurs who had no home-base from which they could draw new settlers.

Settlements needed settlers who, as strangers, had no support in the local community. They would therefore be dependent on their patron and available for defence if there was trouble with the native Irish. Some migrants were recruited by the local landlords from Scotland or the west coast of England. In the 1650s many were ex-soldiers seeking to establish a new life. In the 1690s some were Protestants, fleeing renewed persecution in Europe, who brought industrial and commercial skills.

Boroughs and Parliament

Boroughs were extremely important in the English, Irish and Scottish parliaments. The unicameral Scottish parliament had numerous burgh members and they increased in the Irish parliament as new boroughs received charters. They had to consent to taxation, and they used the opportunity to influence general government economic policy and to push private bills for their particular interests. Even where the towns sent local gentry rather than their own burgess, they had the means of ensuring that their interests were taken into account. In this way, in 1604–8 in England, parliament saw a bitter struggle over the issue of 'free trade' between London interests and those of the outports. In the Restoration period, English towns, concerned about Irish competition, undoubtedly influenced the restrictive acts which were passed. Town representatives regularly had bills to push, from modest proposals for improvements such as uniting churches or making provision for orphans to controversial issues such as the construction of piers.

The borough representatives far outnumbered the knights of the shire in England and Wales and their political attitudes were important. It is not therefore surprising that monarchs attempted to interfere in elections. It was quite common for one MP to be elected by the commons and the other by 'the mayor and his brethren' in the Middle Ages and attempts to change this to a more restricted franchise were usually unwelcome, although a move to the joint election of both was not uncommon. The occasional survival of the behind-the-scenes correspondence shows that the towns valued a member who could be relied on to promote its interests. James II's meddling in the 1685 Lichfield election shows how independent even a small town could be in such a critical matter. The town was most reluctant to accept his candidate and so, clearly, were most of the voters. The result was confusion and a manipulated result.[27]

The weakness of towns in England, Wales and Ireland *vis à vis* the Crown was the absence of a common voice. Disputes could be regulated only by the monarch or by the highest courts of the realm and they had no formal meetings to agree on a common policy. In Scotland, however, the towns regulated themselves through the Convention of Royal Burghs. This permitted representatives of the towns to decide common policy and settle disputes between their members. It possessed judicial functions from the start and early acquired legislative powers. Towns in the sixteenth century were forbidden to go before the lords of the sessions until the Convention had heard the case. New burgh grants reduced the value of the existing privileges so the Convention marshalled all royal burghs to oppose such grants. By the early seventeenth century this powerful agency met several times a year and used its influence to oppose the use of monopolies to bring in new or improved manufacturing. It achieved what Michael Lynch has called a discreet agreement with the Crown because of the power of the purse which it controlled.[28]

Conclusion

The principal cities in Britain were an essential element in the implementation and extension of central government policy. This gave the town authorities potential leverage in achieving central support for their own objectives. From the monarch's viewpoint, towns were a potential form of resistance. This could take various forms from passive failure to implement central legislation to active opposition. The precarious balance between royal and urban interests broke down at various times and in various places up until 1688 and the wars which followed. Thereafter, as urban autonomy became less critical to the town oligarchs, a fragile consensus emerged.

8

THE TOWN IN ITS REGION

The history of towns cannot be divorced from the wider history of the area in which they are found. Although towns were self-sufficient in certain ways, they nevertheless served their hinterland. A town depended on those for whom its services and products existed. It had varying symbiotic relationships with other local authorities, such as the landed classes and the church, who both needed the town and sought to control it. Changes over time in social and economic circumstances, however, led to changes in the services the town supplied and its degree of autonomy; changes in its relationship with its hinterland, in the size of that hinterland, in its relationship with other towns and with central government.

The commercial role of the town was becoming its dominant feature. The number of townspeople whose occupation was agricultural had still been significant in 1500; by 1700 they were fewer and more peripheral. The town fields which, even though towns were rarely self-sufficient, had been of major significance in 1500 had a diminished agricultural role by 1700. The autonomy of the town was diminishing. The facilities it offered were increasingly seen as a common benefit to the area and as the period progressed there were successful de-mands for the county to contribute to the maintenance of those facilities.

The Town and its Hinterland

The average size of a town's hinterland varied in its extent and permeability. There was probably never a time when the hinterlands of neighbouring towns did not to some degree overlap but one model of town development would start from a point at which each town was the centre of an impermeable area, thus making each town a virtual replica of its neighbour. Over time, this evolved so that a series of superimposed hinterlands emerged in which towns were linked to other towns by mutual service.

The position in Britain in the sixteenth century still tended towards the earlier situation. Most towns had a limited hinterland, more or less impermeable depending on geography and the available transport system; drew the bulk of their apprentices from the immediate locality and did the bulk of their business within a day's journey. Dublin, Waterford, Limerick and Cork, for example, remained comparatively isolated from one another by land until more bridges were built in the seventeenth century, and their hinterlands did not overlap. But Ireland had a less developed urban system than the rest of Britain in 1500. A few towns with a large catchment area served the state and merchant capital, otherwise there were only a few ports, and religious centres like Armagh. Towns for more economic purposes were rare.[1]

Most towns elsewhere in Britain were primarily market towns which had developed for the convenience of small-scale local producers on the borders of different production areas between which exchange would be natural. The average hinterland they serviced in England was approximately 45 square miles or a radius of just under four miles. In Wales it was nearer 100 miles. In Scotland the situation is complicated by the monopoly rights of the royal burghs. The notional hinterland of these burghs was vast but in the sixteenth and early seventeenth century local markets without the privileges of the burghs in reality served farming needs. Ireland had few market towns in 1500 outside the English area of the Pale and the South East but colonisation in the seventeenth century saw the growth of markets for every 70 to 80 square miles.

Such averages can be misleading, though, and are no measure of urban health or market effectiveness. The period saw significant shifts in town and hinterland size and number within every kingdom. While the South and East in England were highly urbanised by 1500, the South West after a period of initial difficulty and adjustment saw increasing urbanisation in the seventeenth century as trade, legal and illegal, with the colonies in America and fishing off Newfoundland gave employment to increasing numbers of sailors and stimulated local industry. In Ireland the spread of towns and markets in the less populated Gaelic areas grew unevenly but steadily. Only the Scottish Highlands and islands remained townless.

Spread of Towns

Most towns had medieval origins but between 1500 and 1700 towns were established in areas where there were previously few. The process illuminates the interdependence of town and hinterland. Westmorland and Cumberland had been a backward frontier area with largely military settlements until the accession of James to the English throne cut back on border raiding. Commercial interests in the seventeenth century with the assistance of determined entrepreneurial individuals like the Lowther family promoted new towns. Coal and iron mining in the hinterland could only be profitable if there was a convenient port. There were several potential ports which could have been developed but the Lowthers, who wanted complete control, poured money with government help into the creation of an adequate pier at Whitehaven. It was a calculated risk as at first there was only trade in coal to Ireland. Trade to France, and eventually across the Atlantic for tobacco, slowly grew, consolidating the town's position. Local industries developed as a corollary.

Lancashire industries benefited from the opportunities to exploit the safer northern route to America through Chester and Liverpool when the more southerly English and Welsh ports were affected by war. Shipping from such ports, however, was not confined to serving its own hinterland. When in 1671 the English parliament passed an act prohibiting the Scots from trading directly with America, they then freighted ships from Liverpool and Whitehaven to avoid the embargo.[2]

Development of towns in areas of Ireland which had previously been poorly supplied was integral to the growth of its commercial and economic prosperity. They provided the infrastructure of a market-oriented economy. The development of a harbour serving Mayo saw increasing and increasingly diversified trade in commodities such as iron, linen cloth, woollen cloth and apples and the area began to prosper even though the live cattle trade was destroyed by the cattle acts in the 1660s. Both the population and the standard of living rose.[3] Mistakes were made. The conscious attempt to imitate the English pattern in Ulster and Munster did not fit the different economic structure very well. Many towns did not prosper. Older strategic sites like Derry which were re-used had the best chance of success despite the mixed fortunes of war and the dominance of imported English and Scottish merchants.[4]

Scotland also saw an infilling of towns between the established royal burghs, despite the efforts of the Conventions of Royal Burghs to impede this. Ayrshire illustrates the pattern whereby a royal burgh was increasingly hemmed in by burghs of regality belonging to powerful individuals like the Earls of Cassilis. Irvine, Newton, Mauchline and Maybole were competitors. When in 1599 the Convention instructed Ayr to oppose at law the inhabitants of Maybole for usurping the liberties of a free borough Ayr obtained a court of sessions decree but at ruinous expense.

Relations with the Hinterland

The degree of autonomy which towns possessed affected their relationship with the powers about them, but all towns had a close love/hate relationship with the local lords and gentry. The more prosperous and powerful merchants were often the younger sons of minor local landed families. Successful merchants frequently invested in local rural estates and sometimes, especially in Scotland, intermarried with the landed classes. Many issues led the local landowners to meddle in urban politics especially when ideological differences over religion aggravated territorial issues. The ability to influence the town's behaviour was of major importance to the gentry. In Cardiff, for example, the Earls of Pembroke who held the castle, had long had influence but the town resented the Herbert family's assumption that it was exempt from ordinary town rules. In 1595 when royal officials, who were Herbert clients, were imprisoned for assault and refused bail, a struggle between Herbert retainers and town resulted in a death. In the following year another dispute broke out in which the town mustered 500 or 600 soldiers to maintain its cause. When the Cardiff bridge collapsed, however, the town refused to shoulder alone the burden of its rebuilding and with the support of the Earl of Pembroke advanced a number of arguments to oblige the county to contribute.

Towns were frequently the focus for a struggle between different county interests. In Beaumaris a struggle between the Bulkeleys and their opponents ended only with the Bulkeleys' victory.[5] Such county factional struggles which could take place under the very eyes of the justices and over which the central government had little control commonly centred on towns. Violence was endemic in the sixteenth century. In the 1520s fighting in Leicester between the Hastings and Grey factions became so intense that Wolsey forbade their attendance at assizes, with little effect. In 1534 York suffered a fight at the assizes between the Northumberlands and their brother-in-law. Such outbreaks continued throughout the century, and although they were generally declining, examples of such quarrels can be found quite late in the century. In York in the early seventeenth century, in fact, the weakening of the council in the North allowed an upsurge of rioting.

Mutual dependence did not necessarily make relationships between town and country amicable particularly where the townsfolk were seen to have 'foreign' origins as in Ireland and Wales. Nolan describes the 'mutual antagonism' which he perceives to exist in Ireland between town and hinterland as 'almost endemic'.[6] Thoroughly exasperated Scottish towns could mete out violence to lords, as Perth did in 1594 to Robert Bruce of Clakmannan.[7]

Too high a level of disorder could threaten urban autonomy. Sometimes local disorder reached a point at which the only way of reducing a whole area to comparative peace was direct royal intervention. In ungovernable areas like the south-west of Scotland, which the rest of Scotland regarded as barbaric, and who had their own customary law, this was a periodic remedy. When the Burgh Courts summoned individuals they might, like Thomas Rovesone at Dumfries, turn up dressed for a fight. Outlawing of the Border 'surnames' was usually unproductive.[8] Occasionally in Scotland the king turned up in person and held an ayre or criminal court to deal with cases in which local lairds and sheriffs were the culprits. The impact was transitory. More regular interference was resisted. The sheriff of Ayr had sought to hear cases between the Ayr burgesses. In 1547–8 the queen forbade this. In April 1557 Sir Hew Campbell, sweetened by a gift of £2000 from the burgesses, frankly admitted in a 'band and obligation' that they had full jurisdiction within their freedom over 'Slauchteris mutilationis bluidis thiftis spulzeis and uthairis crymes'.[9]

Underlying tensions in the relationship of most towns with powerful neighbouring lords and patrons might break out in conflict if badly handled. Political patronage, political influence and opposition were all endemic. The struggles between Leicester and the Earl of Huntingdon in 1601, which drew in matters relating both to parliamentary elections and town officials, are a case in point. Normally the town was punctilious in its relations and the Earl in turn promoted their interests. Mutual assistance was more valuable to both sides but protocol had to be observed.

In Ireland, men like the Earl of Cork played a critical intermediate role with a number of long-established Irish towns such as Cork and Waterford who none the less preserved their autonomy. Smaller towns without charters or small chartered towns with few prospects, were bound to be more subservient to those who might help them. Landlords frequently supplied the necessary capital, entrepreneurial skill and drive which established a successful town. The rise of Castlebar was largely due to the patronage of the Bingham family. They saw benefits for the whole area in promoting such a town, as the organisation of the linen cloth and yarn trade would thereby be improved and profits increased. Most Irish towns were traditionally dependent and never enjoyed any real degree of autonomy. In the fifteenth century Derry, despite bishopric and monastery, was in decay but when the O'Donnells regained control and built a small castle it began to recover and in the early sixteenth century the town enjoyed a brief resurgence, particularly under Manus O'Donnell whom Brendan Bradshaw sees as a Renaissance prince.

The assistance of the local gentry could also be critical in Wales. Llanrwyst had been devastated by Glyndwr and did not really start to revive until, in the early seventeenth century, the Wynn family took the town under its wing. The ford was replaced by a bridge, a chapel added to the church, and almshouses and finally a new townhall were erected.[10]

In Scotland, at their best, arrangements with lords were mutually beneficial as that of Renfrew with Argyll. If there was a risk of noble feuds spilling over into the burgh, the burghs themselves had feuds in which they might need noble help. Both Perth and Dundee sought such assistance at the 1568 parliament. The involvement of such a third party in the relationship between royal burgh and Crown was a symbiotic relationship in which each party had powers and expectations. Trouble mainly arose when more than one local lord aspired to be that third party. Disputes mainly focused on the provostship. Aberdeen saw numerous bloody factional fights. When the Earl of Huntly as the dominant local lord sought to replace the Mengies family in the 1540s the dispute spilled over into national politics. Perth was the prize in a similar struggle between Lord Gray and Lord Ruthven, and Stirling between Erskines and Livingstones.[11]

Aristocratic dominance of most towns was not necessarily unacceptable to merchants who were fully occupied in making a comfortable living and who possibly did not want to take time off for administrative and judicial work. The voice and indeed strong right arm of an aristocratic representative at court had a distinct value. Protection and intercession were valuable considerations. On the other hand the towns provided their landed patrons with useful services – a centre where their children might attend schools, where they might find a tailor and other tradesmen, a suitably impressive church in which they might be buried, a supportive voice in parliament.

Transport and the Changing Role of the Town

In this period a number of towns were ceasing to provide all the functions needed by their immediate hinterland. Although they were always at once centre, consumer and supplier they were beginning to find it better to abandon the production of all local requirements since it was cheaper and easier to import specialised goods and to concentrate on manufacturing others for export. This affected their occupational structure, their social function and their commitment to self-government. While it had always been possible to describe a town as having a primary function, an increasing number of towns could now be classified in terms of that function. Hinterlands became less and less impermeable as they drew different goods and services from a wide range of towns. This was made possible partly by improvements in transport systems, which made the importation of bulky goods from a long distance less expensive, partly by increased production leading to increased consumption.

After 1590 internal trading networks grew as increased grain supplies were carried coastally and by river. Improvements to land transport further extended the range. While pack-animals that can be taken over rough and hilly terrain continued to be important, roads and bridges suitable for carts, which were rare everywhere in 1500, were improved and towns built stone causeways to ease the animals' burdens.[12] This gave England a comparative advantage since roads in all the other kingdoms remained poor or non-existent. Ireland, Wales and Scotland still in most parts depended on the packhorse and transport by water was still the cheapest. Thus merchants from Clonmel, Kilkenny and Cashel traded through Waterford while Youghal's hinterland stretched as far as Tipperary.[13]

The concurrent development of a regular system of carriers using carts which by the seventeenth century was extended to most parts of England and some parts of Wales was erratic but significant. The way stations, terminals and nodal points of this transport service which had a regular timetable and clearly defined responsibilities were the great inns. These came to fulfil in the country towns the role that the Exchange and later the coffee houses played in London, adding to it warehousing and occasionally banking.

The sketchy outline of a regular nationwide transport network stimulated by demand from London had already reached quite remote areas by 1600. The development of regular articulated local networks came in the seventeenth century linking individual towns across country. Both of these developments were slow. It was only in the 1690s that a regular postal service linked Exeter and Bristol. When these services were critically interlinked, towns could draw a range of goods and services from the most appropriate provider.

Capital Investment and the Growth of Towns

The central government, Crown and Parliament, recognised that there were some problems which were of more than local significance and intervened to assist privileged towns. Collections, authorised by the Crown, obliged other towns to contribute to such things as the rebuilding of Dover Pier. Trinity House interested itself in the sailing difficulties at the mouth of the Humber, the East Anglian Ouse and the Wash. Lighthouses and buoys which had been, and to a considerable extent still were, local responsibilities were gradually becoming a national concern. Assistance to towns devastated by fire or flood was more routinely demanded from their more fortunate neighbours.

All these things helped some town authorities to improve their facilities so that the capital investment was enough to outweigh any advantage to the merchant of shifting to a town which lacked such facilities even if it otherwise possessed the same or greater advantages. By the seventeenth century Bristol, for example, possessed a tollzey where the merchants could meet to do business as they did in the London Exchange,[14] and an Association of merchants with the power to control foreign trade which dominated the town government and was able to promote essential developments in the port such as the building of a new quay and a graving dock. Similarly, Exeter town authorities promoted credit and banking facilities, which not only helped reduce the trading costs of its merchants *vis-à-vis* the London merchants who could get better rates, but also helped consolidate its position as the centre for credit dealings in the area.[15]

As a result, the pattern of towns even in Wales was undoubtedly changing in the sixteenth century. As George Owen of Henllys commented of Wales in 1598 – 'such of those towns as stood convenient either to serve as a throwfare or a convenient place for a market town or else had som good port or harborow fytt for trading by see, those towns fell to some good trade and so florished and dothe yet uphold themselves in some resonable welth, the rest being placed in wild and obscure places inapt for any trade fell into ruin and utter decay'.[16] Owen was commenting on a process of sorting and shifting which was giving an advantage to towns which provided trade and manufacturing.

The evidence for the development of a regional pattern as the period progressed is strong. Competition between towns established a pecking order. The winners in such a competition usually had a geographical advantage, but the decisive factor was often human power politics. Dartmouth lost ground to Plymouth as the main port of the far South West, possibly because Plymouth had better access to the hinterland but also because it had effective and powerful individuals to push its interests and to make better arrangements with the admiralty.[17] The expansion of facilities in a larger town with better commercial services could reduce the attractiveness of a smaller one. The position of Howth *vis-à-vis* Dublin is typical. Despite the protection of the St Lawrence family who owned the castle and who were usually on the Irish council, and its convenient position with a quay for rapid communications to England, it gradually lost ground and became little more than a fishing village.

Market towns within a short travelling distance of one another, competed with one another for business and either consolidated their position or declined. In an area like north-eastern Derbyshire, Bawtry, Chesterfield, Sheffield, Rotherham, Mansfield,

Alfreton, Wirksworth, Bakewell and Tideswell served the region as market towns, each with approximately a ten-mile diameter but overlapping hinterlands. The dominance in the area of the Earl of Shrewsbury gave him considerable control over the development of each. His insistence on lead passing his weigh beam and wharf at Bawtry shaped trading patterns. The development of specialist metal industries in the countryside around the towns was affected by his preferences. Consumer activities, too limited to be provided in every small town, gravitated to those with greater local spending power, reinforcing the pattern. Industrial development gave an advantage to a centre like Sheffield.

Towns whose original position was under threat sometimes compensated by finding a specialist niche. Lichfield, which even in the Middle Ages had always struggled to maintain its position as a cathedral town, was being slowly outstripped by nearby manufacturing towns like Birmingham. It developed instead as a social and educational centre, with small specialities of its own such as bone lace-weaving, tobacco pipe manufacture and, in 1691, a linen factory.[18]

Similar developments in Scotland and Ireland were not far behind. The seventeenth century saw the development of a range of specialist ports in the Forth and market systems inland. Unlike England, where the process involved subordination of some existing towns to others, Scotland's regional networks developed largely as a process of infilling as new burghs, always less independent than the old burghs, were established by the lords.

Trading links in Ireland grew first in the South and East where individual merchants in the smaller towns did business with Dublin or one of the larger ports, although rivalry between ports limited the links between them. Elsewhere it developed after the setback of the Civil War as resident merchants in the larger towns became the agents for communication between the small towns and the wider world. New industries like the linen industry replaced the prohibited traffic in live cattle. Belfast, Newtonards, Newry and Carrickfergus developed sophisticated and complex functions as administrative, trading and residential centres, while other towns became regional centres and those less well placed remained local market towns.[19] The patterns were by no means stable, however. The improvement of roads and the increasing pull of Dublin was affecting the prosperity of some of the less well-placed ports like Sligo while smaller inland towns were growing quite fast.

Wales remained less linked by land, as the mountains offered few passes and so each valley looked to the town which sat at the entry to the coastal plain. Some towns such as Monmouth survived because they were the only ones reasonably placed even though they were inconvenient. Monmouth was the centre for local gentry and the town families closely associated with them.[20]

As regional interaction became more established it looked as if there was a quid pro quo in a partial surrender of town authority over its citizens. A structure of town self-government which was based on the exclusive rights and privileges of freemen subject to their obedience to town policy was undermined by the increasing willingness of freemen to act as agents for foreigners and the benefits in increasing trade which such activities produced. A town could really only be part of a network if it had such regular links with those in other towns to their mutual benefit. Inevitably, this accelerated the breakdown in gild control over craftsmen.

Defining a Region

Can these hinterlands, in their broadest sense, be equated with distinct regions? The question is important if some cities are to be identified as regional capitals. It is also important if they have a different economic, social and cultural history which affects the behaviour of those who live there. Region is, however, a slippery concept. There is considerable argument about the existence of clearly articulated regions in the period. As R. A. Butlin has said, we 'create and recreate our own regions and regional structures'. Regions do not, that is, have a constant identity. Perceptions of regions are largely a political and economic construct. They have both visible and invisible attributes. A major shift in perspective, such as the discovery of the American continent, can shift the focus of the previously known landmasses.

The durability of regions can thus vary considerably. Visible attributes such as particular farming characteristics, mining or fishing potential are one aspect which may at some point define a region, but beyond this there are man-made elements and of these one may be doubtful if contemporaries were not conscious of their existence. Underdown's classic analysis of the South West, in terms of the correlation of farming areas and different customs, speech-patterns, political and religious affiliations, needs the testimony of seventeenth-century scholars interested in the phenomenon to give it legitimacy.[21] The South East has more hearths and more towns grouped closer together. Does this make it a region?[22] Closer attention to interpreting differences is required. Variations between regions and between town and country within regions needs attention. Does a region necessarily have a central city?

Characterising a region depends on the purpose of the classification. Historians uniformly acknowledge the role of the shire in English political and social life at all levels, and have shown how in many areas it defined such things as the pool from which even the gentry drew their marriage partners and have written with confidence of the county community as a body which had common attitudes and objectives. There has been debate, however, as to whether this parochial awareness overrode or obliterated awareness of more national interests or indeed whether, for the individual, local patriotism overrode personal advantage.

Shire boundaries were often arbitrary. Social and cultural ideology was not bounded by a county; most counties overlapped economic areas, contained more than one geographical area, and sometimes linguistic dialect. People who lived in one county shared religious beliefs with many in other counties; shared a common educational curriculum; shared, perhaps to a lesser extent, ideas about child-rearing and family structures, kin responsibilities and ideas about community cooperation. The centrality of the county in contemporary English thought about space and time is evident in the form which early writing on localities took from Lambarde's *Perambulation of Kent* (1576) and Camden's *Britannia* (1586) onwards but do not comfortably fit the definition of a region.

Nevertheless in England they provided one focus in the period and bore a clear relationship to at least one town in each area. Administrative requirements meant that each shire had a 'county town' whose area determiners were the county boundaries. A town like Buckingham developed few functions beyond administration, while in a county like Kent, Canterbury and Maidstone both made claims to the central role and in Sussex transport problems virtually required a division between East and West for most administrative purposes.

The English monarchs introduced shires to Wales and Ireland as part of the process of extending their government in the areas but for a long time they did not have any local resonance. Choice of a county town was often constrained by political circumstances: as a rule, only where the town already had an established position did it have a strong pull in the area. The different evolution of royal power in Scotland meant that shires had less relevance, at least before 1603.

In all three kingdoms, however, there were areas larger than shires, which contemporaries defined as regions whose inhabitants had a strong sense of separate identity. A distinctive immediately identifiable speech-pattern was an important characteristic. Often based on distant smaller kingdoms or principalities and, in Scotland, frequently associated with the surviving regalities, they did not invariably have a town focus. In Scotland Lothian did focus on Edinburgh and Aberdeen dominated its region, but Fife had many small prospering towns and the South West was ruled from the hereditary sheriff's residence, not from Dumfries. The inhospitable terrain meant that most of the Highland zone had virtually no towns except for a few little local ports.

Regions in Scotland and Ireland are more readily identified in terms of persisting areas with long-established language, political and social differences but often they are not focused on a town. Scottish and Irish historians have not placed a similar emphasis on the idea of regional capital, but towns like Cork or Galway, Aberdeen and Perth may qualify as regional capitals in the sixteenth century and Glasgow may be seen as supplanting Ayr as the centre for south-west Scotland in the seventeenth century.

Was There Such a Thing as a Regional Capital?

Regions, therefore, could exist without a central dominant town; did important towns, therefore necessarily have an identifiable region which looked to them for most of its services? If so, how and when did that region appear? Many historians writing about England assume that there was a recognised regionalisation by the early sixteenth century by speaking of certain large towns as regional capitals which dominate the area.

This makes for a much cruder identification of region than Underdown attempted, if indeed it makes one at all. It assumes that areas larger than counties, but otherwise ill-defined, should typically have a single central town which served as a regional capital acting as an entrepôt, a place providing specialised services and a source of luxuries. Gradually, as more goods pass through this market economy, the area from which they are drawn is enlarged until areas further and further away become dominated, and accept the prices established in the 'regional capital'. More recently, as the ambiguities of the term regional have become more apparent the word provincial has been substituted, although it has the same implication of an area – a province – delimited usually by administrative boundaries. Provincial boundaries may exist incontrovertibly for some of the more outlying areas but not for the hinterland of all proposed towns.

Possible Characteristics of a Regional Capital

English historians have thus both expanded and adapted the idea of provincial or regional when naming towns for this distinction. The English towns currently described as provincial capitals, commonly include York, Norwich, Bristol, Exeter, Chester, Newcastle, Salisbury. They were large in 1500 and with the exception of Salisbury, remained large. Bristol, Norwich and York had probably reached 20 000 inhabitants by 1700 while Exeter had 14 000 and was growing. Demonstrating that these large towns had common distinctive and exclusive functions in 1500 different from those of other towns such as Worcester or Ludlow is more problematic.

Historians have confined themselves to listing characteristics which their chosen towns probably shared with others they exclude. There is a lack of clarity in the criteria. Should the towns have all or only some of the characteristics and how many should be present? Pound sees Norwich as a regional centre by the mid-sixteenth century, saying that it was 'in effect a lesser London', with the residence of the Duke of Norfolk, quarter sessions, resident gentry, a grammar school and fairs – a social capital with a demand for luxury goods.[23] If one confines oneself to his specific criteria of an aristocratic resident, administration, school and fairs, however, one could certainly add to the list of 'regional or provincial centres' such unlikely places as Leicester.

One may propose the following characteristics as ones commonly listed, some or all of which may be expected of a town which focused the identity of an area large enough to be described as a province or region:

1. It would be situated at a key strategic point which would give military control of an important geographical area. Possession of the town by a hostile force would be a damaging blow to the central government because it would remove a large segment of the countryside from central control. In the Civil War, therefore, one would expect a regional centre to be one of the towns seen as key places to be controlled.

2. It would probably have the right to muster its own militia.

3. Uprisings which involved such towns would be a great danger to the central government.

4. It would combine administrative and ecclesiastical functions with trade and industry.

5. Effective road systems regularly used by carriers and merchants would focus on it.

6. It would be the centre of significant social and cultural activities.

7. The area from which it drew its main clientele would have a distinctive language or dialect and speech patterns, a sense of separate identity and history. The town itself would have a strong sense of its own position, dignity and independence.

One early identifier might be whether it had reduced any nearby urban settlements to dependency. A powerful town tends to attract all business away from other independent settlements in its area. It is noticeable that there were few major independent settlements closer to London than St Albans and that Kingston-upon-Thames, which had potential as a strategic road/river crossing with the first bridge over the Thames outside the city, was kept fairly firmly under royal supervision with bailiffs and a steward. This also seems to be the case with Edinburgh. Paradoxically, another aspect of a regional capital may well be that once it is established, it stimulates dependent growth in other settlements within its orbit.

Applying these Criteria

In 1500 the most obvious candidate for the role of an English regional capital would be London. Its position as a national capital conceals a more local role in a more restricted hinterland. In the sixteenth century its courts were more often frequented by suitors from nearby counties than from the more distant ones. Indeed it might be suggested that in 1500 the central government's powers only intermittently extended to some of the border areas. Edinburgh had a similar local role in Lothian. Dublin equally was in 1500 no more than a local focus for English government in Ireland. York also seems to qualify because the geographical constraints of the North East made it a natural focus for an area which was culturally different from the southern parts. York also had strategic importance, as the Pilgrimage of Grace demonstrated. Norwich had some significance for the control of the eastern counties as did Exeter for the South West. The Irish towns of Cork and Galway were centres from which their hinterland could be controlled. Galway enjoyed virtual independence as the loyal key to Connaught.[24] Controlling them was critical for the assertion of English control over Ireland in the seventeenth century.

An important supra-county administrative role applies to some towns. Exeter undoubtedly benefited from the business the council in the West brought for a brief time. In this it was similar to York where there were at least 1–2000 cases a year which required the attendance of many lawyers, juries, witnesses and the like. Ludlow's claim to be a regional capital on these grounds is compelling. The council in the Marches brought a wide range of cases to it from all the Welsh and border counties before the Civil Wars, creating a similar region to York. Chester also had an extended palatinate jurisdiction. Durham was similarly a totally self-contained area for both administrative and ecclesiastical affairs. This sets them apart from the remaining towns, however, which were never more than counties that raised their own militia and had castles and effective town walls. A town like Newcastle seems to be within an area centring on Durham, which raises the problem of 'multiple' capitals within a single province or region.

Most of the nominated towns had a bishopric but the significance of their ecclesiastical function varied. York was a metropolitan see; Durham was a palatinate in which ecclesiastical and secular functions were combined; the see of Exeter covered the whole of the South West. As for the rest, Norwich was the centre of a weak, impoverished see, Bristol and Chester were sees created by Henry VIII, and Bristol was combined with Gloucester for much of the sixteenth century, while Chester was ineffective and Salisbury was in decline.

The two elements on which historians have placed most stress are the social and economic functions. Did these functions help create regions which had not existed before or reinforce a regionalisation which had been of little significance? The most powerful magnet which perhaps created a region where one had not existed before was trade. At the beginning of the period, Bristol's economic hinterland already stretched into the southern Welsh district as well as the Severn and its tributaries but its commercial role in the first half of the sixteenth century was depressed by London's dominance of the broadcloth trade. While the size of the area which depended primarily on the Severn for its outlet grew thereafter to encompass parts as far afield as Leicester its influence was not dominant. The big Worcester clothiers went regularly directly to the capital. Leicester merchants also dispatched goods via King's Lynn. Bristol does not seem to have established a dominant regional pull before 1600. Ensuring that the Cotswold towns habitually looked to Bristol for their services rather than to London was critical to this and was helped by the eventually successful canalisation of the Avon in the mid-seventeenth century.[25]

Exeter had an existing commercial role in 1500 as an outlet for tin from the Devon stannaries and as the main inlet for the wool for local manufacture, but it did not establish secure pre-eminence until the mid-seventeenth century. By 1600 it had a regular carrier service to London but the network of local carrier links was not extensive and the majority of its trade was in a single market. Its relations with its hinterland were not always harmonious: its local pre-eminence was limited to an industrial cloth-producing area of about 200 square miles drained by the Exe and Culm and cut off by hill and moor. Its neighbours, principally Tiverton and Cullompton which prospered on kersey manufacturing, were tied into a network of cloth-handling.[26]

In Scotland the development of the Atlantic trade enabled Glasgow merchants to grasp the opportunity to extend Glasgow's interests and also its hinterland until by 1700 it could claim to be the capital of a region in which Ayr was reduced to dependency. Other regions remained largely unchanged – the old regalities of the medieval period.

If trade and industry provided a basis for towns to become capitals of some new economic regions, it did little to extend the claims of towns like Norwich whose cloth manufacturing was in difficulties throughout the period, or York whose local cloth industry had moved and whose trading power had increasingly to be shared with Hull, despite all its authorities could do as conservators of the Ouse to improve the river facilities and to control the important trade in lead.

The increasingly important function was undoubtedly the towns' social focus. Here York was an early leader. In 1500 gentry and local nobles already came regularly for assizes. The men who ruled the North – the Scropes, Eures, Constables and others – had houses in the city. They were consumers of luxury goods and promoters of a wide range of entertainments including horse-racing and cockfighting. Merchants from the smaller towns met in York. By the Restoration, York's position as the social centre of the North was confirmed by the presence of the second Duke of Buckingham. Exeter was also, from the late Middle Ages, the social centre for the ordinary gentry of the area who had town houses which they used in the winter. Bristol, Norwich and Newcastle also had a significant percentage of better-off residents for whom, by the end of the sixteenth century, the service functions of a provincial centre such as attorneys, doctors, surgeons, numerous apothecaries and the like were available. By the Restoration the towns were exerting themselves to improve the streets and provide even more amenities such as libraries, museums, aviaries and botanical gardens. These immediately and obviously distinguished the important city from the struggling town. In Ireland and Scotland only the capitals provided all such amenities, so that the lesser centres slipped behind.

Conclusion

One may conclude that not every region that can be identified had a capital, and that not every town which developed a strong economic and social pull had a region with common speech patterns and a sense of single local identity. Not all regions which existed at some point in the period 1500–1700 survived. Some, like the region centring on Ludlow, were not cohesive enough to survive the loss of administrative unity. New regions based on economic or social pull appeared. The factors which put a town in the first rank in one period did not necessarily keep it there in another. There is no common basis upon which a town achieved hierarchical primacy and dominated the urban network in its area – most had a mixture of strengths and weaknesses.

9

TOWNS AND URBANISATION

Urbanisation, the process by which more and more people lived and worked in large towns, has been the major preoccupation of urban theorists who also see it as critical for the growth of nation states and a world-wide system of economic interdependence. The issue of when urbanisation began has become contentious and underlies much recent work on towns in Britain. The characteristics of the particular settlements which were called towns between 1500 and 1700 must be the basis for any such general conclusions. The fundamental characteristics of towns must be distinguished from the variable characteristics of a particular town such as its topography, its primary function and the mix of activities which developed within its boundaries.

Defining a Town

Theorists tend to assume that the important features do not change with time. It is possible that some features may vary from period to period, differentiating one from another. What constitutes a list of essential characteristics, however, has never been agreed. This is because historians are reluctant to impose retrospective categories which would have been unintelligible to contemporaries. If a settlement lacks one or more of the agreed characteristics of a town and yet was considered a town in the period, then historians will not accept the criteria as absolute. Some urban historians see population size and density as the sole criteria, others prefer heterogeneity, division of labour, share and diversity of non-agricultural occupations, both commercial and industrial, presence of full-time specialists and administrative functions.

Most people believe they can recognise a town when they encounter one, but in fact what constitutes a town in the period 1500–1700 may differ from the medieval and modern town both in terms of size and role. The importance of different aspects of urban functions can shift quite radically in a relatively short period. Contemporaries usually expected a town to possess certain identifiable institutions. James I's government, when setting up the rules for the Ulster settlement, specified church and churchyard, market place, public school and gaol as public conveniences and at least twenty stone burgages inhabited by artificers. In other words, a town was a religious and educational centre, a market and manufacturing centre. Other features might include central administrative functions, assizes and, rather more doubtfully, a charter of incorporation, that is, government and central law enforcement. Robert Brady, writing just after 1700, acknowledged that a town might not possess a charter and saw two principal urban roles: 'a place of strength or a place of Trade.' Towns without charters had the same roles, paid the same taxes and were also free from toll all over the kingdom, free from contributing to the wages of knights of the shire and free from suit to hundred and county court.[1] This was true even in Scotland where burghs of barony or burghs of regality established by the aristocracy flourished alongside the royal burghs.

A town, basically, is a node of population concentration and density. To strike settlements under a certain size from the list of towns in this period is impossible, however. Many towns, particularly in Ireland and Wales, were no larger than 500 in the early modern period. Size can hardly be the sole criterion. Historians therefore look for other urban characteristics; this makes generalisations more difficult.

Most historians end with a 'working definition' of a town and some rough rules for assigning it to a particular category.

Mumford's now classic definition is still useful: 'The city in its complete sense, then, is a geographical plexus, an economic organisation, an institutional process, a theatre of social action and an aesthetic symbol of collective unity.'[2] The definition, however, takes its criteria from towns in areas influenced by Rome. Recent attempts to look at the rather different history of non-Roman areas have disagreed on alternative definitions but serve to emphasise the potential variety of town forms.[3]

Clark and Slack define the English pre-industrial town as having:

1. an unusual concentration of population;
2. a specialist economic function;
3. a complex social structure;
4. a sophisticated political order;
5. a distinctive influence beyond its immediate boundaries.

They also talk of a more overtly stratified social pyramid than was to be found in the countryside, sharp differences of wealth and status but also elites and a greater turnover of personnel than their village counterparts.[4]

This is not a definition which has been uncritically adopted by historians of the other kingdoms and underlines the problems of agreeing upon basic common features of all towns. Scottish historians like Helen Dingwall have been distinctly more demanding in the characteristics they require before a settlement can be taken as urban. Size, access to professional services and specialised occupations are all demanded.[5] These requirements would not only exclude a number of English towns, but most of the small Irish towns. Many Irish historians use largely morphological definers – walls, castles, bridges, cathedrals, quays and suburbs. Others use a combination which stresses commerce, legal independence, communal organisation, social hierarchy and specialist activity. Graham expresses this as 'a morphologically distinctive settlement form possessing a distinguishing array of redistributive, administrative, cultural and military functions combined with a population concentration characterised by an occupational structure not wholly dependent on agriculture'.[6]

Attempts to refine this lead to longer and more intricate statements like Bradley's 'a settlement occupying a central position in a communications network, represented by a street pattern with houses and their associated land plots whose density is significantly greater than that of the settlements immediately around it . . . it incorporates a market place and a church and its principal functions are reflected by the presence of at least three of the following – town walls, a castle, bridge, cathedral, a religious house, a hospital or leper house close to the town, an area of specialist technological activity, quays, a large school or administrative building and/or suburbs'.[7] Bernadette Cunningham adds perhaps less universal but nevertheless in some places noticeable characteristics: the inhabitants spoke a different language and had a different legal system, inheritance practices and concepts of ownership.[8] In the days before the acts which united Wales to England this might also have been true of Wales where the native Welsh were not permitted to become freemen of the boroughs. To this basic list others have added more peripheral attributes, charities such as alms houses, and symbols of 'urban time' like a town clock.

There has been little discussion of whether these definitions are primarily appropriate to towns in the period 1500–1700, that is, whether some characteristics specific to the period become irrelevant later. One candidate for specificity is defence. Contemporary definitions of what a town or city was usually stress both walls and a charter. Mackenzie certainly stresses that burgh settlers and fortifications were necessary for such an institution in the Middle Ages – a burgh was a protected place. At Aberdeen it has been said 'even the architecture of the burgh's houses with their high walls and low entrance gates enclosing a series of small courtyards was incorporated into the defensive system of the burgh'.[9] By the nineteenth century the defence of a town was not a specifically urban responsibility. Similarly the nineteenth-century legal reforms reduced the significance of the town law courts.

In this period, moreover, distinguishing a small town from a large village is ultimately subjective. Most towns had town fields and a percentage of individuals who earned their living wholly or partly from agriculture. While historians attempt to draw the line in terms of whether the farmers were the dominant element, the distinction does not work well in very small towns where many individuals undoubtedly had multiple occupations and at the least kept a cow or two for household needs. Llantwit Major in the vale of Glamorgan had 500 people – bigger than some unquestioned towns at the time, particularly in Wales. It is denied urban status, however, by Matthew Griffiths, because although it had a Monday and Wednesday market and two fairs, the inhabitants whose living was won from the soil far outnumbered craftsmen.[10] While villages did not have walls, neither did all towns, and some villages have a distinctively defensive layout.

Historians in consequence have worked pragmatically, first identifying settlements contemporaries regarded as towns, and then looking for common features. There is rough but not perfect agreement. Clark and Slack think there were about 700 towns in England in the sixteenth and seventeenth century; Everitt thinks in 1558 there were less than 750 market towns; and Chalklin thinks there were 600 in 1700. The number of Welsh towns has been estimated as 105, of which 71 were planted by the monarch or a local lord. There were over 60 royal burghs and at least 100 burghs of barony or regality in Scotland. By the end of the seventeenth century there were an estimated 150 in Ireland. This would mean one town for every 4000 people in England in 1500, dropping to one for 8000 in 1700 even after new towns are included; one for every 5000 in Wales dropping to one for 6000 if decayed towns are eliminated; and one for 6000 in Scotland where new foundations outweigh any population rise. Ireland, where towns were so scarce and unevenly distributed in 1500 that a calculation can hardly be attempted, had by 1700 approximately one for every 12 000.

There are, then, two basic aspects of a town: its function and its morphology. Function can be divided into nature and stature. There are a variety of different categories under which towns have been listed for this period. One lists country towns, new towns, provincial capitals, and capital; another divides towns into commercial towns, regional capitals, provincial capitals and metropolis. Neither of these analyses by functions. A division by functions into ports, market towns, religious or administrative centres, industrial towns, tourist centres, overlaps them. Many towns, particularly the larger ones, combined one or more of these functions while also being, for example, a country town. A town's stature depended on its role in the region and its position in a wider urban field.

Urban morphological studies show us distinctive land use, layout, plan and buildings. In an established town land has already been structured by size and earlier planning. Redevelopment shows growth and change, the need for further planning and modification, all of it resulting in a distinctive townscape. A town is thus morphologically identifiable. Most towns in Britain by the sixteenth and seventeenth century were affected by earlier settlement patterns such as Roman fortified camps, monastic settlements or the settlements of native princes in Ireland and Wales. Some, however, were new and some, established to provide services to a particular community, perhaps an isolated mining community, disappeared with the resource. Permanence and durability do not have to be urban characteristics although most towns in Britain have a long pre-history.

Identifying urban communities and the population they served is only the first step in considering the role that towns played in human history, particularly between 1500 and 1700. Not everyone sees urbanisation as a key variable in history. Sociologists like Hohenberg and Lees see the town as part of the wider system but occupying a strategic position within it.[11] Some Marxists go further and argue towns were merely locations in which otherwise significant events occur and are worth studying primarily to shed light on wider social and economic trends. The only useful studies become detailed 'total histories' of individual towns which represent the state of human culture at a particular time and place.

The Role of the Town in History

The founding father of urban studies in Britain, H. J. Dyos, had a wider vision of urban history.[12] He saw it as more than the study of individual communities. It was, instead, the investigation of broad historical processes and trends. He expected interpretations which made a fruitful use of theory. The Urban History Group, which he founded, fostered much that was valuable but as it refused to establish a clear agenda, preferring the principle of interdisciplinary approaches, historians focused on different issues. Dyos's unwillingness to engage in establishing a premature orthodoxy resulted in the emergence of numerous subgroups concerned with aspects of urban studies rather than general theories.[13] As a result, specific arguments in the early modern field at present for the most part relate only loosely to theory so that the period is lost between the well-mapped medieval scene and the modern. British historians, with the exception of Wrigley, have been slow to set British towns in a global context. This is unfortunate since, as Wrigley has pointed out, if we can rely on the work of Jan de Vries the pattern of England's development within the European trend was distinctive.

Theory has nevertheless shaped many of the questions which historians of the period have been asking. The most obvious and important of these is whether 1500–1700 or perhaps 1800 was a key period of urban change. Sjoberg's influential book made the pre-industrial city largely static and undifferentiated despite its varying political, social or economic settings, divided between 'folk' and 'feudal'. He suggested that the changes which occurred in the period between 1500 and 1700 were only random fluctuations of little long-term significance. Significant change came only with the coming of the Industrial Revolution and then in parallel with, rather than causing changes in political circumstances.[14] In this theory there were only two significant points of change in urban development, the first, the prehistoric emergence of towns in Europe, Asia and the Americas, and the second, that associated with the Industrial Revolution in the eighteenth and nineteenth centuries.

Support for this view came from anthropologists and pre-historians. To them the appearance of towns was a measure of civilisation in the pre-historic 'urban revolution', a necessary part of the evolution of complex societies. The appearance of towns was inextricably associated with the development of hierarchies and a complex pattern of economic exploitation and religious symbolism and the critical means of exploiting and circulating resources.[15] Until the industrial city of the nineteenth century, nothing that seemed critical to them changed significantly. This idea also gained support from historians like Pirenne and Postan. Although they thought the medieval town promoted the growth of capitalism they also believed towns lost importance in the early modern period when capitalists turned to rural areas for a proletarian labour force, leaving towns to stagnate until the coming of the Industrial Revolution. The assertion that structural change occurred only in the nineteenth century seemed evident from the dramatic rise in urban population.

Geographers sought to examine these developments by isolating urban characteristics which they considered measurable, and graphing them in such a way as to produce a constant pattern which might be 'predictable'. They explain the varying fortunes of particular towns either by locational theory or central place theory. In doing so, they sought to use rigorously some of the same explanations that historians have used pragmatically. If nature prepared the site, man organised it to meet his wants. Transport was critical, and sites at the juncture of transport routes particularly favoured. The physical distribution of economic and social systems govern their growth. Central place theory also seeks to understand patterns of distribution by tying them to physical measurements. The hypothetical spatial distribution of towns is seen as a function of the services they provide and the distances that could be travelled in an hour. A network of ascending sized towns arises from the smallest to the largest with the size also governed by the network.[16]

Not everyone accepts the two-fold division of urban history. Gutkind argued that it was the Renaissance which broke the older mould of narrow municipal self sufficiency, as the state extended its power and took over many functions which had been the concern of individual towns.[17] Jan de Vries argued strongly against the Sjoberg school, that 'an urban system is not a product of industrialisation and modernisation but is itself a precondition for those phenomenon.' The development of a system from what was at best only a loosely articulated semi-disassociated collection of areas, was in de Vries's view the major and critical dynamic development of the period between 1500 and 1800.[18] He and others have recently attempted a synthesis of central place and network approaches designed to re-assess the significance of the geographers' graphs. The questions they seek to answer are: 'how do urban hierarchies (or systems, or networks) develop over time? By which methods and with which sources and dimensions (i.e. population, function, infrastructure) should the hierarchies be defined and measured? How should the patterns of urban arrangements revealed by these methods be categorised? And finally, what meaning can be attributed to the varying patterns that emerge from these studies'.[19] This invites historians to review the relations between cities, looking at administrative hierarchies, trade and communication flows, migration patterns, and similar phenomena.

This gives meaning to the question on which recent historical attention has been focused: whether towns in the period 1500–1640 were economically dependent and derivative or a dynamic influence. Clark and Slack argue for dependence, Wrigley for towns as the engine of growth.[20] Evidence for dependency would suggest de Vries is wrong. Much hangs on a long debate between Rigby and Bridbury over the existence of a late medieval urban decline, whether it continued into the sixteenth century and if so, when and why it ended. If it is agreed that there was a decline, was it absolute or can we, with David Palliser, see some useful 'restructuring' going on?[21] A recent book dealing with the decline and rise of towns saw the recovery starting in 1570 as did Phythian-Adams. Clark and Slack see no recovery until the seventeenth century. Most historians agree that conditions improved after 1650 but disagree as to the cause. Did the smaller towns generate their own recovery or was it the result of a dominant metropolis as Clark and Slack suggest?

One reason for disagreements is the patchiness of the sources for interpreting change in towns. Municipal records, registers, accounts, apprenticeship records, testaments and wills, and deeds provide a good institutional framework but shed only indirect light on the size and population structure of towns. Additional sources used in more recent studies include parish registers, census returns, taxation assessments, central court records. The reliability of these sources of course depends upon the purpose for which they are being interrogated and the theoretical stance of the historian. Most are only a proxy for the information that the historian is seeking; they are not a direct evaluation and the extent to which they can be adapted is problematic.

If leading citizens avoided office, was it because their town was wrestling with deep-seated problems or because their social conscience was not enough to persuade them to divert their time and attention from their own profitable business? The percentage of the population on the poverty line is an important measure of the quality of life but historians do not agree on a measure of poverty. The numbers on poor relief rarely reach one in twenty but do not represent all working poor. Historians, preoccupied with these issues of proof, have tended to avoid the grand theory but many, like Derek Keene, have none the less been influenced by ideas about significant moments of change.[22]

Urbanisation

Urbanisation in these theories has a very specific meaning, distinct from the existence of towns in themselves. It has been described as a process of concentration whereby all non-agricultural activities were drawn into high-density areas of population, increasing productivity so that the pull of the central place became self-reinforcing, leading to constant expansion in town size. It is not a simple percentage increase in the number of people living in small towns closely linked to their immediate hinterland but one in which the size and scale of a comparatively small number of cities divorced the inhabitants from any rural roots. Historians like de Vries and Bairoch are interested only in towns over an arbitrary figure such as 5000 or 10 000.

Such concentrations arguably have characteristics that are distinct from those which related to smaller towns including the size of the household and the number of households which were wealthier than average. Another underlying assumption is that the growth of such towns is related to distinctive ways of organising work so that structural changes taking one from feudal relationships through those of 'mercantile capitalism' to 'proto-industrialisation' may be identifiable. This assumes that capital is the most significant element in developing towns beyond a certain point and that not only did production, trade and banking benefit from proximity but the growth of cities produced 'a spiral of change' in the surrounding districts and so in the city itself.

Population Figures

The question of when urbanisation occurred thus divides historians. Some identify the massive increase in the percentage of the population living in towns, preceded by necessary changes in the relationships and functions of towns, which had started before 1700. Others see urban growth and decline at that time as largely cyclical and due to external uncontrollable events. Part of the answer lies in attempting to establish the size of the population at large and the numbers of town dwellers as a percentage of that population between 1500 and 1700. To verify or disprove de Vries' claims really requires figures on whether the urban population was growing, whether it was increasing in wealth and which categories of towns were growing.

Even benchmark figures for total population are unreliable. Depending on the means of calculation, the same original figures can produce an English population in 1541 of between 3.11 and 5.05 million.[23] The figures suggest, however, that between 1540 and 1640 population was rising, then there is a drop and oscillation around a norm. In 1541 the estimate is 2 700 000 which rose to just over 4 million in 1601 and 5 million in 1701. Even at the end of the period, the basis on which the calculations have been done leaves room for sizeable error in particular cases. Clark's calculation for Lynn would give a population of c.5745 in 1691. Alternative calculations based on the poll taxes paid at that time could reduce that to 3931.[24]

Taken separately the population of Wales was probably around 207 000 in 1540, perhaps climbing to 250 000 by the mid-sixteenth century. By 1670 there may have been 371 000 people. Significant further rises did not occur until after 1710. One reason may have been a tendency for the Welsh to migrate to English towns such as Bristol and Chester, Hereford, Shrewsbury and London.

While evidence for England and Wales is slight and hard to interpret, evidence for Scotland and Ireland is even trickier. Surviving Scottish parish registers are rare and the basis for calculations before 1697 difficult to interpret. The most accepted figure for 1700 is about 1 million; in 1560 it may have been 800 000 suggesting much slower growth than in England, although there may have been a decline in the seventeenth century from a higher point in 1600.[25]

O'Dowd has described the inability adequately to calculate Irish population as 'one of the greatest weaknesses of early modern Irish history.'[26] Connell's original estimates, that the population of Ireland in 1600 was 1.4 million and by 1687 it was 2.2 million[27] have been revised[28] using the assumption that Irish households were larger than English. Nicholas Canny, however, thinks that Ireland was sparsely populated in 1600 and that the 1600 figure must be lowered to 1.1 million. Since, if a figure of 2.2 million stands, this would result in a faster rate of growth than was experienced anywhere else in Europe, Clarkson has suggested that the 1687 figure needs to be revised downwards to 1.7 million, sharply reducing the difference but increasing the percentage of those living in towns. Earlier figures are even more problematic. With great caution the total population of Ireland in 1500 has been estimated at somewhere between 500 000 and 750 000.

Changing Urban Numbers and Size

The fundamental question of urbanisation, the changing size and importance of different towns, is subject to the same problems. This could only be known for certain if figures of town inhabitants at different periods can be calculated, preferably from common and comparable data, which is rarely available. The absence of census data drives historians to use sources such as parish registers, local censuses, religious counts of communicants, muster returns, hearth taxes and the like. Recording baptisms, marriages and funerals in the established church is not, however, a direct measure of population; musters are concerned with adult males available for military training, hearth taxes counted fireplaces in houses which may not be a direct indication of either wealth or residents. Moving from these to a possible total population is a delicate and intrinsically unreliable process. What seems clear is that the nationwide sources for any of the kingdoms cannot on their own supply a secure answer on the size of any individual town. Not only do they have problems of reliability and frequent gaps, they are also unevenly spread across the period and the countryside. Only detailed work by local historians which can integrate other indicators of growth or decline can build a total picture. One such source which is a likely indicator of moments of growth is a housing boom or evidence of multi-occupancy of existing property. Where rentals survive, increasing numbers of houses suggests growth as at Burford where in 1552 a survey showed 140 houses which in the 1596 rental had risen to 180. This also requires caution, however, as houses can be unoccupied. Archaeological work can help here by showing infilling or redeveloping and, on the other hand, places abandoned. The detailed work on Winchester is one example of this.

Precise figures for any town, in short, are impossible. Only indications can be obtained. The crude counting of baptisms has been used to give some idea of town size in terms of a possible birth rate within the known demographic limits. For every thousand people, the maximum crude birth rate is 55 and the minimum 22 and at this time was probably towards the upper end. The effect of different assumptions, however, can be seen in the following table. The aggregate decade-corrected count of London baptisms in seventeenth century suggests a doubling of population across the century and a higher population than is usually accepted even if the lower birthrate is taken.

Detailed work on parish records, however, suggests that birth rates fluctuated considerably from decade to decade depending on such factors as the average age of the woman at marriage. Crude calculations must be used with caution.

Table 9.1 The effects of differing assumptions on estimates of London's population in the seventeenth century

Decade	Baptisms in London	Population if birthrate 33 per 000	Population if birthrate 40 per 000
1610	86 405	261 800	216 000
1620	97 517	295 500	243 800
1630	121 121	367 000	302 800
1660	115 339	349 500	288 347
1670	133 335	404 000	333 337
1680	155 660	471 096	389 150
1690	164 641	498 912	411 600
1700	164 474	498 060	411 185

Sources: Valerie Fildes (ed.), *Women as Mothers in Pre-industrial England* (London, 1990), table 6.

Other sources such as taxation records are even more suscep- tible to error. Most of them demand a 'multiplier' to arrive at a comparable figure and the average multiplier is not set in concrete; at certain times and places it may be wrong. It is not, therefore, surprising that fierce debates can rage over the conver- sion of taxation material into population figures. The main multipliers now accepted are: for houses (or housefuls) 5.75; for households/families 4.25; for communicants (male) 3.00; for communicants (male and female) 1.5. In Scotland Whyte and Lynch both use a different household multiplier of 4.5, in Ireland the houseful may have been 6.5. The differences which can arise from different assumptions about the same evidence can be seen from comparing Clark's figures for two Gloucestershire towns with independent estimates by David Rollison.

For the end of the seventeenth century overviews may be obtained from the works of Petty, King and the Compton census but understanding them requires consideration of the political circumstances in which they were produced. Gregory King's contemporary estimates are a common starting point. He sees 530 000 living in London in 1695–6 and 870 000 in other cities or 1 400 000 of a total population of 5.183 million including Wales, that is 28 per cent of the population lived in towns. He

Table 9.2 Varying calculations from similar data

		Rollison	Clark	Rollison	Clark
Year	1551	1603	1603	1676	1676
Bisley	668	1008	1350	2010	1800
Wotton-under-Edge	668	2030	1820	2692	2570

Source: I am grateful to Dr David Rollison and Professor Peter Clark
    for permission to use their figures.

arrives at these figures by saying there were 1 212 663 houses in
England excluding London and 77 921 houses in Wales and
using multipliers to produce a population of 4 583 000 for
England and 315 000 for Wales.

In general, British historians, while arguing fiercely over the
details of assessing pre-census data, concur in the claim that over
the period as a whole the size of the urban population was
increasing and so were the numbers of large towns. The pattern
varied, however, from one part of the country to another. Norfolk
towns, for instance, were experiencing a rise while Essex towns
were in general decline. The evidence suggests that in the South
West larger towns like Plymouth and Dartmouth, Tiverton and
Cullompton, doubled in size between the 1580s and 1640 while
the smaller towns were declining.

General conclusions suggest that in 1500 there were probably
15 towns over 4000 representing 6 per cent of the population;
while by 1700 there were 30 towns over 5000 representing
15 per cent of the population.[29] Although different historians
give somewhat different figures these include three towns
above 20 000: Bristol (*c.*20 000), Norwich (*c.*28 881) and New-
castle-upon-Tyne (*c.*20–25 000). York was probably approaching 20 000, Exeter 14 000, Sheffield, Shrewsbury, Chester,
and Yarmouth were probably around 10 000, Colchester (9500),
Cambridge and Plymouth (8500–9000), Manchester and Oxford
were just below with a string of 15 or so more towns including
Kings Lynn, Liverpool, Leeds, Tiverton and Birmingham above
5000.

In 1700, therefore, 10 per cent of the population lived in
London alone, about another 4 to 5 per cent in towns over or

around 10 000 and a further 2 to 3 per cent in towns above 5000, a major increase in the experience of large urban life. This tends to support de Vries' argument. The hundreds of small towns would add no more than a further 4 to 5 per cent of the population to town dwellers, making the larger towns already far more important for urbanisation.

Despite the ambiguity of much available evidence, Ireland was clearly experiencing a similarly rapid growth of urban population although at a lower level. The only approximately comprehensive guide for small Irish towns is the 1659 census and parish registers hardly survive for periods before 1660. Counts of houses are the closest to population that one can usually get before 1687 when Sir William Petty's calculations provide a starting point. It is clear that Irish towns in the sixteenth century were still small, few in number and concentrated mainly in the South East. Only Dublin meets the minimum requirement of 5000. The population of major centres like Cork, Limerick, Galway, Waterford and Carrickfergus were not much more than 2000; county centres like Drogheda, Carlingford, Wexford, Youghal, Kinsale, Sligo, Bantry, Dundalk, Dungarvan, Kilkenny, Rosscarbery, approached but were mostly well under 2000. On these figures the percentage of people living in towns is probably not much more than 5 per cent.

In the seventeenth century, population and towns were both growing, and the percentage of urban dwellers was increasing, but was still low by European standards. In Sligo in the 1670s the total town population was still well under 2000 or not much more than a tenth of the county population.[30] With the new settlements in 1611 there were notionally 76 borough towns and numbers continued to rise but before 1660 most of the plantation towns remained tiny. In the 1630 muster even the larger towns were under 1000. The 'census' of 1659 shows that towns were still quite small – just 20, all of them large corporations, had taxable populations of over 500.

Many of the new townspeople were not Irish-born. Between 1580 and the 1680s about 100 000 people migrated from Britain to Ireland, many of whom were expected to settle in towns. Dublin already needed migrants to replace its failing population

Table 9.3 Irish town sizes in the seventeenth century

Year	1600	1660	1680	1700
Dublin	15 000	25–30 000	45 000	62 000
Galway	4200		5–6000	6000
Limerick	2400			11 000
Waterford	2400		5–6000	6000
Cork	2400	5000	10 000	25 000
Belfast				2000
Derry		586	*c.*2000	3000
Drogheda			10 000	

Source: From L. M. Cullen's original figures as modified by Raymond
    Gillespie, *The Transformation of the Irish Economy 1550–1700*,
    Studies in Irish Economic and Social History, Vol. 6 (Cork, 1991).

as burials exceeded baptisms by over two to one, indicating that
immigration was the major source of population growth. While
some of this was from Dublin's Irish hinterland, much of it came
from Britain, especially Wales and North West England. This
suggests that 8 or 9 per cent of the population lived in towns over
5000 by 1700 and another 6 or 7 per cent in smaller towns. This
was a major shift on the position in 1600 when only Dublin had
classified and represented only about 1 per cent of the total
population.

Scotland's urban growth was more variable. The sources
available for estimating size in sixteenth-century Scotland are
again taxation based, supplemented by some local counts of
houses and households. In the seventeenth century there is an
assessment for tax in 1639 for the covenanters and in 1691 a
hearth tax, both of which are hard to interpret. It is also
unfortunate that the 1639 figures were probably affected by a
recent plague and the 1691 figures by the recently ended political
struggle and may represent the trough of temporary fluctuations.

Despite the general paucity of evidence there seems agreement
that most towns nearly doubled in size in the long sixteenth
century. Numerous new towns were also established in the
period, mostly as burghs of regality or baronial burghs. Although
only 25 per cent took root, 17 were significant, but none reached
the 5000 figure. Musselburgh with over 3000 was probably the

largest.[31] Town fortunes in the seventeenth century were more mixed. Whyte and Lynch disagree as to whether between 1639 and 1691 most towns were growing or declining, mainly because Lynch's estimates for 1639 are higher than Whyte's. Lynch believes that the medium sized were declining and only Stirling and Linlithgow were actually rising against the trend. Stirling was recovering from the loss of long-established trades and from 1500 –2000 people in 1544 had grown to 3000 in 1691.

The old royal burghs were largely maintaining their dominance affected only by Glasgow's rise and Perth's decline. The continuing dominance of the four great towns, Edinburgh, Aberdeen, Perth and Dundee, is clearly seen in their tax payments. In the next rank were Linlithgow, and Haddington; then Ayr, Rothesay, Montrose, Wigtown, Dumbarton, Irvine and Stirling. In the seventeenth-century Edinburgh, Glasgow, Aberdeen, Perth and Dundee were probably the only cities over 5000 and the ten or so next centres such as Dumfries, Ayr and Inverness were well under. Twenty-five towns were under a thousand population and another 11 under 2500. Clearly, while towns had grown both in size and number only 9 to 10 per cent of people lived in towns unambiguously large while another 8 to 10 per cent lived in small towns.

Global Urban Population Figures

Until recently the start of the process whereby a relatively smaller number of larger towns developed and their growth became self-reinforcing was located somewhere in the eighteenth century. De Vries and Bairoch, however, agree that in Europe as a whole the absolute numbers of people living in towns over 5000 and even more over 10 000 increased and so did the percentage of the total population that they represent before 1700.

Bairoch claims that this urban growth was 'in countries previously only slightly urbanised, especially Britain and the Netherlands'. This he associates with new patterns of trade centring on the Atlantic.

He shows a marked growth in England's and the Netherland's level of urbanisation in the period compared to other areas

Table 9.4 Urban population growth in 1300–1750

Year	Total Pop.	Urban millions	Pop. annual variation%	Level of total pop.	Urbanisation annual variation%
1300	75	7.9		10.4	
1500	76	8.2	0.02	10.7	0.01
1600	95	10.9	0.29	11.5	0.07
1650	(98)	(11.6)	0.12	(11.8)	0.06
1700	102	12.6	0.16	12.3	0.08
1750	120	14.7	0.31	12.2	−0.01

Source: Paul Bairoch, *Cities and Economic Development: from the Dawn of History to the Present*, trans. Christopher Braider (Chicago, 1988), p. 177.

with England moving from below to above the European average.

Figures such as these are the result of heroic assumptions, Bairoch and de Vries' calculations are markedly different for 1600 (10.8 per cent (de Vries) or 12.9 per cent (Bairoch)) and producing more detailed assessments is now the subject of a

Table 9.5 Urban population percentages by nations 1300–1700

Year	1300	1500	1700
Austria–Hungary	4–7	5–8	5–8
Balkans	8–11	7–12	7–12
Belgium	25–35	30–45	26–35
England	6–9	7–9	13–16
France	9–11	9–12	11–15
Germany	5–8	7–9	8–11
Italy	15–21	15–20	14–19
Netherlands	8–12	20–26	38–49
Portugal	8–11	11–13	18–23
Scandinavia	5–7	5–8	5–8
Spain	13–18	10–16	12–17
Switzerland	5–7	6–8	6–8
Europe	9–12	10–12	11–14

Source: Paul Bairoch, *Cities and Economic Development: from the Dawn of History to the Present*, trans. Christopher Braider (Chicago, 1988).

major international team project. In 1800 they agree that 13.5 per cent of the population of Europe lived in towns of this size and that most of this rise is attributable to Britain. Continental Europe saw little increase in urbanisation between 1600 and 1800 – or even between 1400 and 1800.[32]

The figures calculated above for England suggest that between 1500 and 1700 the percentage of people living in towns over 5000 has certainly risen above the European norm, while Scotland and Ireland although enjoying, particularly in Ireland's case, considerable growth are only approaching the minimum. As de Vries noted England does not fit his claim that in Europe between 1500 and 1650 urban growth was centred in the small cities and in the larger cities from 1650 and 1750. It is England and Wales, however, which conform to the geographer's expectations.

If one includes all towns, in the later seventeenth century at least 20 per cent, perhaps as much as 25 per cent of England's population lived in towns compared to 59 per cent in the Netherlands and 16 per cent in France. This is a clear rise on 13–14 per cent in 1500. Even in Wales, where no towns were above 5000 in 1700, the growth of some towns such as Cardiff, Newport, Abergavenny and Denbigh made up for the disappearance of Bere, Disuth, Sefnllys and Kenfig. The percentage of urban dwellers, although it had grown, was much lower in Ireland and Scotland than in England. In 1687 one in 26 or 4 per cent of people in Ireland lived in Dublin, and one in 17 in a town of over 5000, only 5 to 6 per cent of the total. Towns between 2500 and 5000 at most number another 20, housing 60–80 000 people, another 4 to 5 per cent. The growing number of smaller towns do not add all that much to the urban population, a maximum of perhaps 25 800 taxable people in such towns gives a total of less than in the whole of Dublin. All town dwellers in Ireland still number at most one in nine – perhaps between 12 and 15 per cent.[33] The smaller towns of Scotland in 1700 may have added 6 or 7 per cent to the total of 8 to 10 per cent in large towns, making 16 to 17 per cent. The percentage in cities over 10 000 is noticeably different. Whyte presents a comparison between England and Scotland in a table to which I have added my own calculation for Ireland.

Table 9.6 Percentage of population living in British towns of over 10 000

	1500	1550	1600	1650	1700
Scotland	1.6	1.4	3.0	3.5	5.3
England	3.1	3.5	5.8	8.8	13.3
Ireland	0	0	0.1	1.2	4.9

Source: Ian D. Whyte, 'Urbanization in Early Modern Scotland: a preliminary estimate', *Scottish Economic and Social History* Vol. 9 (1989).

Density of Towns

One of the criteria for urbanisation is not simply size but density of population. In the Middle Ages many cities in Europe had densities of 150 400 per hectare within a range of 70 to 770. A very small town covering six hectares with a minimum density would thus have over 420 inhabitants; at medium density 1140 and maximum 2400. Density, however, is doubly hard to establish. Not only must population be established but also area and often only the size of the parish in which the settlement lay is known, not the built-up area or boundaries of the town. The parish of Chesterfield in Derbyshire, for example, covered 45 square miles and comprised not only the town but numerous rural settlements.[34] Even walled towns present problems since the area may include fields within the walls and the areas they enclosed have also been variously calculated. Thomas estimates Winchester as 33 hectares, Turner as 55 hectares. Turner gives 52 hectares and Harvey 60 for Great Yarmouth. Some small English towns were below the minimum density level and many Irish towns probably had not reached minimum density by 1640.

Most known town areas in Britain were small, however, and while density may have been initially low, fairly small increases in population could build up to unacceptable levels. When London's population reached 52 000 in the mid-sixteenth century it was already at maximum density. Dublin in 1600 had a high density of 281 per hectare. Bristol in the early sixteenth century had a density of 250 a hectare, which is high, but growth by 1700 would have pushed it to 700. In these growing cities people were moving to the liberties or suburbs outside the walls, one of the signs of growing urbanisation which can be observed in all the major cities in Britain.

Fluctuations

If the period saw the start of significant urbanisation it was far from a constant upward trend. Much work is still required to fit this into a framework of chronological fluctuations within the period which varied from kingdom to kingdom and from region to region. There is a general sense that the first part of the sixteenth century was a period of decline for provincial towns in England and that recovery only began some time in the second half of the century as the English provincial ports started to recover. Important inland towns like Worcester appear to have lost population between 1538 and 1570 and then to have recovered significantly. Ireland saw little urban change in the sixteenth century while Scotland saw significant growth. With the 1590s famine, plague and war there was a general setback, followed by a recovery in the early seventeenth century, difficulties in the 1620s and an uneven development in the 1630s as overseas trade continued to be affected by the Thirty Years War. The 1640s saw the devastations of civil wars but the Restoration then brought substantial recovery and expansion until the 1690s in England, Wales and Ireland while in Scotland urban growth was more mixed and less stable.

Problems in Explaining Growth

One unresolved problem about urban population is the manner in which any rise was achieved. Usually, more died in towns than were born there, and so town populations did not replace themselves. Moreover, individual town-dwellers on average died younger so that net migration from rural areas was essential to prevent town population from dwindling away to nothing. The impact of disease on urban size was often horrendous. In the 1550s York lost one third of its population. In 1604 one in six inhabitants of Salisbury died, one in five of Leicester in 1610–11. These were not single disasters. Leicester suffered 11 plague attacks between 1558 and 1639.

Alan Sharlin has suggested that the natural decrease is more apparent than real, the excess of deaths over births being mainly attributable to the death of recent migrants who were not immune to the endemic viruses and bacteria in the towns and who were perhaps also resident in the most overcrowded and less salubrious areas.[35] It may be that the smaller towns had less natural decrease and some clearly had an excess of births over deaths. The main problem to be resolved, however, is the massive rise in London which in the sixteenth century required an average of 4800 migrating a year or 40 per cent of the estimated rural surplus and more in the seventeenth century when the rural surplus was less.[36] From 1650, indeed, the natural increase in England was not sufficient to meet London's requirements and migrants must have come from elsewhere.[37]

It is generally assumed that external sources of additional population were probably not statistically significant. Nevertheless there is a tendency to 'balance the books' with reference to such migration, and shifts between the kingdoms may be underestimated. In England in some decades there was significant migration from the continent. In the 1680s and 1690s many of the larger towns in Britain accepted refugees mainly from France. Bristol alone received over a thousand despite the lack of enthusiasm on the part of the authorities.[38] Whether these counterbalanced the numbers who were leaving for colonies in America is less clear. Irish historians are inclined to think that migration to Ireland more than counterbalanced the numbers of Irish who migrated to England and Wales, although Welsh writers spoke of one in every four or five households in some Welsh towns being Irish and in London 8 per cent of recorded crime was attributed to Irish people.

Urbanisation in Britain

The surge in numbers of those living in large cities between 1500 and 1700 is a phenomenon largely produced by the capitals.

Between 1500 and 1700 London rose from tenth to first place in Europe. The surge in Dublin's population in the seventeenth century at an average annual growth rate of 1.5 per cent to a total of nearly 70 000 in the early eighteenth century was equally amazing. By 1700 both were probably bigger than all the larger provincial towns put together while the number and size of large provincial towns had also risen.

What supports the suggestion that this was urbanisation is that all the prosperous English towns were developing specialised functions in a range of areas including education, leisure activities, trade and manufacturing. Manufacturing in the older towns like Coventry and Leicester was rising again. Towns like Bath were exploiting leisure. Those ports which were able to attract manufacturers dealing in the growing re-export trade, especially in sugar and tobacco, grew; those which controlled a raw material like coal, for which there was an increasing demand, grew. Towns beginning to develop an industrial base, like Cardiff, grew.

Shifts in town ranking did not necessarily indicate a drop in absolute levels of prosperity; Dartmouth although losing ground, comparatively to Plymouth in the late seventeenth century was still expanding and prospering.[39] Those which prospered reinforced their attractiveness by upgrading their facilities. Even towns with only local administrative or local market functions and a stable population of between 2000 and 3000 were doing what they could. The smaller towns were beginning to suffer from the greater pull of larger centres, and some, such as Burwash or Ditchling in Sussex, virtually disappeared as their function was absorbed by a neighbour. Small settlements nevertheless still accounted for a significant percentage of townspeople. Clark believes that in the early eighteenth century 54 per cent of townspeople lived in towns of under 5000 – many in towns of under 2500.[40]

The slower growth of Scottish towns may be associated with a failure to develop dominant craft specialties although the manufacturing of spirits was making an appearance. The only remotely single-industry towns in 1600 were Dysart for salt, Crail for coal, Pittenweem for fish and Culross on the Forth as a small mining town and Leadhills. Significantly, some of the more prosperous towns as the seventeenth century progressed were developing new industries. Greenock became a centre of fish-curing and soap-making; Glasgow of tobacco manufacture, sugar-refining and minor goods such as paper. The town council promoted a woollen factory in Drygate so that by 1700 it was claimed that three companies producing wool and linen cloth were employing 1400 people.[41]

Ireland's rapid urban growth was not at first associated with specialisation. Here it was a question of catching up and the small size of the towns produced less rather than more specialisation. By the late seventeenth century, however, it was beginning to appear in some smaller towns in the form of linen and other manufactures while silk manufacture in Dublin was becoming important. Wales remained comparatively backward. Most Welsh towns before 1700 remained undifferentiated, their inhabitants still closely involved with rural occupations. They had few of the amenities which made some English towns visibly wealthy. Words like unhygienic have been applied to them. Nevertheless, an increasing number of lawyers, doctors and schoolmasters were taking up residence in the bigger towns and signs of future development were appearing. Demand for the products of Welsh mines was growing, shipbuilding was increasing and Carmarthen became a specialist centre of beaver and felt hat manufacture while Wrexham developed lead smelting and a paper mill.[42]

Conclusion

Two conditions usually assumed necessary for sustained urban growth were an increase in agricultural output so that a smaller percentage of the population could produce enough for the whole, and a substitute for organic fuel. Both of these have been shown for the period. Necessary conditions, however, are not sufficient conditions and a number of other factors are seen as coming together to encourage urban growth in the period, particularly in London. One was the major demand of the growing transatlantic economy which made increasing calls on European manufacturing and supplied in return a burgeoning number of tropical and semi-tropical products. Another was the role of London as what Fisher called an 'engine of growth' and Beier an 'engine of manufactory', stimulating demand for domestic goods. The timetable of growth is seen to reflect the history of capital. The third factor which is usually accepted is the centralising role of government.

The extraordinary growth of London and Dublin produced a situation in which in 1700 one in nine English people – 500 000 – lived in a city larger than the total population of Wales and at least one in 30 inhabitants of Ireland lived in Dublin. Edinburgh housed perhaps one in 22. If one adds to these numbers those living in the other towns with populations over 5000, the percentage of people whose experience of urban life was in large and diverse communities rises to perhaps one in seven in England, one in 20 in Ireland and one in 15 in Scotland. By 1700 'town' dwelling as a distinct way of life was coming to mean the big town experience as opposed to the small town life. The urban experience was spreading even further than that. Society was increasingly becoming involved in urban activities even if most people were still not permanent town residents. Temporary residents greatly expanded the total number of people to whom town life was familiar.

10

NETWORK AND HIERARCHY

Theorists interested in urbanisation believe that the process involves more than simple increase in size and that what is important is not a pyramid locating towns in terms of wealth and size but the development of a hierarchy. For a pyramid to become a hierarchy more is required. A hierarchy implies more than simple ranking. It requires more than the replacement of one settlement by another as, for example, Totnes slowly lost ground to Dartmouth as the Dart became choked with tin mine debris. It requires the development of an interlocking structure in which one town services another. The different levels should not simply measure riches but also functions, so that specialisation at every level links individual towns to those above and below them. Goods would thus not simply pass through a single town to the immediate consumer but pass up and down the hierarchy through a number of towns.

The further up the hierarchy the town was, the wider the hinterland to which it related. An integrated network in which communication and specialisation overrode the self-sufficient impulse of earlier towns also implies that towns at the same level but with specialised functions developed links with their neighbours. This required improved transport facilities and made likely the disappearance of small unspecialised towns at the lowest level and other towns with no surviving *raison d'être*.

Changing Rank Order of Towns

The existence of a pyramid locating towns in terms of their wealth and perhaps size goes back to the Middle Ages. Different lists ranking towns by size at various dates have been produced. Dyer, relying on tax payments for England starts from 1377 while de Vries operates retrospectively from the 44 towns which in 1800 had reached 10 000. This may help establish which towns were flourishing at different periods but does not in itself explain why, still less establish the existence of a hierarchy. While Dyer lists people, the records really measure wealth rather than population and the reliability of the conversion is doubtful. Coventry's population from the 1524 subsidy is given as 4712, for example, but a full local census in 1520 showed a population of 6001. They are at best indicators which in any particular instance may be affected by specific problems. External disasters could temporarily cause the appearance of decline and affect rankings. In 1625 when Exeter's population was perhaps 12 300, 2300 died from plague, possibly 1000 able-bodied men were kidnapped by pirates and more were taken by the press gang.[1] Tiverton, whose population had doubled between 1560 and 1590, suffered two disastrous fires in 1598 and 1612.[2] Bristol in the early seventeenth century suffered from a plague in which 2956 died so that when the mayor counted the population in 1607 it was only 10 549, a drop of a fifth. York, in 1604, lost 3512 in an epidemic – perhaps 30 per cent of the total population.

If one accepts the lists as a rough guide, however, a comparison of the two suggests significant shifts. De Vries' list contains 13 towns whose main expansion was in the eighteenth century. Dyer's list of the top 50 for 1377 contains 31 towns not over 10 000 in 1800.[4] Of those ranked below 35, only Reading reaches de Vries' list. None of the 13 new names in the top 50 in 1524 are over 10 000 in 1800, although towns like Tiverton and Crediton were prosperous and comparatively populous throughout the period.[5] Four of the new names in the top 50 for hearth tax in 1662 also remain under 10 000.[6] If de Vries' list represents the future of urbanisation, therefore, Dyer's at first sight suggests a time when change was due to more random factors. Dyer's list, however, has weaknesses. It does not include towns not taxed centrally before the Restoration. Some towns are missing by accident, and others which were already quite large possibly because they are not distinguished in the tax lists as they did not have royal charters. The position of his top 50 in 1377 is no indication of their later fortunes. Of the 24 defined as declining, 16 are in the top 30 in the 1662 hearth tax and 12 had a population of over 10 000 in 1800. Of the 22 towns that improved their position between 1377 and 1524–5 only six are in the top 30 in 1662 hearth tax and two over 10 000 in 1800, while of Dyer's marginal 11, eight are in the hearth tax top 30 and four over 10 000 in 1800. Carter's list for Wales also shows a shift in the position of particular towns over the period 1500–1700. Denbigh and Caernarvon, originally at the top, slipped, while Cardiff, Swansea and Abergavenny moved to the top, and towns like Aberystwyth and Welshpool moved up from the third rank.[7]

While Dyer's lists would seem at first sight to support the idea that fluctuations between 1377 and the late seventeenth century had largely localised explanations, looked at more closely it suggests that there were about 20 towns whose location was such that they could recover from any temporary misfortunes and share in urban growth and that a further 12 towns at least were emerging from the ruck during the period, which would seem to suggest that the basic requirements for urbanisation were being realised in the period. Matching the towns which moved up the ranks at different periods also suggests that there were common factors at work. This may help pinpoint which sources of prosperity were most significant at different periods. Those which had risen between 1377 and 1524, for instance, were mainly market towns serving inland trade, rising at a time when the big ports were suffering from competition with London.

Thus, although random variation played some part, there is an underlying pattern which is self-reinforcing. Dramatic declines at the top are rare. Of the top 10 towns in 1524, or 11 if one includes Newcastle for which the 1524 records are missing, seven are in the top 10 in 1662. The top 10 in 1662 are all amongst the towns with a population of over 5000 in 1700.[8] Moreover, the four which lost rank by 1662 include Coventry which later recovered to find a new base for prosperity in the manufacture of shoes; the monastic town of Bury St Edmunds which suffered from the dissolution and proximity to London, and two inland cathedral towns, Salisbury and Lincoln, which had only the religious and administrative role to sustain them. Both were in long-term difficulties. Salisbury's population had halved by the 1690s.

The other top towns were growing in the second half of the seventeenth century, and the 15 to 20 new towns which were rising to join them rested either on the transatlantic trade like Liverpool which reached 10 000 by 1720, or like Sheffield and Manchester on the metal industries. This rise in the larger towns fits de Vries' proposed British pattern, as does the evidence that the great majority of the smaller towns were not rising after 1660. Indeed, it seems possible that some of London's growth may have come from the losses of the smaller towns, especially those in her immediate orbit.

Geographical Distribution

Another indicator of growing urbanisation is the size distribution of settlements across the country. Mapping the distribution of towns by size can show how the natural hinterlands which they serve change and come to overlap. If this is done for 1500–1700, the size distribution is starting to show a pattern with a main centre surrounded by smaller satellites. If the hinterland of some of the towns is measured in terms of the circuit from which vendors and purchasers come to the markets and fairs – the main places from which apprentices are drawn and from which other townspeople may come – the conclusion must be the same. Improvements in transport affected the distribution and created new roles for particular places. Two similar towns which were closer than the norm, rarely both prospered without some exceptional reason.

Mapping also shows the spread of towns to new areas. Towns in Ireland had become markedly more accessible to the majority of people. Large tracts of Gaelic Ireland which had lacked towns

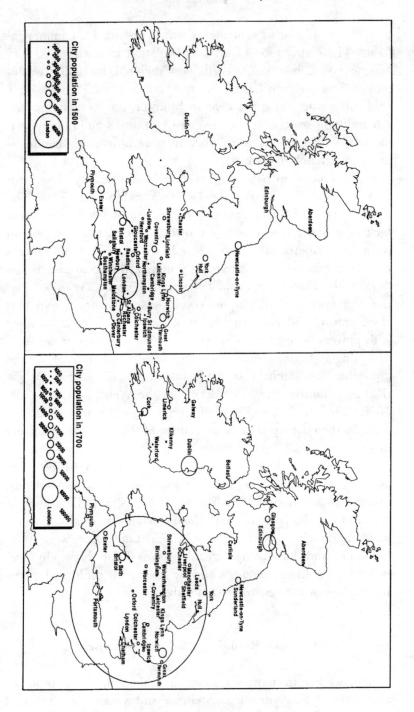

in 1500 by 1700 had settlements which provided a commercial focus. The distribution of urban population in towns with over 500 taxpayers, however, was still very regional. In 1659 it was at most 3.2 per cent in Ulster, 4.5 per cent in Connacht, 11.5 per cent in Leinster, 11.8 per cent in Munster, an average between 7.6 and 9.6 per cent. While the density of towns had not reached the level of England most inhabitants were now within comparatively easy reach of a town.

In Scotland there was also great regional diversity. The Firth of Forth had numerous towns with specialised functions. The South West and South East saw the establishment of new small burghs and after the union of crown a modest improvement in prosperity. Aberdeen, which had effectively kept its entire area free from competitors, was seeing the growth of coastal baronial burghs like Fraserburgh and Peterhead. Urban development in the highlands and islands, however, was still rare, a sign that royal control did not extend into areas still governed by lords with powers of regality from centres which were not urban.

In England, small market centres were much thicker on the ground in the South West, the South Midlands and East Anglia than in Cumbria, the North East and the Welsh border. In the 1670s Essex, Suffolk and Norfolk were among the most urbanised areas in the country with about a third of their inhabitants living in towns while Leicestershire had only 20 per cent and Lincolnshire 15 per cent. This pattern was changing between 1660–1700 as new towns started expanding rapidly in the West Midlands, South Lancashire and West Riding of Yorkshire.[9] The north of England was thinly populated, which worried the English government, although Durham, Yorkshire and Lancashire were more populous and had some sizeable towns. The hierarchy was therefore far from complete and by no means uniform but the bare bones of the system were mostly in place.

Factors Bringing About a Network

A network was in many ways incompatible with complete urban autonomy. A kingdom-wide system inevitably took a good deal of the action away from the control of individual towns, even London. Many of the changes had their roots in the fifteenth century and first manifested themselves in England's dominant export trade. The business of cloth manufacturing was large-scale and complex. The merchants of the staple had become the intermediaries who bought and mixed the wool, put it out to be spun and sold it to the clothiers. The management of the cloth and its finishing was in the hands of very wealthy clothiers because the process required access to considerable credit. No one town could dominate the business of its own hinterland. The London clothiers in the sixteenth century went from fair to fair buying cloth and arranging for it to be processed. In this way the big London merchants were able to dominate the overseas market by maintaining factors abroad which ensured them better information about market opportunity, and better access to insurance, loans and bills of exchange.

This early dominance of London in England's principal export trade and government actions often taken for political not economic reasons accelerated the breakdown of urban isolation. It did not happen without resistance. The dominance of London in the regulated companies resulted in great struggles between the outports and London. The exclusion of non-London-based merchants from the influential inner group of 'assistants' meant the outports had little leverage when it came to policy and for a time little role in overseas trade.

The development of a system whereby wholesale purchase could be by sample at Blackwall Hall and Leadenhall and sale by commission, with the goods going directly to the final market, restored a role to the provincial ports. Cooperation benefited both parties. Part of the recovery of the ports like Hull, Lynn, Exeter and Great Yarmouth lay in the specialisation of their merchants in handling the distribution of a diversity of imports, acting as agents for London cloth merchants and so sharing the benefits of long-distance trade without having to generate all the capital required to participate in a risky venture. The ports regained their prosperity by becoming part of a wider network.

The other trading companies also helped to break down urban

isolation. The success of the protection company convoys in providing for trade from politically sensitive areas like the Baltic was their justification for monopolising trade in particular areas. Britain needed imported manufacturing essentials, such as timber, hemp, flax, pitch and tar, wax and iron from the Baltic. Much did not need to pass through London. Ships from Hull, Newcastle and Ipswich regularly represented more than half of those sailing to Elbing. The company pursued its own interests, not those of any one town. Not even London had much leverage. The market was, therefore, national and its traders formed their own links to merchants in other towns.[10]

The process was advanced by the growth of banking and credit facilities. Individual firms, frequently scriveners, in London began to provide money management services. Again, government had a role. From the mid-century royal treasurers managed the transfer of money from and to distant areas by providing money in one place for merchants in the other. Merchants could settle bills by a paper transfer in London. By 1600 Whitby fish dealers who sent fish to London drew bills on London dealers. Landowners were not slow to follow suit.[11] Some of the larger provincial towns like Norwich established local facilities by 1615. What Kerridge is prepared to call a banking network began to link towns all over England.[12] The London businessmen had correspondents and agents in numerous country towns. The extent of this development should not be exaggerated. Trade from Hull and elsewhere to the Baltic was a simple bilateral affair which employed few agents and rarely involved bills of exchange. Nevertheless, the increasing mobility of capital must have reduced the ability of the town corporations to regulate the structure of trade in their areas. Increasing use of inland bills tied provincial towns to London. A central bank would serve to regulate interest rates and the availability of short-term loans. Earlier private banks like Backwells had many of the functions of the Bank of England, which was finally established in 1694.

Evidence for the development of a market network which linked different areas also comes from prices. When all prices, apart from surcharges produced by costs of carriage, are determined in a single centre a common market area exists. Kerridge argues that this is happening in England in the sixteenth century.[13] Such evidence as has been put together for provincial prices suggests that, just as wages varied in different parts of the country, so a single common price even for fairly standard goods did not exist before the second half of the sixteenth century except where it was the product of traditional regulation.

As the century progressed, however, the elimination of price differentiation from one locality to another was slowly occurring.[14] London prices were set at a level which attracted goods from an ever-widening hinterland. Provincial towns had to match them or lose the resource. This was particularly obvious with corn, where the insatiable appetite of the London corn market affected prices in west coast towns which might export corn to Wales, Ireland or Scotland. The small local markets which were close enough together to offer rural producers a choice were thus driven into competition, keeping prices fairly standard across the country. A domestic overland network developed. A dyer in a small inland market town and modest manufacturing centre for cloth, Chesterfield, in 1588 was dealing with merchants from Kendal, Shrewsbury, Leeds, Rochdale, Marsfield and Newbold. This was not uncommon. By the seventeenth century, dealers there and in many such towns frequently had links to London.[15]

An improved land transport system needed to keep pace with this, but although adequate roads were slow to come, and river improvements did not develop until the later seventeenth century the construction of more extensive stone causeways around a great many towns enabled bigger and better carts in part to replace packhorses. The appearance of a regular network of common carriers also assisted. By the mid-seventeenth century the effects of this were becoming apparent. The first directory to these services appeared in 1637 (John Taylor's *Carriers Cosmographie*) showing that over 200 towns had at least in principle, a weekly service and from some there was a local service to towns off the main routes. In a town like Exeter it was the period after 1630 which saw the start of change as the traditional economy broke down and both Exeter's commercial role and the work of its cloth-producing hinterland changed.[16]

Differentiation Between Towns

The volume of trade required to establish these links, however, started to highlight the difference between towns where there were substantial merchants with these facilities and small market towns without them. Towns specialising in particular manufacturing processes became collecting centres for goods such as cloth. Norwich, Tiverton, Exeter, Shrewsbury, Kendal, Rochdale, Manchester, Leeds, Ipswich, Sudbury, Bury St Edmunds were some of the towns which prospered in these ways.[17]

Increasing use of bonds or formal contracts also favoured those towns which had courts able to deal rapidly with disputes under mercantile law. The unincorporated towns were disadvantaged because their courts, adequate perhaps for most matters had more problems with mercantile matters. The effect of these strong links between towns was inevitably to reduce the autonomy of the provincial communities and to increase their use of central courts and services. The growth of local newspapers made information more rapidly and widely available. The 1640s and 1650s marks a further big change in urban economics and attitudes. It may have to do with the big shift in the form and incidence of taxation, in particular the introduction of the excise taxes and changes to customs regulations. Towns no longer saw themselves as really autonomous or exempt from regulations which affect others.

Ireland after 1660 was drawn into the English network. Irish merchants were rarely able to be specialists in a single market or product, internal trade still relied on cash or barter, but merchants dealing on any scale overseas increasingly required exchange and discounting facilities available primarily through Dublin or Cork. Thus they were drawn into a widening circle of English commerce.[18] The network was still fragmentary but the powerful pull of Dublin was already drawing industry away from some of the provincial towns by the later seventeenth century.

In Scotland, Lynch sees a typical network developing despite Edinburgh's comparatively small size, the binary role of Glasgow and the difficulty of distinguishing province from region. At the bottom are the small-scale marketing and industrial centres. The growing towns were the satellites of Edinburgh and Glasgow, the small specialist ports, the old established inland markets and the border burghs.[19] As the Scottish economy recovered from the devastations of the Interregnum, however, Edinburgh and Glasgow were being drawn into London's orbit. Despite the English Parliament's various Acts which curtailed the rights of both Ireland and Scotland to share the benefits of the growing colonial trade, the Scottish towns were obtaining credit from London. It was the pull of London that stimulated business in both Wales and Scotland. By the 1680s so great was the volume of cattle and sheep driven to London that it provided the basis for bills of exchange in all business activities and controlled the exchange rate between England and Scotland.[20] The restrictive rules of the mercantile system designed to give England a monopoly of colonial trade while it produced a cat's-cradle of complex illicit deals between the three kingdoms served its purpose. Ireland, which had once traded as much directly with Europe as with England, Wales and Scotland, was now forced into predominantly trading with England, in English-owned ships.[21] The hierarchy was reinforced when the smaller Irish ports in the South and East were severely set back by the end of the live cattle trade. The substitution of salt beef in barrels, mainly sold to the navy or the East India company, benefited those ports that could develop the additional facilities required and that meant those which were part of the growing British credit network.

The idea that hierarchy might mean that some towns shed some of the trades within them is not borne out by events. In East Anglia nearly all the 28 market towns seem to have developed a greater range of occupations by the end of the seventeenth century, offering their hinterland double or treble the choice available in 1500 and of the few which declined, like Thetford, most could point to some physical problem.[22]

Welsh towns do not seem to have participated in this urbanisation before 1700. Of the 105 places in Wales which have been described as towns, 35 had a population of under 100 and seem unlikely to meet any normal urban criteria and the larger ones like Cardiff were only a few hundred strong. A decline in the fourteenth and fifteenth centuries undoubtedly reduced these numbers. Most do not seem to have grown substantially after 1500 and suffered their fair share of epidemics and famine which kept the population low. Cardiff did not grow substantially until the nineteenth century. Monmouth in 1610 had a population of perhaps 2000. Ruthin, Builth, Abergavenny, Cowbridge, Presteigne and Welshpool, although described as good market towns, certainly had under 1000 inhabitants. Pembroke had about 630 inhabitants and Beaumaris 555, Wrexham, the largest town was about 2300. Shifts in the pyramid occurred, however, which suggest that it was the pull of trade or industry which governed the changes. Denbigh and Caernarvon, originally in the first rank, declined, while Cardiff, Swansea and Abergavenny moved from the second rank to the first, and towns like Aberystwyth and Welshpool moved up from the third rank. The small size of the ports and their undifferentiated trade, moreover, early reinforced the long-established links to larger centres, South Wales to Bristol and Redcliffe, which was their outlet for fish, North Wales, to Chester or Liverpool.

The new towns in Ireland were linked from the start into a network because colonial towns, as they struggled to establish themselves, needed goods and services which could only be provided from the outside. The early Munster town merchants did business with Dublin and Cork; Ulster merchants after 1660 were the necessary link in the flow of goods from the region to Belfast or Dublin. In Scotland, Lynch and Whyte both perceive a major change which was beginning to link towns that were still isolated in 1500. They stress the development of a network in which Edinburgh, while losing some of its trading monopoly was strengthening its role as judicial and administrative centre drawing business from lesser provincial administrative towns. At the same time the smaller ports on the Forth with specialised trades were flourishing and inland towns were growing on the returns from inland trade and the border boroughs on increasing trade with England. At the other end they see many small towns declining into villages. The links between Edinburgh and towns like Dumfries are already evident by the 1600s.[23]

Conclusion

Distance and isolation which had once provided some protection for small towns was being broken down. The resulting competition favoured the wealthier, better-patronised and best-located towns. Especially as transatlantic traffic increased, there was a cumulative advantage for those able to improve the services they had available which smaller ports with more limited inland trading links and resources could not provide. Increasing numbers of specialist service agencies providing credit, banking and insurance, increasing numbers of specialist areas of production that could be supported within the town itself, attracted potential customers from a ever wider hinterland. Medium-sized towns in their catchment area became linked settlements with local functions. Small non-competitive places dwindled into villages. A mixture of trade and industry remained the winning combination. Newcastle upon Tyne rose to the top in the period 1500–1700 mainly on the coastal trade in coal. Its salt production, its second staple, depended on cheap coal while glass, its third, relied on abundant supplies of good quality sand and fuel while its position gave it an advantage in European trade.

Although market demand did not necessarily follow a similar cycle in the different countries the increasing pull of the English markets and especially the London market drew all four kingdoms into a more regular network towards the end of the seventeenth century. The development by 1700 was by no means complete. The broad outline was visible but much detail remained to be filled in and many changes were to result from later industrial developments. Whether the hierarchy which resulted was an exact reflection of the pyramid of wealth may be more doubtful. Position in a hierarchy depends more on the services and functions provided than on wealth, although the two might go hand-in-hand. Specialist towns, however, might achieve a relatively high level of wealth while remaining comparatively peripheral in the network. The network was as yet less complete than the hierarchy. Cross-country routes which would provide a more dense network as every town developed direct contact with every other, without the need to pass through London, were still only partially developed.

CONCLUSIONS

Cities and towns were social constructs, made by the people who built and lived in them. Like many human institutions they acquired a momentum of their own, a dynamic which makes focusing attention on the town as an object worthy of study in its own right desirable. A town was certainly a geographical location but it was not only a location in which the events of human life occurred, it was a structure created to facilitate economic, social and political intercourse which affected the way in which economic, social and political life was conducted. Beneath the particular identity of the individual town, moreover, there are recognisable generic features.

Towns by 1700 were playing a somewhat different role from the one they had played in 1500. The services which they were providing the people had altered in some respects quite markedly. Some functions which had been quite critical like defence were fading, other functions like banking and credit were becoming essential. The proportion of the total population which lived in towns, moreover, had risen significantly. Britain was not yet as urbanised as Holland but she was much less rural than she had been. As many as one in four people in England lived in towns and although the percentage was lower in the other kingdoms it was rising. Since a number of people who resided in towns for part of their lives did not remain there, the urban experience was even more widespread than these figures suggest.

Assessing the importance of these changes, however, is a delicate matter and terms like rise and decline must be handled with some care. The long-term shifts which were to come could not have been predicted from the start. The early fortunes of towns differed from kingdom to kingdom. A loss of vitality has been postulated on the grounds of their weakness and ineffectiveness as communities in the maintenance of cultural, political and religious practices. The lack of enthusiasm of the rich for prestigious office has been interpreted as demoralisation, the unwillingness of the poor to participate in processions and pageants as a sign of alienation from the community. The degree to which these pointers to the problems of some towns can be extended to all, however, may be questioned. Poverty might be indicated by the dilapidation of the town fabric, obliging people to live in houses inappropriate for their needs. While the lavish and large-scale town planning of the Renaissance clearly passed Britain by, rebuilding can be identified in some towns, clearly indicating a modest level of prosperity.

There can be little doubt that many towns in England were in some difficulties in 1500 whether or not the percentage of people living in towns had risen or declined. Some of the functions previously carried out by some towns were threatened. In some areas parts of the clothing manufacturing process were moving to villages or the countryside, some ports were suffering from the diversion of trade to London. The basic functions of administration, government and religion were not affected, and neither was the local demand for trading and market centres but the loss, temporary as it turned out, of some economic functions has led to the assertion that towns were economically dependent and derivative at least until 1640. Evidence for the continuing importance of the role of towns as a pivot in trade, government and society makes the definition of dependence problematic. Some towns recovered their prosperity in the second half of the sixteenth century when adjustments to both trading and manufacturing processes stimulated a new demand for urban services and drew people back to the locations which could provide them, particularly the ports. Towns which had had a reduced role for a time now began to provide new services. This was not true of all towns. Some were losing ground permanently by 1500. Others remained more or less unchanged as they fulfilled a static local role for a limited population which was neither growing in size nor wealth.

Welsh towns were markedly less prosperous than the English. Even so, as the sixteenth century progressed, the ports in the South West were developing both on fishing and on illegal trade and the racial distinction between the English townsfolk and the rural Welsh was submerged by the movement of Welsh into the towns. The Welsh experience of town life, however, was more likely to come from English towns as they migrated in some numbers to Bristol, Hereford, Chester and other nearby places.

Irish towns, too, in the sixteenth century were largely unchanging. Small, few in number and primarily located in the South East, ethnically distinct from the native Irish, intensely loyal to the Crown and primarily sea-coast trading communities, they were apparently unaffected by long-term fluctuations. Scottish towns which were also concentrated in a small part of the kingdom were, on the contrary, growing in numbers and in size.

It is hard to find a turning point in the sixteenth century around which improvements in the well-being of all towns cluster. Differences between the levels of prosperity in the still largely regional societies and economies of the divergent parts of the kingdoms resulted in a variety of local patterns, so that when the South West was recovering from its difficulties the North East was facing other problems. While attempts to divorce the prosperity of towns from the general movement of the economy are misplaced, since the fortunes of both are ultimately interlinked, they do not rise and fall at precisely the same moment, with precisely the same speed and timing, and the distribution of resources between town and country can vary considerably.

Evidence for urbanisation in the sixteenth century depends very heavily on the growth of London and perhaps Edinburgh. Most of the other English towns were at best keeping pace with general population, and even in Scotland where many doubled in size, there were only a few large towns. The tentative development of a hierarchy was also very much the result of the pull from London which drew an increasing number of provincial towns into its orbit.

The movement accelerated in the seventeenth century, at least in England and Ireland. The capitals continued to increase their lead over their nearest rivals, but a significant number of other towns at least doubled their size. Scottish towns were having greater problems but even there, west coast ports like Glasgow were developing new roles. There is an increasing amount of evidence for steady and permanent links between the merchants in different towns and in different kingdoms and for an improving and regular transport network which was supplying a wider range of goods to all parts of the country. Merchants no longer needed to be constantly on the move to buy and sell goods but could operate at a distance from the bigger towns which offered the convenience of information networks, credit and insurance. The manufacturing pattern was becoming equally complex. While parts of some trades remained small and local – the shoemaker, the blacksmith, the wheelwright – larger-scale enterprises which required specialised ability were becoming more important.

This economic development could not have taken place without the institutional framework of the towns which maintained and improved the facilities available. The effectiveness of town government has perhaps been underestimated, as has their commitment to the community. In the midst of the daily struggle to regulate domestic matters such as provision of schooling, welfare problems dominated by poverty, planning and control of the building processes, health and hygiene, coping with disasters such as famine, plague and fire, the silting up of ports and the encroachment of the sea (for all of which they had inadequate resources), they did what they could to develop facilities that would attract business to the town. The very real problems all towns faced periodically when struck by disaster or recession should not be used as a criticism of their underlying success. There seems general agreement that the Restoration saw a shift of attitude on the part of the larger town authorities which were becoming less parochial and inward-looking and more aware of national and international events.

Growth of the larger towns is the main reason for an overall increase in the percentage of the total population living in towns in all three kingdoms. The greater towns already had resources to enable them to recover from temporary difficulties. Older towns which had experienced some decline eventually recovered. Those towns that grew were primarily the capitals, ports able to take advantage of the new trade routes or specialise in particular trades like coal, new industrial settlements and towns geared to the new demand for leisure facilities. The evidence suggests that these towns were indeed beginning to pull non-agricultural activity towards them, concentrating the control of wealth and power. Specialisation, particularly in manufacturing or trade, was becoming an obvious characteristic of most larger prospering settlements. There is no evidence that small towns, as defined by historians, played any significant role in urbanisation in this period.

The developments which occurred between 1500 and 1700 mark the beginning of a shift towards a more integrated system in which individual towns are linked into a network which could draw on goods and services from a considerable distance. The development by 1700, however, was neither complete nor uniform. Many small towns would not have seemed very different in 1700 to a revenant from 1500. Survival of 'Elizabethan' town centres reflects an incapacity rather than an unwillingness to rebuild in 1700. Even they, however, could be drawn into the wider transport and communications system by the simple fact of location on the carrier routes.

Considering all four kingdoms together reveals a complex process of interaction which was bringing the towns of all the different kingdoms into a single economic system. It was also bringing people of diverse cultures into proximity. There was a complex pattern of migration from one kingdom to towns in another: the Welsh went to Ireland and to neighbouring English towns, the Irish went to Wales, to London and to west Scottish towns, the Scots went to Ireland and increasingly to England; the English to Ireland. If one adds to this mixture the refugees from France and the Low Countries, some towns were becoming increasingly cosmopolitan.

NOTES

1 INTRODUCTION

1. Paul Bairoch, *Cities and Economic Development: from the Dawn of History to the Present,* trans. Christopher Braider (Chicago, 1988).
2. E. A. Gutkind, *Urban Development in Western Europe,* Vol. I, (London, 1971), p. 49.
3. Lewis Mumford, *The City in History* (London, 1961).
4. Charles Tilly, *Coercion, Capital and European States, AD 990–1992* (Oxford, 1993), p. 17.
5. Yi-Fu Tuan, *Topophilia: a Study of Environmental Perception, Attitude and Values,* 2nd edn., (New York, 1990) and *Space and Place; the Perception of Experience* (London, 1977).
6. Paul Bairoch, 'Urbanization and the Economy in Preindustrial Societies: The findings of two decades of research', *Journal of European Economic History,* 18, pp. 239–90.
7. Lucy Toulmin Smith (ed.), *Leland's Itinerary in England and Wales* (London, 1964) Vol. 2, p. 34-7.
8. C. L. Kingsford (ed.), *A Survey of London, reprinted from the text of 1603,* 2 vols, (Oxford, 1908).
9. W. H. Richardson (ed.), *The Annals of Ipswich; the lawes customes and government of the same collected out of ye Records and writing of that town by Nathaniell Bacon serving as recorder and town clerk in that town Anno Domini 1654* (Ipswich, 1884).
10. There is an interesting survey of the 'vision' of the early writers in Peter Clark, 'Visions of the urban community, antiquarians and the

English city before 1800' in Derek Fraser and Anthony Sutcliffe (eds), *The Pursuit of Urban History* (London, 1983), pp. 105–14.

11. John Throsby, *History of Leicester* (Ipswich, 1791), pp. 108–9.

12. James Thompson, *History of Leicester* (Leicester, 1849), pp. 278–80.

13. E.g.William McDonald, *History of the Burgh of Dumfries* 3rd edn. 1906 (Dumfries, 1867).

14. Walter Thornbury, *Old and New London; a narrative of its History, its People and its Places illustrated with numerous engravings from the most authentic sources The City, Ancient and Modern*, 6 volumes, (London, 1883).

1 PLACE, SPACE AND TIME – THE BUILT ENVIRONMENT

1. Raymond Gillespie, *Colonial Ulster: the Settlement of East Ulster 1600–1641*, Studies in Irish History (Cork, 1985), p. 173.

2. J. V. Beckett, *Coal and Tobacco: the Lowthers and the Economic Development of West Cumberland 1660–1760* (Cambridge, 1981), pp. 182ff.

3. R. G. Hillier and J. Hanson, *The Social Logic of Space* (Cambridge, 1984).

4. E. A. Gutkind, *Urban Development in Western Europe*, Vol. I (London, 1971), p. 39.

5. Brian Lacey, *Siege City: the Story of Derry and Londonderry* (Belfast, 1990), p. 88.

6. M. W. Barley (ed.), *European Towns: Their Archaeology and Early History* (London, 1977), p. 495.

7. R. Butlin (ed.) *The Development of the Irish Town* (London, 1977), p. 72.

8. Hilary L. Turner *Town Defences in England and Wales: an Architectural and Documentary Study 900–1500* (London, 1971), pp. 15–16; Alfred Harvey, *The Castles and Walled Towns of England* (London, 1911), p. 191.

9. Keith Kissack, *Monmouth: the Making of a County Town* (London, 1978), p. 22.

10. D. M. Palliser, *Tudor York* (Oxford, 1979), pp. 25–6.

11. Peter Clark, *The English Alehouse* (London, 1983), pp. 16–20.

12. R. J. Hunter, 'Ulster plantation towns 1609–1641' in David Harkness and Mary O'Dowd (eds), *The Town in Ireland* (Belfast, 1981), p. 60.

13. W. G. Hoskins, *Essays in Leicestershire History* (Liverpool, 1950), p. 108.

14. Michael MacCarthy-Morrough, Chapter 6, in Cieran Brady and Raymond Gillespie (eds), *Natives and Newcomers: Essays on the Making of Irish Colonial Society* (Dublin, 1986), pp. 182–9.

15. Ian Hodder, *The Domestication of Europe* (Oxford, 1990), p. 31.
16. Keith Kissack, *Monmouth: the Making of a County Town* (London, 1978), p. 48.
17. Mary O'Dowd, *Power, Politics and Land: Early Modern Sligo 1568–1688* (Belfast, 1991), p. 160.
18. Eurwyn Willan, '"Let use be preferred to uniformity" Domestic architecture' in Gwynfor Williams (ed.), *Class, Community and Culture in Tudor Wales* (Cardiff, 1989).
19. M. P. Smith (ed.), *Cities in Transformation: Class, Capital and the State* (Sage, 1984), pt v.

2   SOCIAL STRUCTURE AND SOCIAL EXPERIENCE IN THE TOWN

1. Matthew Griffiths, '"Very wealthy by merchandise"? Urban fortunes' in J. Gwynfor Jones (ed.), *Class, Community and Culture in Tudor Wales* (Cardiff, 1989), p. 197.
2. John Walter and Roger Schofield, 'Famine, disease and crisis mortality in early modern society' in John Walter and Roger Schofield (eds), *Famine, Disease and the Social Order in Early Modern Society* (Cambridge, 1989).
3. D. M. Palliser, *Tudor York* (Oxford, 1979), pp. 15–20.
4. Anthony Streehan 'Irish towns in a period of change 1558–1625' Chapter 4, in Cieran Brady and Raymond Gillespie (eds), *Natives and Newcomers: Essays on the making of Irish Colonial Society* (Dublin, 1986), pp. 100–1.
5. Mary O'Dowd, *Power, Politics and Land: Early Modern Sligo 1568–1688* (Belfast, 1991), p. 162.
6. Henry Thorpe, *Lichfield: A Study of its Growth and Function* (Collections for a History of Staffordshire edited by Staffs Rec Soc for 1950 and 1951 (1954)), p. 184.
7. Matthew Griffiths, '"Very wealthy by merchandise"? Urban fortunes' in J. Gwynfor Jones (ed.), *Class, Community and Culture in Tudor Wales* (Cardiff, 1989), p. 216.
8. David Harris Sacks, *Trade, Society and Politics: Bristol c.1500–1640* (New York, 1985), p. 220.
9. Quoted in W. Nolan (ed.), *The Shaping of Ireland: the Geographical Perspective* (Cork, 1986), p. 75.
10. J. P. Pound, *Tudor and Stuart Norwich* (Chichester, 1988), p. 109.
11. F. Kevin Shurer, 'Variations in household structure in late 17th century: Towards a regional analysis', Chapter 12 in Kevin Schurer and Tom Arkell (eds), *Surveying the People* (Local Population Studies, Oxford, 1992).

12. Percy Russell, *Dartmouth* (London, 1950), p. 82.
13. David Underdown, *Fire From Heaven: The Life of an English Town in the Seventeenth Century* (London, 1992), chapter 3.
14. A. L. Beier, 'Poverty and progress in early modern England' in A. L. Beier, David Cannadine and Janus M. Rosenheim (eds), *The First Modern Society: Essays in Honor of Laurence Stone* (Cambridge, 1989), p. 203.

3 TOWNS AND RELIGIOUS CHANGE

1. C. L. Kingsford, (ed.) *A Survey of London, reprinted from the text of 1603*, 2 vols (Oxford, 1908), Vol 2, p. 197.
2. James D. Marwick, *Early Glasgow: A History of the City of Glasgow from the Earliest Times to the Year 1611* (Glasgow, 1911), p. 62. This comes from the Diocesan registers Protocols no 498n503 504
3. R. S. Ferguson & W. Nanson (eds), *Some Municipal Records of the City of Carlisle viz the Elizabethan Constitutions, Orders, Provisions, Articles and Rules from the Dormont Book and the Rules and Orders of the Eight Trading Guilds,* Cumberland and Westmoreland Antiquarian and Archaeological Society, (Carlisle 1887), pp. 26–7.
4. A. D. Dyer, *The City of Worcester in the Sixteenth Century* (Leicester, 1973), p. 187.
5. J. H. Thomas, *Town Government in the Sixteenth Century* (London, 1933), pp. 22–3.
6. Graham Mayhew, *Tudor Rye* (Chichester, 1987).
7. Percy Russell, *Dartmouth* (London, 1950), p. 92.
8. D. M. Palliser, *Tudor York* (Oxford, 1979), p. 211.
9. M. Claire Cross, *The Free Grammar School of Leicester,* (Department of English Local History Occasional Papers, ed. H. P. R. Finberg (Leicester, 1953), p. 10.
10. J. P. Pound, *Tudor and Stuart Norwich* (Chichester, 1988), p. 115.
11. Keith Kissack, *Monmouth: The Making of a County Town* (London, 1978), pp. 34–7.
12. See 'The reformation in the Cities: Cork, Limerick and Galway 1534–1603' in John Bradley (ed.), *Settlement and Society in Medieval Ireland: Studies presented to F. X. Martin* (Kilkenny, 1988), pp. 445–9.
13. Allan White, 'The Impact of the reformation on a Burgh Community: the case of Aberdeen' in *The Early Modern Town in Scotland* (London, 1987), pp. 85–6.
14. White, *The Early Modern Town in Scotland*, pp. 90–1.
15. White, *The Early Modern Town in Scotland*, pp. 87, 94–5.

16. Louise B. Taylor, Aberdeen Council Letters, Vol. 1 (1552–1633) (London, 1942), p. xlii.
17. Annie I. Dunlop (ed.), *The Royal Burgh of Ayr* (London, 1953), pp. 106–7.
18. Sir James D. Marwick, *Early Glasgow; A History of the City of Glasgow from the Earliest Times to the Year 1611* (Glasgow, 1911), pp. 194–5.
19. Pound, *Tudor and Stuart Norwich*, p. 135.
20. Michael MacCarthy-Morrough, *The Munster Plantation: English Migration to Southern Ireland 1583–1641* (Oxford, 1986), p. 151.
21. David Underdown, *Fire From Heaven: the Life of an English Town in the Seventeenth Century* (London, 1992).
22. Dyer, *The City of Worcester in the Sixteenth Century*, p. 236.
23. Pound, *Tudor and Stuart Norwich*, p. 88.
24. P. Clark, 'The Ramoth-Gilead of the Good' Urban change and political radicalism at Gloucester 1540–1640' in P. Clark, A. G. R. Smith and N. Tyacke (eds), *The English Commonwealth 1547–1640: Essays in Politics and Society presented to Joel Hurstfield* (Leicester, 1979).
25. Geraint H. Jenkins, *Protestant Dissenters in Wales 1639–1689* (Cardiff 1992), pp. 10–13, 31.
26. Jenkins, *Protestant Dissenters in Wales 1639–1689*, pp. 36, 41.
27. Russell, *Dartmouth*, pp. 94–5.
28. Peter Jackson, 'Non-conformity in Devon' in Kevin Schurer and Tom Arkell (eds), *Surveying the People* (Oxford, 1992), chapter 7.

4   URBAN WEALTH, TOWNSMEN'S WEALTH

1. A. D. Dyer, *The City of Worcester in the Sixteenth Century* (Leicester, 1973), p. 157.
2. See generally Peter Borsay, *The English Urban Renaissance: Culture and Society in the Provincial town 1660–1770*, Oxford Studies in History, ed. Keith Thomas, (Oxford, 1989).
3. David Underdown, *Fire From Heaven: the Life of an English Town in the Seventeenth Century* (London, 1992), p. 4.
4. Phyllis Hembry, *The English Spa 1560–1815 A Social History* (London, 1990), pp. 27, 53.
5. David Harris Sacks, *Trade, Society and Politics in Bristol c.1500–1640* (New York, 1985), p. 71.
6. John Pound, *Tudor and Stuart Norwich* (Chichester, 1988), p. 100.
7. J. F. Hadwin, 'From dissonance to harmony on the late medieval town', *Economic History Review* 2nd ser. XXXIX 3 (1986), pp. 423–6.

8. N. R. Goose, 'In search of the urban variable' *Economic History Review* 2nd ser. XXXIX 3 (1986), pp. 165–85.

9. Ralph Davis, *The Trade and Shipping of Hull 1500–1700* (East Yorkshire Local History Society, 1964), p. 4.

10. David Rollison, *The Local Origins of Modern Society: Gloucestershire 1500–1800* (London, 1992), pp. 25–30.

11. W. B. Stephens, *Seventeenth Century Exeter: A Study of Industrial and Commercial Development 1625–1688* (Exeter, 1958), p. 32.

12. Glanmor Williams (ed.), *Glamorgan County History* Vol. IV, (1974), p. 156.

13. Matthew Griffiths, 'Very wealthy by merchandise'? Urban fortunes in J. Gwynfor Jones (ed.) *Class, Community and Culture in Tudor Wales* (Cardiff, 1989), p. 217.

14. Raymond Gillespie, Chapter 7, and Anthony Streehan, Chapter 4, in Cieran Brady and Raymond Gillespie (eds), *Natives and Newcomers: Essays on the Making of Irish Colonial Society* (Dublin, 1986), p. 111. See also R. A Butlin (ed.), *The Development of the Irish Town* (London, 1977), p. 70.

15. Arnvid, Lillehammer, 'The Scottish and Norwegian timber trades in the Stavanger area in the sixteenth and seventeenth centuries' in T. C. Smout (ed.), *Scotland and Europe 1200–1800* (Edinburgh, 1986), chapter 6.

16. W. B. Stephens, 'English wine imports *c.*1603–1640' in Todd Gray, Margery Rowe and Audrey Erskine (eds), *Tudor and Stuart Devon: the Common Estate and Government, Essays Presented to Joyce Youings* (Exeter, 1992), pp. 134–5.

17. Patrick McGrath, *The Merchant Venturers of Bristol: A History of the Society of Merchant Venturers of the City of Bristol from its Origins to the Present Day* (Bristol, 1975), p. 33.

18. Raymond Gillespie, *The Transformation of the Irish Economy 1550–1700*, Studies in Irish Economic and Social History, Vol. 6, (1991).

19. Mary O'Dowd, *Power, Politics and Land: Early Modern Sligo 1568–1688* (Belfast, 1991), pp. 151–2, 160.

20. L. M. Cullen, *Anglo-Irish Trade 1660–1800* (Manchester, 1968), pp. 14–5.

21. T. C. Smout, *Scottish Trade on the Eve of Union*, (Edinburgh, 1963).

22. D. McNiven, 'Merchants and traders in early seventeenth century Aberdeen' in J. Stevenson (ed.), *From Lairds to Louns. Country and Burgh Life in Aberdeen* (Aberdeen, 1986).

23. Allan White, 'The impact of the Reformation on a Burgh community: The case of Aberdeen' in Michael Lynch (ed.) *The early Modern Town in Scotland* (London, 1987), p. 81ff.

5 CONTROLLING TOWNS; TOWN SELF-GOVERNMENT

1. Roger Howell jr, 'Resistance to change: the political elites of provincial towns during the English Revolution' in A. L. Beier, David Cannadine and Janus M. Rosenheim (eds) *The First Modern Society: Essays in Honour of Laurence Stone* (Cambridge, 1989), p. 433ff.

2. D. M. Palliser, *Tudor York* (Oxford, 1979) p. 46.

3. Raymond Gillespie, *Colonial Ulster: the Settlement of East Ulster 1600–1641*, Studies in Irish History, (Cork, 1985), p. 186.

4. John Pound, *Tudor and Stuart Norwich* (Oxford, 1988), p. 93.

5. Keith Kissack, *Monmouth: the Making of a County Town* (London, 1978), p. 12.

6. Mary Vershuur 'Merchants and craftsmen in 16th c Perth' in Michael Lynch (ed.), *The Early Modern Town in Scotland* (London, 1987), p. 45.

7. David Harris Sacks, *Trade, Society and Politics in Bristol c.1500–1640* (New York, 1985), p. 18.

8. Alfred Neobald Palmer, *History of Town of Wrexham* (Wrexham, 1893), chapter 3.

9. *VCH Gloucester*, Vol. VI, pp. 142–165.

10. Palliser, *Tudor York*, pp. 62–4.

11. J. H. Thomas, *Town Government in the Sixteenth Century* (London, 1933), pp. 24–5.

12. Heather Swanson, 'Artisans in the urban economy: the documentary evidence from York' in Penelope J. Corfield, and Derek Keene (eds), *Work in Towns 850–1850* (Leicester, 1990), pp. 42–3.

13. N. S. B. Gras, *The London Corn Market*; J. Pound, *Tudor and Stuart Norwich*; Jean Vannes, *Bristol at the Time of the Spanish Armada* (Local History Pamphlets no. 69. 1988), p. 12.

14. Annie I. Dunlop (ed.), *The Royal Burgh of Ayr* (London, 1953), pp. 268–9.

15. A. D. Dyer, *The City of Worcester in the Sixteenth Century* (Leicester, 1973), p. 167.

16. Kissack, *Monmouth: the Making of a County Town*, p. 30.

17. Robert J. Naismith, *The Story of Scotland's Towns* (Edinburgh, 1989), pp. 73, 87.

18. J. W. Horrocks (ed.), *The Assembly Book of Southampton* Vol. 1 (Southampton, 1917), p. xxii.

19. Thomas, *Town Government in the Sixteenth Century*, p. 26.

6 THE CAPITALS

1. Raymond Gillespie, 'Describing Dublin: Francis Place's Visit, 1698–9' in Adele M. Dalsimer (ed.), *Visualizing Ireland: National Identity and the Pictorial Tradition* (London, 1993).
2. Vanessa Harding, 'The population of London 1550–1700, a review of published evidence', *London Journal* 15(2) (1990).
3. Peter Earle, *The Making of the English Middle Class: Business, Society and Family Life in London 1660–1730,* (London, 1989), p. 240.
4. Peter Somerville-Large, *Dublin* (London, 1979), p. 89–90.
5. Colm Lennon, *The Lords of Dublin in the Age of Reformation* (Dublin Press, 1989), p. 61.
6. John A. Inglis, *Sir Adam Otterburn of Redhall, King's Advocate 1524–38* (Glasgow, 1935), pp. 1, 8–9.
7. Michael Lynch, *Edinburgh and the Reformation* (Edinburgh, 1981).
8. Richard M. Wunderli, 'Evasion of the office of alderman in London 1523–1672' *London Journal* 15(1) (1990), p. 3ff.
9. Helen Dingwall, *Late 17th-Century Edinburgh: A Demographic Study,* (Edinburgh, 1994), p. 105.
10. Ian W. Archer, *The Pursuit of Stability: Social Relations in Elizabethan London* (Cambridge, 1990); Steve Rappaport, *Worlds Within Worlds: Structures of Life in Sixteenth Century London* (Cambridge, 1987).
11. Howard Clarke (ed.), *Medieval Dublin: the Living City* (Dublin, 1990), pp. 190–6.
12. Dingwall, *Late 17th-Century Edinburgh*, p. 91.
13. For much of this I am indebted to Raymond Gillespie who has sent me a copy of his as yet unpublished paper on Dublin; cf. also Lennon, *The Lords of Dublin in the Age of Reformation*.
14. Lynch, *Edinburgh and the Reformation*, pp. 9–10.
15. Susan Brigden, *London and the Reformation* (Oxford, 1989) provides a fascinating and detailed study of a complex story.
16. J. T. Gilbert, *A History of the City of Dublin* (Dublin, 1859), pp. 57–9.
17. Earle, *The Making of the English Middle Class*, pp. 32–3, 85–6.
18. For a full discussion of this see Robert Brenner, *Merchants and Revolution: Commercial Change, Political Conflict and London's Overseas Traders 1550–1653* (Cambridge, 1994).
19. Earle, *The Making of the English Middle Class*, pp. 18–19.
20. Michael J. Power, 'The East London working community in the 17th century' in Penelope J. Corfield, Derek Keene (eds), *Work in Towns 850–1850* (Leicester, 1990), p. 105.
21. Penelope J. Corfield and Derek Keene (eds), *Work in Towns 850–1850,* (Leicester, 1990) p. 7.

22. Philip Banbury, *Shipbuilders of the Thames and Medway* (Newton Abbot, 1971), pp. 33–4.

23. H. A. Gilligan, *A History of the Port of Dublin* (Dublin, 1988), pp. 10–13, 246. The Ouzel Galley was built in the 1690s and went trading to the Mediterranean.

24. R. Butlin (ed.), *The Development of the Irish Town* (London, 1977), p. 95.

25. E. Gillespie (ed.), *The Liberties of Dublin* (Dublin, 1974), p. 30.

26. L. M. Cullen, *Anglo-Irish Trade 1660–1800* (Manchester, 1968), p. 12.

27. Mary O'Dowd, *Power, Politics and Land: Early Modern Sligo 1568–1688* (Belfast, 1991), p. 160.

28. D. Stevenson, *The Scottish Revolution 1637–1644* (Newton Abbot, 1973).

29. Dingwall, *Late 17th-Century Edinburgh*, pp. 100–1, 154, 162, 165, 180.

30. Dingwall, *Late 17th-Century Edinburgh*, pp. 144, 203–5.

7 THE PLACE OF THE TOWN IN THE KINGDOM

1. C. L. Kingsford, (ed.), *A Survey of London, reprinted from the text of 1603*, 2 vols (Oxford, 1908), Vol. 2, p. 197.

2. Raymond Gillespie, *Colonial Ulster: the Settlement of East Ulster 1600–1641*, Studies in Irish History, (Cork, 1985), p. 167.

3. Ian Soulsby, *The Towns of Medieval Wales, A Study of their History, Archaeology and Early Topography*, (Philimore, 1983), p. 1.

4. Sir James D. Marwick, *Early Glasgow: A History of the City of Glasgow from the Earliest Times to the Year 1611* (Glasgow, 1911), p. 36.

5. Marion M. Stewart '"A sober and Peeceable Deportment": The court and council books of Dumfries 1561–1661' in Alison Gardner-Medwin and Janet Hadley Williams (eds), *A Day Estivall: Essays in the Music Poetry and History of Scotland and England in Honour of Helen Menme Stir* (Aberdeen, 1990), p. 152.

6. Kingsford, (ed.), *A Survey of London*, p. 199.

7. Craig Muldrew, 'Credit and the courts: Debt litigation in a seventeenth-century urban community', *Economic History Review*, 2nd ser. XLVI 1 (1993) pp. 23–38.

8. David Harris Sacks, *Trade, Society and Politics in Bristol c.1500–1640*, (New York, 1985) pp. 182–4.

9. Percy Russell, *Dartmouth* (London, 1950), p. 57; Todd Gray, 'Fishing the commercial world of Early Stuart Dartmouth' in Todd Gray, Margery Rowe and Audrey Erskine (eds), *Tudor and Stuart Devon: The*

Common Estate and Government, Essays presented to Joyce Youings (Exeter, 1992), p. 177.

10. John Davidson and Alexander Gray, *The Scottish Staple at Veere* (London, 1909); Matthijs P. Rooseboom, *The Scottish Staple in the Netherlands An account of the Trade Relations between Scotland and the Low Countries from 1292 till 1676 with a Calendar of Illustrative Documents* (The Hague, 1910).

11. Public Record Office, State Papers Elizabeth 12/270/27.

12. A. D. Dyer, *The City of Worcester in the Sixteenth Century* (Leicester, 1973), p. 209.

13. Jean Vannes, *Bristol at the Time of the Spanish Armada* (Local History Pamphlets no 69, Bristol 1988), pp. 21–2; Lindsay Boynton, *The Elizabethan Militia* (London, 1967), pp. 58–9.

14. J. W. Horrocks (ed.), *The Assembly Book of Southampton Vol. 1, 1602–1608,* (Southampton, 1917), p. xv.

15. Mark Charles Fissel, *The Bishops' Wars: Charles I's Campaigns against Scotland 1638–1640*, Cambridge Studies in Early Modern British History (Cambridge, 1994), p. 186n38.

16. Boynton, *The Elizabethan Militia*, p. 54.

17. David Harris Sacks, 'Celebrating authority in Bristol 1475–1640' in Susan Zimmerman and Ronald F. E. Weissman (eds), *Urban Life in the Renaissance* (Newark, 1989), pp. 209–10

18. Patrick McGrath, *Bristol and Civil War* (Local History Pamphlets no. 50, Bristol), pp. 7–8

19. Robert J. Naismith, *The Story of Scotland's Towns* (Edinburgh, 1989), pp. 68–9.

20. Roger Howell jr 'Resistance to change: The political elites of provincial towns during the English Revolution' in A. L. Beier, David Cannadine and Janus M. Rosenheim (eds), *The First Modern Society: Essays in Honor of Laurence Stone* (Cambridge 1989), p. 433ff.

21. Henry Thorpe, *Lichfield: A Study of its Growth and Function*, Collections for a History of Staffordshire edited by Staffs Rec Soc for 1950 and 1951, (1954), p. 181.

22. Brian Lacey, *Siege City: The Story of Derry and Londonderry* (Belfast, 1990), p. 119.

23. Malcolm and Edith Lodwick, *Story of Carmarthen* revised and rewritten by Joyce Lodwick and Victor Lodwick (Carmarthen, 1972), pp. 52–3.

24. Anthony Streehan, 'Irish towns in a period of change 1558–1625' Chapter 4 in Cieran Brady and Raymond Gillespie (eds), *Natives and Newcomers: Essays on the Making of Irish Colonial Society* (Dublin, 1986), p. 108.

25. Paul Courtney 'Feudal hierarchies and urban origins in SE Wales' in Peter Addyman and Steve Roskans (eds) Vol. 1, *Urbanism: Medieval Europe* (London, 1992), pp. 215–18.

26. R. J. Hunter 'Ulster plantation towns 1609–1641' in David Harkness and Mary O'Dowd (eds), *The Town in Ireland* (Belfast, 1981).

27. C. H. Josten 'Elias Ashmole and the 1685 Litchfield election: An unpublished episode' Staff Rec Soc Collections (1952), pp. 215–27.

28. Michael Lynch 'The Crown and the Burghs' in Michael Lynch, (ed.), *The Early Modern Town in Scotland* (London, 1987), p. 62.

8 THE TOWN IN ITS REGION

1. See John Bradley (ed.), *Settlement and Society in Medieval Ireland: Studies presented to F. X. Martin* (Kilkenny, 1988), p. 246.

2. V. Beckett, *Coal and Tobacco: the Lowthers and the Economic Development of West Cumberland 1660–1760* (Cambridge, 1981), pp. 104–5.

3. Raymond Gillespie, 'Lords and Commons in 17th century Mayo' in Raymond Gillespie and Gerard Moran, '*A Various Country*': Essays in Mayo History 1500–1900* (Cork, 1987), pp. 44–53.

4. Brian Lacey, *Siege City: the Story of Derry and Londonderry* (Belfast, 1990), p. 115–16, 149.

5. Matthew Griffiths, ' "Very wealthy by merchandise"? Urban fortunes' in J. Gwynfor Jones (ed.), *Class, Community and Culture in Tudor Wales* (Cardiff, 1989), p. 215.

6. W. Nolan (ed.), *The Shaping of Ireland: the Geographical Perspective* (1986), p. 75.

7. Michael Lynch (ed.), *The Early Modern Town in Scotland* (London 1987), p. 21.

8. Marion M. Stewart ' "A sober and Peeceable Deportment": The court and council books of Dumfries 1561–1661' in Alison Gardner-Medwin and Janet Hadley Williams (eds), *A Day Estivall: Essays in the Music, Poetry and History of Scotland and England in Honour of Helen Menme Stir* (Aberdeen, 1990), pp. 146–7.

9. Annie I. Dunlop (ed.), *The Royal Burgh of Ayr* (London, 1953), p. 26.

10. Ian Soulsby, *The Towns of Medieval Wales, a Study of their History, Archaeology and early Topography*, (Philimore, 1983), p. 172.

11. Mary Verschuur 'Merchants and craftsmen in sixteenth century Perth' and Michael Lynch 'The Crown and the Burghs', Allan White 'The Impact of the Reformation on a Burgh Community: The case of Aberdeen' in Michael Lynch (ed.) *The Early Modern Town in Scotland* (London, 1987), p. 83.

12. D. F. Harrison, 'Bridges and economic development 1300–1800' *Economic History Review second series* XLV 2 (1992), pp. 240–6.

13. Michael MacCarthy-Morrough, Chapter 6, in Cieran Brady and Raymond Gillespie (eds), *Natives and Newcomers: Essays on the Making of Irish Colonial Society* (Dublin, 1986), p. 175.

14. Patrick McGrath, *The Merchant Venturers of Bristol: A History of the Society of Merchant Venturers of the City of Bristol from its Origins to the Present Day* (Bristol, 1975), p. 28.

15. W. G. Hoskins, *Industry, Trade and People in Exeter 1688–1800 with Special Reference to the Serge Industry* (Manchester, 1935), p. 25.

16. Quoted in J. E. Lloyd (ed.), *History of Carmarthenshire* vol. 2 (London Carmarthenshire Society, 1939), p 13.

17. Percy Russell, *Dartmouth* (London, 1950), p. 60.

18. Henry Thorpe, *Lichfield: A Study of its Growth and Function*, Collections for a History of Staffordshire, edited by Staffs Rec Soc for 1950 and 1951 (Birmingham, 1954), p. 187.

19. Raymond Gillespie, 'The small towns of Ulster 1600–1700,' *Ulster Folklife* vol. 36 (Belfast, 1990), pp. 28–9.

20. Keith Kissack, *Monmouth: the Making of a County Town* (London, 1978), p. 13.

21. David Underdown, *Revel, Riot and Rebellion* (Oxford, 1985), pp. 55–6.

22. For a detailed study see Kevin Schurer and Tom Arkell (eds), *Surveying the People* Local Population Studies (Oxford, 1992), pp. 67–77.

23. John Pound, *Tudor and Stuart Norwich* (Chichester, 1988), p. 55.

24. R. Butlin (ed.), *The Development of the Irish Town* (London, 1977), pp. 70–1.

25. David Harris Sacks, *Trade, Society and Politics in Bristol c.1500–1640* (New York, 1985), p. 46.

26. W. B. Stephens, *Seventeenth Century Exeter* (Exeter, 1958), pp. 40–5, 51–3, 85–8.

9   Towns and Urbanisation

1. Robert Brady, *A Treatise of English Burghs or Bouroughs* (London, 1711), pp. 3, 163, 166.

2. Lewis Mumford, *The Culture of Cities* (New York, 1938), p. 428.

3. see H. B. Clarke and Anngret Simms (eds), *The Comparative History of Urban Origins in non-Roman Europe. Ireland, Wales, Denmark, Germany, Poland and Russia 9th–13th Century* (Oxford, 1985), pp. 97, 417.

4. Peter Clark and Paul Slack, *English Towns in Transition 1500–1700* (London, 1976), p. 5.

5. Helen Dingwall, *Late 17th-Century Edinburgh: A Demographic Study* (Edinburgh, 1994), p. 10.

6. Graham in *Journal of Historical Geography* 5 (1979), pp. 111–25.

7. H. B. Clarke and Anngret Simms, *The Comparative History of Urban Origins in non-Roman Europe* (Oxford, 1985), p. 420.

8. Raymond Gillespie and Gerard Moran (eds), *'A Various Country': Essays in Mayo History 1500–1900* (Cork, 1987), p. 11 ff.

9. Allan White, 'The impact of the Reformation on a burgh community: The case of Aberdeen' in Michael Lynch (ed.), *The Early Modern Town in Scotland* (London, 1987), p. 84.

10. Matthew Griffiths, ' "Very wealthy by merchandise"? Urban fortunes' in J. Gwynfor Jones (ed.), *Class, Community and Culture in Tudor Wales* (Cardiff, 1989), p. 201.

11. Paul Hohenberg and Lynn Hollen Lees, *Making of Urban Europe 1000–1950* (Cambridge, Mass, 1985).

12. H. J. Dyos, 'Agenda for urban historians' in H. J. Dyos (ed.), *The Study of Urban History* (London, 1968).

13. David Cannadine 'Urban history in the United Kingdom: The Dyos phenomenon and after' in David Cannadine and David Reeder (eds), *Exploring the Urban Past: Essays in Urban History by H. J. Dyos* (Cambridge, 1982).

14. G. Sjoberg, *The Pre-Industrial City Past and Present* (New York, 1960).

15. William Sanders, Henry Wright, Robert McCAdams (eds), *On the Evolution of Complex Societies: Essays in Honor of Harry Hoijer* (Malibu, 1984).

16. A. Losch, *The Economics of Location* (Yale, 1954).

17. E. A. Gutkind, *Urban Development in Western Europe* Vol. I (London, 1971), p. 23.

18. Jan de Vries, *European Urbanization 1500–1800* (Harvard, 1984), chapter 6.

19. A. D. van der Woud, Akira Hayami, Jan de Vries (eds), *Urbanization in History: A Process of Dynamic Interactions* (Oxford, 1990), p. 1.

20. E. A. Wrigley, 'Brake or accelerator? Urban Growth and Population Growth beforre the Industrial Revolution' in A. D. van der Woud, Akira Hayami, Jan de Vries (eds), *Urbanization in History: a Process of dynamic Interactions* (Oxford, 1990), pp. 101–13.

21. David Palliser, 'Urban decay revisited' in J. A. F. Thomson, *Towns and Townspeople in the Fifteenth Century* (Stroud, 1988), pp. 17–18.

22. Derek Keene, 'Continuity and development in urban trades: Problems of concepts and the evidence' in Penelope J. Corfield and Derek Keene (eds), *Work in Towns 850–1850* (Leicester, 1990), pp. 1–3.

23. E. A. Wrigley and R. S. Schofield, *Population History of England 1541–1871* (London, 1981), p. 161.

24. Sheila Cooper, 'Household form and composition in Kings Lynn: A reconstruction based on the poll taxes of 1689–1701' Chapter 10, in Kevin Schurer and Tom Arkell (eds), *Surveying the People* Local Population Studies, (Oxford, 1992).

25. M. W. Flinn et al., *Scottish Population History: from the 17th century* (Cambridge, 1977).

26. Mary O'Dowd, *Power, Politics and Land: Early Modern Sligo 1568–1688* (Belfast, 1991), p. 63.

27. K. H. Connell, 'Population trends in seventeenth century Ireland', *Economic and Social Review* vol. 2 (1975), pp. 149–65.

28. L. A. Clarkson, 'Irish population revisited 1687–1821' in J. M. Goldstein and L. A. Clarkson (eds), *Irish Population, Economy and Society: Essays in Honour of the late K. H. Connell* (Oxford, 1981), p. 13.

29. Clark and Slack, *English Towns in Transition 1500–1700*, p. 8.

30. O'Dowd, *Power, Politics and Land: Early Modern Sligo 1568–1688*, p. 65.

31. Ian D. Whyte, 'Urbanization in Early Modern Scotland: A preliminary analysis' *Scottish Economic and Social History* 9 (1989), p. 31.

32. E. A. Wrigley, 'The great commerce of every civil society: Urban growth in early Modern Europe' *Scottish Economic and Social History* 12 (1992).

33. I am most grateful to Dr Raymond Gillespie for permitting me to see the paper he has written for Peter Clark's forthcoming book on small towns before it appears in print, from which many of the figures are drawn.

34. J. M. Bestall and D. V. Fowkes (eds), *Chesterfield Wills and Inventories* (Derbyshire Record Society, vol. 1 1977), p. xiii.

35. T. Sharlin, 'Natural decrease in early modern cities: A reconsideration', *Past and Present* 79 (1978), pp. 126–38.

36. Robert Woods, Chapter 5, in Richard Lawton (ed.), *The Rise and Fall of Great Cities: Aspects of urbanization in the Western World* (London, 1989).

37. E. A. Wrigley and R. S. Schofield, *Population History of England 1541–1871* (London, 1981), p. 166.

38. Ronald Mayo, *The Huguenots in Bristol*, Local History Pamphlets no 61 (Bristol), pp. 2, 8, 10–11.

39. Percy Russell, *Dartmouth* (London, 1950), p. 93.

40. Peter Clark and Jean Hosking, *Population Estimates of English Small Towns 1550–1851* Centre for Urban History, University of Leicester Working Papers no 5 (Leicester, 1993), pp. i–iv. Under the CNRS–

ESRC Franco-British program in conjunction with Professor J. P. Pousson of the Sorbonne, Professor Clark has been working since 1985 on data-collection.

41. Robert J. Naismith, *The Story of Scotland's Towns* (Edinburgh, 1989), pp. 78–9.

42. Geraint H. Jenkins, *The Foundations of Modern Wales 1642–1780* (Oxford, 1987), pp. 115–16.

10 NETWORK AND HIERARCHY

1. W. B. Stephens, *Seventeenth Century Exeter: A Study of Industrial and Commercial Development 1625–1688*, (Exeter, 1958), p. 13–14, 43–4.

2. W. G. Hoskins, *Industry, Trade and People in Exeter 1688–1800 with Special Reference to the Serge Industry* (Manchester, 1935), p. 13.

3. D. M. Palliser, *Tudor York* (Oxford, 1979), pp. 126–7.

4. In A. D. Dyer, *Decline and Growth in English Towns 1400–1640* (Basingstoke, 1991). In his rank order from top to bottom Lincoln*, Salisbury, Boston*, Beverley*, Canterbury, Winchester, Bury St Edmunds, Gloucester*, Hereford*, Ely, Northampton, Scarborough, Stamford*, Newark, Ludlow, Southampton, Pontefract, Lichfield, Newbury, Huntingdon, Hadleigh, Wells, Bridgnorth, Bridgewater, Barking, Chichester, Peterborough, Maidstone, Doncaster, Cirencester, Louth . * means rank declined 1377–1524. The others either improved or the information is missing.

5. Rochester, Crediton, Saffron Walden, Beccles, Taunton, Tiverton, Wymondham, Bodmin, Basingstoke, Windsor, Alton, Wisbech.

6. Dover, Sandwich, Ludlow, Warwick.

7. Howard Carter, *The Towns of Wales: A Study in Urban Geography* (Cardiff, 1965), p. 35.

8. Birmingham, Bristol, Cambridge, Chatham, Chester, Colchester, Coventry, Exeter, Hull, Ipswich, Leeds, King's Lynn, Leicester, Liverpool, Manchester, Newcastle upon Tyne, Norwich, Nottingham, Oxford, Plymouth, Portsmouth, Preston, Sheffield, Shrewsbury, Wigan, Yarmouth, York.

9. Peter Borsay, *The English Urban Renaissance: Culture and Society in the Provincial Town 1660–1770* (Oxford, 1989), p. 11.

10. J. K. Fedorowicz, *England's Baltic Trade in the Early Seventeenth Century: A Study in Anglo–Polish Commercial Diplomacy* (Cambridge, 1980), pp. 1, 14–16, 20, 50–2, 61.

11. Eric Kerridge, *Trade and Banking in Early Modern England.* (Manchester, 1988), pp. 49, 52–4.

12. Kerridge names London, Ipswich, Norwich, Great Yarmouth, Hull, York, Wakefield, Halifax, Ripon, Darlington, Seaton, Newcastle, Berwick, Portsmouth, Bristol, Taunton, Tiverton, Exeter, Plymouth, Dartmouth, Oxford, Coventry, Shrewsbury, Chester, Dublin, Manchester, Rochdale, Kendal, Cambridge, Wellingborough, Leicester, Newark and Southampton. He thinks there were probably more, 'guessing' Barnstaple, Northampton, Nottingham, Sheffield, Bury St Edmunds, Whitby, King's Lynn, Warrington. This list has some surprising omissions like Worcester.

13. Kerridge, *Trade and Banking in Early Modern England.*, pp. 5–6.

14. For a comparison of prices in Worcester and Winchester see A. D. Dyer, *The City of Worcester in the Sixteenth Century* (Leicester, 1973), pp. 49–51.

15. J. M. Bestall and D. V. Fowkes (eds), *Chesterfield Wills and Inventories*, Derbyshire Record Society vol. 1 1977, p. xxii.

16. W. B. Stephens, *Seventeenth Century Exeter: A Study of Industrial and Commercial Development 1625–1688* (Exeter, 1958), p. xix.

17. Kerridge, *Trade and Banking in Early Modern England*, pp. 1–15.

18. L. M. Cullen, *Anglo–Irish Trade 1660–1800* (Manchester, 1968), p. 13.

19. Michael Lynch, 'Urbanization and urban networks in seventeenth-century Scotland', *Scottish Economic and Social History* 12 (1992), p. 32.

20. J. A. Chartres, *Internal Trade in England 1500–1700* (London, 1977), pp. 20–1.

21. Cullen, *Anglo–Irish Trade 1660–1800*, pp. 16, 21.

22. John Pound, *Tudor and Stuart Norwich* (Chichester, 1988), p. 2.

23. Michael Lynch, 'Whatever happened to the medieval burgh' in *Scottish Economic and Social History* 9 (1989).

Further Reading

Archer, Ian W. *The Pursuit of Stability: Social Relations in Elizabethan London* (Cambridge, 1990).

Bairoch, Paul, *Cities and Economic Development: From the Dawn of History to the Present*, trans. Christopher Braider (Chicago, 1988).

Beckett, J. V., *Coal and Tobacco: the Lowthers and the Economic Development of West Cumberland 1660–1760* (Cambridge, 1981).

Beier, A. L. and Finlay, R. (eds), *London 1500–1800* (London, 1986).

Borsay, Peter, *The English Urban Renaissance: Culture and Society in the Provincial Town 1660–1770*, Oxford Studies in History, ed. Keith Thomas (Oxford, 1989).

Brady, Cieran and Gillespie, Raymond (eds), *Natives and Newcomers: Essays on the Making of Irish Colonial Society* (Dublin, 1986).

Butlin, R. (ed.), *The Development of the Irish Town* (London, 1977).

Cannadine, David and Reeder, David (eds), *Exploring the Urban Past: Essays in Urban History by H. J. Dyos* (Cambridge, 1982).

Carter, Howard *The Towns of Wales: A Study in Urban Geography* (Cardiff, 1965).

Clarke, Howard (ed.), *Medieval Dublin: The Living City* (Dublin, 1990).

Clarke, H. B. and Simms, Anngret (eds), *The Comparative History of Urban Origins in non-Roman Europe. Ireland, Wales, Denmark, Germany, Poland and Russia 9th–13th Century* (Oxford, 1985).

Clark, Peter and Slack, Paul, *English Towns in Transition 1500–1700* (London, 1976).

Corfield, Penelope J. and Keene, Derek (eds), *Work in Towns 850–1850* (Leicester, 1990).

Davidson, John and Gray, Alexander, *The Scottish Staple at Veere* (London, 1909).

Davis, Ralph, *The Trade and Shipping of Hull 1500–1700* (East Yorkshire Local History Society, 1964).

De Vries, Jan, *European Urbanization 1500–1800* (Harvard, 1984).

De Vries, Jan and van der Woud, A.D. and Hayami, Akira (eds), *Urbanization in History: A Process of Dynamic Interactions* (Oxford, 1990).

Dingwall, Helen, *Late 17th-Century Edinburgh: A Demographic Study* (Edinburgh, 1994).

Dyer, A. D., *The City of Worcester in the Sixteenth Century* (Leicester, 1973).

Dyer, A. D., *Decline and Growth in English Towns 1400–1640* (Basingstoke, 1991).

Dyos, H. J. (ed.) *The Study of Urban History* (London, 1968).

Earle, Peter, *The Making of the English Middle Class: Business, Society and Family Life in London 1660–1730,* (London, 1989).

Fraser, Derek and Sutcliffe, Anthony (eds), *The Pursuit of Urban History* (London, 1983).

Gillespie, Raymond, *Colonial Ulster: The Settlement of East Ulster 1600–1641*, Studies in Irish History (Cork, 1985).

Gillespie, Raymond, *The Transformation of the Irish Economy 1550–1700*, Studies in Irish Economic and Social History Vol. 6 (Cork, 1991).

Gillespie, Raymond and Moran, Gerard (eds), *'A Various Country': Essays in Mayo History 1500–1900* (Cork, 1987).

Goldstein, J. M. and Clarkson, L. A. (eds), *Irish Population, Economy and Society: Essays in Honour of the late K. H. Connell* (Oxford, 1981).

Gutkind, E. A., *Urban Development in Western Europe* Vol. I (London, 1971).

Harkness, David and O'Dowd, Mary (eds), *The Town in Ireland* (Belfast, 1981).

Hohenberg, Paul and Lees, Lynn, Hollen *Making of Urban Europe 1000–1950* (Cambridge, Mass., 1985).

Jenkins, Geraint H., *The Foundations of Modern Wales 1642–1780* (Oxford, 1987).

Jones, J. Gwynfor (ed.), *Class, Community and Culture in Tudor Wales* (Cardiff, 1989).

Kissack, Keith, *Monmouth: The Making of a County Town* (London, 1978).

Lacey, Brian, *Siege City: The Story of Derry and Londonderry* (Belfast, 1990).

Lennon, Colm, *The Lords of Dublin, in the Age of Reformation* (Dublin, 1989).

Lynch, Michael, *Edinburgh and the Reformation* (Edinburgh, 1981).

Lynch, Michael (ed.), *The Early Modern Town in Scotland* (London, 1987).

MacCarthy-Morrough, Michael, *The Munster Plantation: English Migration to Southern Ireland 1583–1641* (Oxford, 1986).

McGrath, Patrick, *The Merchant Venturers of Bristol: A History of the Society of Merchant Venturers of the City of Bristol from its Origins to the Present Day* (Bristol, 1975).

MacKenzie, William Mackay, *The Scottish Burghs* (Edinburgh, 1949).

Mair, Craig, *Stirling: The Royal Burgh* (Edinburgh, 1990).

Mumford, Lewis, *The City in History* (London, 1961).

Nolan, W. (ed.), *The Shaping of Ireland: The Geographical Perspective* (Cork, 1986).

O'Dowd, Mary, *Power, Politics and Land: Early Modern Sligo 1568–1688* (Belfast, 1991).

Palliser, D. M., *Tudor York* (Oxford, 1979).

Pound, J. P. *Tudor and Stuart Norwich* (Chichester, 1988).

Rappaport, Steve, *Worlds within Worlds: Structures of Life in Sixteenth Century London* (Cambridge, 1987).

Russell, Percy, *Dartmouth* (London, 1950).

Sacks, David Harris, *Trade, Society and Politics: Bristol c.1500–1640* (New York, 1985).

Schurer, Kevin and Arkell, Tom (eds), *Surveying the People* Local Population Studies, (Oxford, 1992).

Sjoberg, G., *The Pre-Industrial City*, (New York, 1960).

Slater, T. R. (ed.), *The Built Form of Western Cities: Essays for M. R. G. Conzen on the Occasion of his Eightieth Birthday* (Leicester, 1990).

Somerville-Large, Peter, *Dublin* (London, 1979).

Soulsby, Ian, *The Towns of Medieval Wales, A Study of their History, Archaeology and Early Topography* (Philimore, 1983).

Stephens, W. B., *Seventeenth Century Exeter: A Study of Industrial and Commercial Development 1625–1688* (Exeter, 1958).

Stevenson, J. (ed.), *From Lairds to Louns. Country and Burgh Life in Aberdeen* (Aberdeen, 1986).

Thomas, Avril, *The Walled Towns of Ireland* (Dublin, 1992).

Tilly, Charles, *Coercion, Capital and European States, AD 990–1992*, (Oxford, 1993).

Underdown, David, *Fire From Heaven: The Life of an English Town in the Seventeenth Century* (London, 1992).

Wrigley, E. A. and Schofield, R. S., *Population History of England 1541–1871* (London, 1981).

INDEX